Weddings for Grownups

WEDDINGS *for* GROWNUPS

Everything You Need to Know to Plan Your Wedding Your Way

Carroll Stoner

CHRONICLE BOOKS
SAN FRANCISCO

Printed in the United States of America.

Library of Congress Cataloging in Publication Data

Stoner, Carroll.
Weddings for grownups / Carroll Stoner.
p. cm.
ISBN 0-8118-0229-9 (pbk.)
1. Weddings – United States – Planning – Handbooks, manuals, etc.
I. Title.
HQ745.S797 1992
395'.22 – dc20 92-21868
CIP

Editing: Judith Dunham
Book and cover design: Robin Weiss
Composition: Ann Flanagan Typography
Cover photograph: Dennis Keeley

Distributed in Canada by Raincoast Books,
112 East Third Avenue, Vancouver, B.C. V5T 1C8

10 9 8 7 6 5 4 3 2 1

Chronicle Books
275 Fifth Street
San Francisco, CA 94103

To Bob, my love

Acknowledgments

Gathering the information for this book was a labor of love. For encouraging my romantic notions and helping me learn about the practical side of things, I am especially grateful to two Chicago florists. Beth Tarrant, of Anna Held Flowers, brings the eye of a painter to her work. She and Virginia Wolff light up rooms when they enter, even when their arms aren't loaded with flowers.

Musicians and bandleaders Peter Duchin, Becky and Don Cagen, Bill Harrison and Marc Perlish were helpful and often made me laugh. To master chef and baker Eric Singer and photographer Marc Harris, who shared my sense of the ridiculous in wedding mania, I'm glad we met. To Roz Paaswell, a wonderful partner and great friend, let's always enjoy the memories.

To literary agent Betsy Nolan, who had recently married and saw the sense to this project from the start, and to Caroline Herter who understood what I was trying to say before I said it, appreciation. For Annie Barrows, who brings intelligence and wit to her work, extra thanks, and to Judith Dunham, whose finely tuned ear for language enhances her skills as a copy editor, thank you. To Robin Weiss, for her impeccable design skills, my gratitude.

To my composer/musician son, Garrick Stoner, who read parts of this manuscript in progress and offered sound advice, and to my daughter Eve Bergazyn, who understood the secrets to good weddings when she was seven, let's dance at many weddings together.

Special appreciation to the many couples, and especially brides, who were open with their wedding memories. This book could not have been done without their generosity.

Table of Contents

INTRODUCTION

Any Kind of Wedding You Want

I called it my year of weddings. In one twelve-month period, six women I know got married.

The women and their weddings could not have been more different from each other. They were affluent, not-so-affluent, and important-to-look-affluent, urban and suburban, Catholic, Jewish, High Episcopalian, and Evangelical Protestant, and included a Jewish-Catholic intermarriage. Five of the six were first marriages, the women ranged from ages 26 to 49, and not one of the brides was casual about her wedding.

Several brides worked with their mothers in the planning process. One couple made the wedding a project and worked together. In every case, the brides did the majority of the planning and were astonished by how time-consuming it was. No matter how the wedding planning was managed, all but one wedding looked incredibly complicated. Several of the brides wondered if they were doing something wrong. Were their standards too high? Was that why they couldn't seem to make up their minds? Was there an easier way to get the work done without becoming traumatized about it? Were they going to enjoy their own weddings, knowing what had gone into them? Why couldn't people get along? And why didn't family members, especially their mothers and mothers-in-law, make the work easier for them?

By the end of the year, I was convinced there had to be an easier way. Weddings are joyous occasions. Why did these seem so difficult?

Each of the six weddings was complicated in a different way. Several brides had problems with parents or in-laws. One worried about how her divorced parents and their new mates would all fit in. And every bride was intimidated by wedding planning logistics.

A 38-year-old acquaintance, Sandy, knew the wedding she wanted was significantly different from what her mother would plan for her. This first-time bride had grown up in the lap of luxury in show business. Tony Bennett sang along with her mother, a dramatic former big-band singer, around the grand piano of their Beverly Hills home. Joey Bishop dropped in for coffee. And when Sandy was 16, she entertained the Beatles around her pool during their first American tour. But

Sandy no longer thought like the rich girl she once was. "I do not want a typical Beverly Hills wedding," she said.

Sandy had hired a wedding consultant, a man who expected her to buy all her wedding goods and services through him and, just as important, to do things his way. Sandy didn't find his resources unusual, cost-conscious, or sophisticated, three qualities that now mattered to her. She found more interesting, less expensive stationery on her own. She didn't like his florist recommendations and instead located a floral designer who was an artist using flowers as her medium. When Sandy said she could not envision her name in white letters on a black stand in a hotel lobby, the wedding consultant did not understand. What kind of wedding did she want? He seemed genuinely perplexed and more than a little annoyed. Sandy quickly decided to fire him before he left her, losing the hefty $750 deposit she had already paid him.

Now add Sandy's mother to the equation. She still wanted "the best" for her daughter and agreed with the consultant that a hotel wedding would be beautiful and foolproof. She, too, was confused. Not hold a wedding in a hotel or private club? What kind of wedding *did* Sandy want?

Just when Sandy was wondering what to substitute for the wedding everyone expected her to have, we ran into each other and renewed an old acquaintanceship. She wanted elegance, she explained, and also intimacy. She wanted sophistication, but a certain kind of opulence no longer fit her definition of what was tasteful. I thought she sounded perfectly reasonable. After a few minutes of conversation, I suggested a mansion or restaurant or private club such as an arts club and gave her some specific suggestions.

Clubs were out. Neither she nor her fiance, Patrick, was a member of one, and she wouldn't feel comfortable using a friend's membership. She liked the idea of a mansion and visited a few, but in the end didn't like the layout of the rooms and the way her guests would be split into groups at dinner. We scheduled lunch at a charming, middle-sized northern Italian restaurant that was at the top of her list, and before dessert she had booked the entire place for a Sunday afternoon wedding reception. Having selected the downtown restaurant for the reception, she chose a suburban synagogue for her mixed-religion marriage ceremony.

During the first stages of planning, Sandy was on the phone constantly with her mother. She didn't mind explaining every decision. But then her mother began to second-guess her, and Sandy began to feel pressured and unhappy. Wasn't having guests drive from the suburb to the city a terrible imposition? Sandy reassured her mother that it was not, and drew up a quick logistical plan of who would ride with whom. "No limousines," she warned her mother, "they remind me of proms." After a heart-to-heart talk, when she told her mother she loved her but didn't want the kind of wedding she knew her mother wanted, she felt better. Her mother backed off.

After eight months of planning, every detail felt right to Sandy, from the ceremony to the beautifully arranged bowls of fresh fruit and nuts served before the wedding cake dessert. The six-course meal was sophisticated and delicious, from the unusual passed hors d'oeuvres to the towering Italian rum cake. Friends raved about Sandy and Patrick's wedding. The cost? Because the couple bought their own champagne and wine and because restaurant food costs were lower than hotel prices, the wedding cost about the same as a less elaborate hotel wedding, $120 per person with 80 guests. The total: $9,600.

The second wedding was that of a close friend's 26-year-old stepdaughter, who wanted a beautiful wedding but didn't want her divorced parents' acrimonious relationship to interfere with it. Her mother requested that her father (my friend's husband) pay a portion of the bills for the suburban Boston wedding. This wedding was fraught with peril for the bride, as every occasion had been since her parents' divorce. Both parents had remarried. There were two stepparents; the bride's brother; my friend's son, who is the bride's stepbrother; and the bride's little half sister (her father and stepmother's daughter), who was dying to be a flower girl. Who would stand under the wedding canopy? Everyone? Who would walk down the aisle? And in what order? All of these details needed to be worked out. A strong-willed grandmother kept track of the arrangements, from the choice of wedding site to the selection of the florist. "I just want a beautiful wedding and I want everyone to get along," my friend's stepdaughter said more than once.

The day of the wedding there were problems. The grandmother publicly shouted at her ailing husband for not being where he should have been, embarrassing everyone. She and the bride's mother screamed at the florist because the centerpieces had "bare spots." The bride's father made the last-minute discovery that his second wife was not included under the wedding canopy, even though the bride's mother and her husband were. Behind-closed-doors negotiations took place and the stepmother was included. To make matters worse, my friend later explained that she felt awkward since she was not dressed appropriately. All the women in the wedding party, including the two mothers, wore white. She had on a dark gray dress. As if picking up on the tension, her normally confident six-year-old daughter, the flower girl, burst into tears just as she was about to walk down the aisle, necessitating a change in the order of the bridal processional. "No one showed me how to drop the petals," she wailed.

The cost: Beyond the high emotional costs, the wedding was not inexpensive. The bride's mother originally thought the wedding would cost between $35,000 and $40,000, an amount her father found high, but turned out to be average for the wedding they envisioned – 200 guests at $200 per person. The wedding actually cost between $30,000 and $35,000 for 160 guests. The $9,000 band fees were paid by the bridegroom's father, and the bride's father agreed, before planning began, to contribute $10,000. About $3,000 was also spent for an engagement party, and another $1,000 for a restaurant prenuptial party for the couple's family and friends.

Then there was my oldest friend from childhood, whose daughter, also 26, wanted an inexpensive wedding so they could use the families' wedding funds for their new home in suburban Minneapolis. This mother of the bride, working with her daughter every step of the way, planned a lovely afternoon wedding that cost about $3,000 for over 200 guests. Most of the food was made at home, and family members helped with everything from the wedding dress to the reception decor.

The bride's gown could have been a designer original that cost as much as the entire wedding, but it was made by her mother, a skilled seamstress. Another family member bought the invitations and stationery wholesale. The family's home church, one of the biggest Lutheran congregations in town, is beautiful and well furnished. But the banquet hall in the newly built, Evangelical Protestant church where the young couple are members is as plain as a high-school gymnasium and required decorating creativity. By the time the bride's mother and her family and friends finished decorating, the simple hall looked festive and pretty. Each table was covered with a floral chintz or pastel tablecloth. Homemade grapevine wreaths wrapped in double-edged satin ribbon were placed at the center of each table, and helium-filled, pastel balloons were tied to the backs of the chairs that filled the huge room. The buffet tables were embellished with flowers combined with tree branches from a family member's backyard. One of the bride's aunts decorated the church pews with oversized white bows and flowers.

The bride's mother and an uncle who loves to cook prepared gallons of turkey and wild-rice salad at several prewedding cooking sessions. Lunch was a combination of delicious homemade dishes served with baskets of tiny, fruit muffins alongside several of the caterer's specialties. Every detail was carefully planned with cost kept firmly in mind. It was a beautiful, loving occasion.

This wedding and a friend's second wedding in a beautiful old Episcopal church outside Philadelphia came off without tears or disagreements or last-minute problems. But even the mature, second-time bride had her qualms. A magazine editor and manager who plans at least ten major corporate meetings a year, she was having 50 friends and family members to an at-home reception immediately following the wedding in the suburb of Chestnut Hill. Two days before her wedding, she said she felt fine about the ceremony but was nervous about the arrangements for the party, because she couldn't watch every detail as she ordinarily would. She asked a friend to do that for her, and because she had given such clear instructions to her caterer, florist, and musicians, the friend had very little to do. "What she did wasn't important," the bride explained. What mattered most was the bride's peace of mind.

The couple's four grown children said they loved the wedding and took part with genuine happiness. They had all known each other for many years, and two of the daughters were longtime best friends. At a prenuptial party, one of the daughters apologized sweetly in the form of a toast for not always being so sweet to her father's "friend." She ended her little speech by saying it was now clear that "father knows best," which drew a laugh from other guests, as much for the wit as for the honesty. Final cost: $4,000 for a lavish cocktail party and dinner for 50 guests, or $80 per person.

The fifth wedding was that of a medical student who had lived with us for a year between college and medical school and with whom we'd developed a loving, familial relationship. The former valedictorian of her high-school class and an honors college graduate, she threw herself into planning her wedding with the same diligence she'd once reserved for her studies. She wanted something special and, on a limited budget, created a lovely wedding that was a bit more lavish than her family might have planned on their own.

The decision to hold the wedding in her fiance's Methodist church rather than her own Catholic parish might have been a source of conflict, but the bride and her fiance took pains to explain every decision to both sets of parents, and thus their wedding came together with few problems. It was a beautiful occasion, with the bride's and bridegroom's many friends from college and their work worlds mixing congenially with family members. Because this couple was such a favorite with everyone, their friends and family seemed eager to meet each other. The couple's outgoing personalities could be felt throughout the wedding and reception. As for problems, the bride expressed some disappointment about her personal flowers and the food service at the suburban catering hall reception. Still, she loved her wedding and refused to dwell on the negatives. Total cost: $7,500 for 150 guests, or $50 per person.

The only terrible situation was that of my friend Alice, who planned every detail of her wedding in the face of her parents-in-law's disapproval. From the start, this wedding was fraught with difficulties. The 28-year-old bride was the first in her family not to be married at the family church with the reception held at her father's golf and country club. Until she left her Ohio hometown, she thought that was the most beautiful kind of wedding you could have. But now, living in a big city, she wanted something else, in her "grownup hometown." She explained to her parents that she would supplement what they would normally have paid. In every category, from her band to her florist, she hired the best money could buy. Her only budget-related compromise was to hold the wedding in the afternoon rather than in the evening.

The day of her wedding was a nightmare, and I watched all her carefully made plans unravel. The society band leader wouldn't listen to her or take her instructions. She confided that they'd met and discussed in detail how she wanted him to do specific things at specific times. Alice had even typed out a schedule with times for the first dance, cake cutting, bouquet toss, and other wedding rituals she knew had to happen like clockwork if the wedding was to be out of the ballroom on time. Alice, a retail manager, was marrying an attorney, but she later complained that the men she hired treated her like a pouty teenage bride rather than an adult client.

The photographer insisted on taking table shots during the meal, because the bridegroom's mother was adamant that this was the only time guests would be there (a good point), even though Alice told him not to, feeling it would be a tasteless interruption of the service. The catering director at the posh hotel rushed the wedding party through the slightly delayed meal because he had another wedding coming for dinner in the same ballroom. With no one to run interference between the bride and the servicepeople she'd hired – the bride couldn't possibly be the woman with the clipboard at her own wedding – she was forced to let the band leader, photographer, and hotel catering manager control her wedding reception.

But worst of all was the way her new parents-in-law seemed to disapprove of everything. They were used to a certain kind of traditional wedding, and this wasn't it. They felt it looked vaguely chintzy. They hated the society band music and thought the all-white flowers looked boring instead of elegant. Most of all they believed that the midday meal and two-and-a-half-hour reception should have been an evening dinner dance with a more exuberant band and a four-hour party that went into the wee hours, overtime costs be damned! Unfortunately, they told the bride exactly what they thought.

Until the day she dies, Alice will believe her father-in-law tripped her while they were dancing. As angry as she was, she had the presence of mind to get up, laugh, and dust off her gown while she kept right on dancing. No one but Alice knew just how upset she was. It was the final humiliation in a day filled with problems.

Alice knew that her father-in-law expected his son to return to their city and enter his successful law practice. She gritted her teeth and said, "Over my dead body." What might have been a smooth relationship with her husband's parents was off to a rocky start. And the wedding was not inexpensive: about $28,000 for 160 guests, or $175 per person.

By the end of my year of weddings, I had begun to develop a philosophy. I believed then, as I do now, that weddings should be glorious occasions that start marriages off with meaningful ceremonies and fabulous celebrations. Here's what I saw in that year of weddings, and why I feel they often look so complicated.

Today's older brides – and by older I mean age 26 or 29 or 45 rather than 21 or 22 – want their weddings to reflect who they are rather than who their parents are. Even when they plan their weddings with their mothers, they must work together as adults, since these brides have their own ideas and no longer crave their parents' or parents-in-law's approval. Parents must recognize this and go out of their way to be supportive.

Families and communities have changed. Today's women grow up, move to new cities to start careers, and end up putting down new roots. Belonging to a religious or ethnic community is the result of choice, rather than inevitability. Even though all couples enter marriage believing they will be successful, family histories are often filled with obvious examples of love gone wrong, and remarriages and stepfamilies unquestionably complicate matters.

Regardless of how evolved women may be, they frequently have deep-seated romantic feelings about their weddings. If they become frustrated, their feelings can be translated into perfectionism, which puts them in conflict with their more practical sides, and with conventional wedding vendors and sometimes their own families as well.

A lack of confidence can inspire brides to stick with outmoded traditions because they don't trust their own instincts. Weddings are important ceremonies and the biggest, most expensive party most brides will ever give. Under these circumstances, breaking the rules takes courage.

There's something wrong with a system that complicates weddings so that the pleasure of planning what should be a joyous celebration is lost. What was desperately needed, I believed then and believe now, is a support system for grownup brides.

The factor that best explained my six friends' weddings and other weddings, is this:

Every wedding is an exception to the rules.

The reasons for today's freedom and independence, and thus for the accompanying conflicts, are both simple and profound. The by-the-book rules that once guided all of life, including the wedding planning process, are not as valid today. More and more people feel comfortable breaking away from ethnic, cultural, religious, and family ties that no longer fill their needs. Women have changed. They still want weddings that express their romantic fantasies, but they also want to fulfill their more practical desires to get what they pay for and have their weddings reflect their independent lives. Thus, every grownup wedding – and by this I mean a marriage ceremony and celebration planned as personal expressions of the bride and bridegroom, and planned by the wedding couple or the bride herself – is bound to be an exception to the old rules.

I had left a career in newspaper management wanting to go into business. Within a year I was the co-owner of a wedding company built around the principles I'd discovered during my year of weddings. With a partner who had a background in business that balanced my experience as a manager, we started The Wedding Company.

Before we opened our doors, we learned about traditional wedding consultants like the one Sandy used, and we decided that today's working women needed something new. We saw ourselves as the bride's advocate, and we built the business around an informative, monthly wedding-planning seminar where we reviewed a wide range of styles and costs for what we called Wedding Components, all the choices made from the beginning of the process until the wedding day. We trained a group of wedding consultants who worked with brides during the planning stages to assure that they got what they wanted and to help keep costs down when that was a priority. While we helped brides develop a framework for making choices, we encouraged them to open their minds to new ideas and to discard old wedding fantasies. Women were more than ready.

Our goals were simple. The most important was to give brides and couples permission to do what they wanted to do, rather than let family or community conventions dictate every choice. We reassured clients that their choices would work out fine, although we discouraged such excesses as brides who wanted to decorate their receptions with acres of palm trees, dress like Nefertiti, and be carried down the aisle on the shoulders of four costumed servants. We passed out wedding checklists that ranged from goods to services and included realistic schedules and budgets. We acted as an idea resource, and we attracted brides and couples who wanted to make their weddings personal expressions of who they are. If clients wanted a blues band, we knew two, as well as jazz, brass, and rock bands, and string ensembles, and everything from wedding sites to resources for flowers, stationery, photographers, and wedding gowns. If clients wanted unusual wedding invitations, for example, we had a book filled with examples that ranged from cartoons to hand-tinted photographs, and we often sent them to graphic artists and the corner quick-print shop for low-cost, original stationery. We provided wedding consultants to run the day of the wedding at a cost of $150–300 and they would either plan every detail or do a minimal amount of work with clients. But in every decision we emphasized freedom of choice and practicality and we encouraged clients to maintain control. "Work with people you like. Trust them. Choose wedding goods that make you feel wonderful," we said again and again.

In the first months of business, we met with unusual success, partially as a result of the national publicity we received. We had no difficulty finding employees. Women love weddings. As for our clients, they were working women, or couples who wanted to plan their weddings together, along with an occasional bride and her mother who wanted to do something original. After their weddings, our clients wrote us appreciative letters telling us how they couldn't have done it without our encouragement. Although we provided help in specific areas of planning, and with ideas and resources, the support was what they remembered.

In the process, we learned a lot about weddings. One of our major discoveries was how women often needed to sort out their fantasies before they could begin planning their weddings. Thus our consultants frequently served as psychologists as well as planners. What women needed from us was clear: Many brides had to think through which decisions were worthy of compromise and which were absolutes, which wedding components meant the most to them and which others didn't matter so much. We warned our clients against obsessing about every detail of their weddings and about having to be in control of everything. That was our instinct before we had much experience, and after a year in business we had several fascist-bride horror stories to prove our point.

We also learned about what we called the clash of expectations and why conflict is sometimes inevitable. We learned why it is difficult for the sophisticated bride to find unusual contemporary goods and services that are tasteful as well as affordable. But we saw, again and again, how much brides enjoy planning their weddings when the process goes smoothly.

Still, after several years in the wedding business, I continued to ask myself why weddings often became so complicated. I knew that they were public declarations of a family's style and status and thus a reflection of different, often unarticulated expectations. I also knew that women had changed and were continuing to grow in independence. I had learned, too, about their exaggerated hopes for these highly romantic occasions.

Some of the answers came from my own wedding story. Twenty years ago there was still a sense of embarrassment about second weddings, which ours was for both of us. I didn't envision a lavish celebration, even though I secretly craved something big and bold and memorable. I wore a suit, rather than the cream-colored lace dress I really wanted. I carried modest, pastel flowers, although I was dying to carry an oversized, loosely tied bouquet of country flowers in vivid colors.

Without ever articulating my fantasy, I envisioned about 25 friends and close family members at a nonsectarian ceremony in front of my living room fireplace. My four-year-old son would have a role, as would my husband's two children, ages nine and eleven, who I thought could read something biblical or poetic about love and family.

Then, waiters would sweep in with trays of champagne, and another 40 or 50 guests would join the celebration. A lavish buffet would be set up throughout the dining room, living room, and breakfast room of my rambling, old Philadelphia apartment. The string quartet that played classical music for the ceremony would add a piano and play Cole Porter and George Gershwin. Maybe my parents-in-law, whom I was fond of before I married their son, would give a toast, along with my two sisters and a much-loved brother-in-law. Here, plans grew hazy. How much ceremony was too much? And what would it all cost? I wasn't sure.

As it happened, it didn't work out that way because my parents-in-law said they wouldn't feel comfortable inviting their friends from New York to attend this kind of occasion. To them, it felt casual, not like a real wedding. In their ethnic group, a wedding was a dinner dance, period. Instead of telling them that I was sorry their friends wouldn't be with them, but that this was the wedding we wanted, I said nothing. I compromised on the very premise of my wedding and planned a late morning ceremony at home and lunch for 15 family members at a nearby arts club.

If I'd been willing to admit it to myself, something deep within me craved romance and ritual and the public acknowledgment that our marriage was forever, that we were marrying for all the right reasons this time, and that our love and partnership were worth celebrating. I should have articulated these thoughts. I still regret that I didn't gently insist on getting what I wanted, although I have long since stopped blaming my husband's parents for their opinion. The real issue is why I didn't defend my wedding idea and fight for what I wanted.

In my own defense, it was the early 1970s (which still felt like the 1960s), when nothing sentimental was considered cool. I was busier than I'd ever been at my job as a newspaper editor and as a divorced mother. I didn't know how I'd find the time to plan a real wedding. Both my parents had died and I didn't have anyone to help with arrangements I sensed might become complicated. What I needed was the moral support I later set up a business to provide. Without it, I backed away from my own dream. Two days before Christmas of 1972, after devoting what I considered an amazing amount of time and money to planning my tiny wedding, we were married.

First weddings are not the only declarations of love and hope. In the long run, all weddings are affirmations of married love, friendship, and hopeful beginnings. They mark our entry into a community, whether it's the same as our parents' or one that's all our own. As partners, we often want to celebrate for the sheer joy of it. It is no accident that weddings have for centuries been celebrations of an important passage.

In over 20 years of life together that surely constitute a happy ending, I have never overcome the disappointment of not having a wedding to mark the beginning of my marriage. Not surprisingly, when people tell me they're tempted to elope, I urge them to work things out and have the kind of wedding they want.

Every year my husband and I order a wedding cake at Christmas. Will it be a killer chocolate cake or a *genoise* with fresh fruit filling or one layer of each? Will it be decorated with fresh flowers or marzipan roses? And how big should it be this year? We take these decisions seriously. The friends who watch us cut the cake and feed each other the first slice know they're witnessing a meaningful ritual. For every friend who thinks it's corny as sin, there's another with wet eyes. It's my small healing gesture.

This book, *Weddings for Grownups,* explores why and how weddings are intended to be memorable declarations of the ageless bond between men and women. All weddings, not just first marriages, are declarations of love and hope, and their rituals are important parts of the occasion, just as budgets and schedules are, because they contribute to peace of mind.

Weddings for Grownups is a personal wedding guide. It gives permission to express as many different styles as there are people who read it. It offers the reflections of brides and couples on what made their weddings special, and what they would change if they had it all to do over again. It is also a sourcebook of creative ideas. It gives a healthy dose of wedding rules, with the idea that you can't move beyond what you don't know. Insouciance and panache can come only when you know the rules and then can flout them.

Weddings for Grownups is for brides and couples who want weddings that fulfill their deepest longings for romance or that eschew sentimentality entirely, or who want something in between. It demonstrates how weddings are worth the time and energy that go into them. Weddings, after all, are expressions of individuals as much as they are reflections of the world they inhabit. Perhaps most important, *Weddings for Grownups* helps us over the hurdle that separates the women we used to be from the women we are today.

CHAPTER ONE

Separating Fantasy from Reality

Why do weddings sometimes look so complicated? Why do brides frequently go through what one wedding-gown designer calls "the 48-hour crazies" a week or two before their weddings? Why do families fight, brides and their mothers argue, and couples lose heart and wish they could elope?

Understanding the sources of the complexities of weddings is the first step toward avoiding stress. It is normal to feel romantic, even to have romantic fantasies, about your wedding. It's understandable to see brides with high standards who want every part of their weddings to be breathtaking, original, unique in all the world. Thus, romanticism can be transformed, with the best of intentions, into perfectionism. It's also reasonable to want to spend both your time and your money wisely. But the resulting combination of rosy sentiment and hard-eyed perfectionism, peculiar to weddings, can cause conflict and stress.

Problems may also be caused by conflicting expectations. You will be dealing with many other individuals when planning even a small wedding. Parents may have their own ideas. The bridegroom may see things differently. And wedding vendors can be difficult, wanting to treat your wedding as just another piece of business, insisting on using their tried-and-true wedding formulas.

Weddings are among the great undefined social rituals in America. Because of the tremendous number of cultural influences in this country, there is simply no one way to be married. You are fortunate if you've attended many weddings over the years, and even luckier if you've helped a sister or a friend organize her wedding. But it's safe to say that until you plan your own, you have no idea of the number of choices and decisions you will need to make, and of the emotional overload attached to many of them.

Knowing the potential source of problems is one step toward making the process less stressful. There *are* ways to avoid conflict and tension. Attempting to separate fantasy from reality is a good first step. More than any other part of the planning process, this can help you understand the sources of problems because it's key to defining your own expectations.

Let's be clear about one thing: Not everyone has problems planning their weddings. But the number of brides who do is substantial enough that an analysis of why problems occur may be helpful in forestalling difficult situations in the first place.

The Best Thing About Our Wedding

"That we made it a surprise wedding. We invited family members and a few close friends to our country house for Thanksgiving, and told them it was going to be a special day. Then, we had a rabbi there with us, and as each family member arrived, the three of us met them at the door and told them we were going to be married. And right before our favorite meal of the year, we did! If we'd made it into a more formal wedding, there would have been too many expectations. What we did was just right."

Judy Baum, 36, first-time bride.

THE BRIDE'S FANTASIES

How perfectionistic do you want to be? Brides who don't believe that every choice has to be drop-dead gorgeous will unquestionably have an easier time making choices. There is less likelihood that they will end up with flowers that look like those at a gangster's funeral, and with other wedding details that look as if they tried way too hard. They won't end the planning feeling exhausted, worried, and anxious about what their weddings will reveal about them. There is no question that, by narrowing the choices and reinventing the fantasy of your own wedding, you can sidestep potential sources of conflict and strain.

As for wedding fantasies themselves, even the most mature women may have unspoken but elaborate wedding images in their minds. These may be clear and easy to articulate, but more often they are as hazy as childhood memories that spring from unspoken feelings about what comprises love and lasting marriages. These idealized wedding fantasies may be in direct contrast with women's definitions of themselves today and thus can cause the worst kind of ambivalence, which is fear based on insecurity and self-doubt.

Mary Beth, in her late twenties, uses her own name in her commercial photography business and her married name in her social life. Mary Beth was married in a memorably beautiful Catholic-Jewish ceremony in the tented side yard of her city house in a changing neighborhood. The wedding combined the two sets of cultural and religious beliefs, and it demonstrated how Mary Beth and her husband want to be seen as a couple: dramatic and a little unconventional, lively and fun.

Mary Beth explains her wedding theory this way: "Too many brides think they should move into another class of society when they have a wedding. They have these amazing centerpieces they'd never have in their homes. Everything is out of time, out of character, and out of reach. They have huge dresses and huge crowds, and think everything has to be on that scale. Then they wonder why they lose control of everything."

A Casual, Unsentimental Wedding

Ellen Mason was someone who knew exactly what kind of wedding she wanted, though finding the right space for it was a challenge. Ellen, an extraordinary businesswoman, had just left a Fortune 500 company, taking her entire department with her to start a new and competing business. The resulting lawsuits were covered in the *Wall Street Journal,* as was the tremendous growth of the business in the first months after their departure. Now, the two managing partners in the venture were becoming husband and wife.

This was a first wedding for Ellen, the second for the bridegroom. The busy bride spent close to a month working with a wedding consultant she paid to accompany her and have contractual details ready as they shopped for the right location for the ceremony and reception.

Neither the bride nor the bridegroom wanted anything even remotely sentimental, reverent, or religious in any part of their wedding. The space they chose was a surprise to everyone. It was a middle-sized party room in a sophisticated downtown hotel. The area was not large and the ceiling was somewhat low for the size of the room. The couple had the means to pay for any kind of wedding they wanted, but their choice meant that the party would have an intimate, somewhat casual feeling, the exact opposite of the more formal atmosphere of the high-ceilinged ballroom with gilt pillars that so many brides crave.

The reception felt exactly as Ellen had specified it should, more like a party than a wedding. About 150 guests rubbed shoulders with each other and talked and moved easily from one table to the next. Wedding rituals were kept to a minimum. There was no tossing of the bouquet. There were a few toasts but no first dance and no one, absolutely no one the bride specified, was to be introduced with a microphone. The sophisticated small band she hired understood completely and looked to her all evening for music cues. They did not attempt to run her wedding.

The food was elegant, the wines carefully chosen. Late in the evening, the couple cut their wedding cake and fed each other a bite, but it was an almost private occasion that was not treated as a photo opportunity.

After her wedding, Ellen explained that she wanted to avoid what she called a "sacred wedding" feeling. She was something of an exception to the rule that women want romance to be a part of their weddings. For Ellen and Robert, their low-key, expensive wedding was festive, stylish, and perfect.

Shaping Your Wedding Image

Without question, the best way to avoid problems while planning a wedding is to be clear about your expectations. This is accomplished by separating fantasy from reality and by communicating well with everyone involved in the process. This exercise will help brides-to-be and couples define and articulate what they envision for their weddings. Choose ten qualities that sound appealing and then eliminate ideas until you can clearly envision four or five qualities that you want to define your wedding.

Warm	Romantic
Lively	Avant-garde
Impromptu	Luxurious
Religious	Intimate
Trendy	Visual
Chic	Family-oriented
Old-fashioned	Casual
Urban	Spiritual
Lavish	Traditional
Polished	Contemporary
Musical	Large
Exuberant	Country-style
Formal	Cool
Relaxed	Small
Nonsectarian	Stylish
Artistic	Witty
Dramatic	

Mary Beth's idea was to create a more extravagant party than she would normally give, but not an event that looked as if she had hired impersonal professionals to do everything for her. "I hate those over-organized, flawless, sterile weddings in impersonal places. All the life is sucked out of them and they end up not being reflections of anyone, much less of the bride and bridegroom." Mary Beth did hire a florist, photographer, caterer, and other professionals to help her plan her wedding. She also worked on an hourly basis with a wedding consultant who helped her think through her plans. She was willing to admit that her wedding for 120 was a fairly complicated event. But she hired people she liked and even used the services of some professionals who did not specialize in weddings, feeling that she would get something new rather than a wedding formula.

"I listened to all kinds of advice, and then I did what I wanted. One friend suggested I have a small table of Challah [a Jewish bread] and wine, and another of Irish tea breads. I helped the caterer make the tables look really beautiful with nice linens and baskets. I loved their symbolism and how they looked. Food is important to us both. My sister wrote out a blackboard menu in colored chalk, like a restaurant menu but prettier. I thought long and hard about the things I cared about and ignored all the rest."

Mary Beth discovered during her planning that setting priorities and recognizing where advice might be needed helped her decide how to spend her time. She hired and paid a friend who is a magazine art director with fabulous taste to help her think through the reception's style and decor. "When the florist came to the house she was saying, 'We can swag this and have different centerpieces on each table,' which were ideas I liked. But my friend said, 'Back up a minute. What do you want this all to look like?' We decided to make everything look like a country garden, and that gave us an overriding theme to work with. And in the house, instead of decorating it, we tried to make it look really beautiful, which is different."

A related source of potential problems is that brides or bridegrooms are often unaware of just how public their choices are when they first begin their planning. Everyone knows, at least in an unspoken way, that rituals such as weddings are important public occasions. But brides and bridegrooms are soon confronted with the intensely public character of inviting friends and family members and perhaps members of their parents' or their own community to a party preceded by a life-changing ceremony. No wonder many couples are intimidated. The fact that few brides have ever entertained as lavishly as they will at their own weddings can cause justifiable worry.

It's wise to remember that, as public as weddings are, they are also intensely personal and private.

Look at it this way: The logistics and practicalities of planning your wedding can be in direct contrast with the feelings of romance generated by wedding fantasies. All of this combined may cause conflict with family, friends, and wedding vendors, who often have strong feelings about your wedding.

However, keep in mind that weddings, unless they are kept extremely simple, are not projects a bride can handle herself. On the wedding day, every task must be delegated.

TIME AND MONEY

Outlining a framework for decision making such as an approximate schedule of deadlines begins to make wedding planning look manageable. Think of time as well as money as an important commodity. Acknowledge that perfection is not possible. This is not a grand opera production with dozens of workers helping to pull together details that will look perfect onstage. In the field of corporate events, special event planners devote days and weeks to planning an evening's worth of dinner, dancing, and entertainment. Furthermore, they are not revealing their personal financial and social stature in their events, and their visions of perfection are not clouded by sentiment. Just as important, they do nothing else and often have support staff to back them up.

Kathy Hartwell, a first-time bride of 34 who planned an elegant dinner-dance wedding for 100 in just two months, says she got exactly what she set out to achieve, and the details were perfect.

She touches on one of the main reasons for wedding-planning overload: logistics. "I ended up interviewing more people than I thought I would," Kathy says, "since I wasn't always comfortable with recommendations. That took time. But I think people who allow themselves a year or more to plan their weddings can give themselves too much time and that's why they get crazy. I knew exactly what I wanted and treated it as if it were a job. I mean how many florists and ballrooms do you have to see?" The owner of her own marketing business, Kathy arranged her work schedule so she could spend time planning her wedding.

Traditions may begin to look appealing, not just because of their appropriate and historic sense of fanfare, but because they reduce the number of choices. The bride who has always wanted to walk down the aisle to "The Bridal Chorus" from *Lohengrin* by Richard Wagner is ahead of the game: That's a decision she doesn't have to think about. Other no-decision-needed traditions help move the process along: wearing your mother's gown, going with traditional readings suggested by your cleric, using the same wedding orchestra or string quartet your friend used, accepting your mother's or a friend's advice on the choice of invitations and stationery.

The best way to get a grip on the actual work involved in planning a wedding is to approach it as if it were a work-related project, as Kathy did. To keep major projects from looking impossible, they are broken down into components. A framework for completing the work is set up, with intermediate deadlines, schedules, and goals. The project thus becomes a series of smaller tasks and is no longer overwhelming. Think of the bride as the project manager.

A Warm, Exuberant Wedding

Jane Konnor wanted permission to live out the fantasy that she and her bridegroom had developed together, which was to invite 250 friends, family members, and colleagues to the biggest, warmest, most fashionable party they'd ever attended.

This was a first marriage for Jane, the treasurer of a brokerage house, and her fiance, a commodities trader. There was, however, a slight inequity between their two families. Jane's father was a high-school science teacher; Frank's family was very well-off, but would never spend money in a flashy way. And neither family would have planned a wedding in the style Jane and Frank wanted.

The couple decided that money, within reason, was no object. They planned their evening wedding for a downtown Catholic church, with the dinner dance held in a small, European-style hotel nearby. The hotel had recently been remodeled and was developing a reputation for good food and stylish surroundings. It happened to have exactly what this couple wanted, a beautiful, authentic art deco ballroom.

The night of the wedding the hotel looked as if it was still the Roaring Twenties, but with a Nineties opulence. Stunning tropical flower arrangements in huge, linear gold vases were placed throughout the room. Tall gold fixtures held the table centerpieces at eye level. When you entered the ballroom, the sight was of candlelit, gilt elegance and breathtaking flowers. The five-tier wedding cake was decorated in gold, art deco cutouts and was set on a tabletop covered with white flowers on black and gold linens. It was in the middle of the spacious dance floor so everyone could admire it. The scene was right out of the movies.

Jane and Frank had spent top dollar on art deco–style invitations and stationery, engraved in gold ink. Menus, also printed in gold, were produced for a lower cost at a neighborhood print shop, and were at every place setting.

Finding resources that could stretch their design capabilities and carry out an overall theme took time and patience. But Jane and Frank had been to dozens of weddings and wanted their own to be different. Everything had to pack a design punch, and the decorations and food had to create an elegant and beautiful atmosphere. The florist, for example, designed and built wooden containers to fit around inexpensive vases and then painted the containers gold. The baker designed art deco cutouts after studying the era's motifs and spent hours creating a special icing for the cake.

The real struggle for Jane and Frank was to make their wedding both extravagant and warm. They managed this with toasts by family members and friends, a sophisticated but lively band, and, the most important ingredient, their own warmth. All night long the couple walked around the ballroom and visited with friends and family. It was a fabulous, albeit costly, wedding.

Most sensible brides keep an eye on costs. Wedding goods are not inexpensive, and wedding budgets can look like a fortune to brides and bridegrooms who have never spent more than $20 on flowers at one time. Creating a wedding budget may be important, but time is an equally precious commodity for today's two-career couples. For example, how difficult should it be to choose a wedding site? As Kathy asked, "How many ballrooms do you have to see?" Ironically, it's the good student, the risk-taking woman who is often successful professionally, who frequently gets trapped by her own high standards.

Some brides and couples (and a few mothers of the bride) catch wedding fever. For every couple who looks at four or five wedding sites (on four or five lunch hours or after-work visits, after scheduling the appointments, after reaching the appropriate person, etc.), there is another who must look at 20. The record is held by a Los Angeles bride marrying an Ohioan in Chicago who looked at 54! The couple made it a six-month-long project and laughed as they confessed, "We got to know all of the city's clubs and ballrooms."

Even buying a wedding gown, which most women look forward to with great pleasure, can be a logistical nightmare if the bride must comparison-shop for style, price, and service at every salon in town, or if she's not sure what she's looking for.

Setting priorities is mandatory. Let's say you love flowers and have decided to make them a priority. How do you learn enough about flowers in a short time to know what to choose? First, I suggest getting a book on flowers. Look for a large-format book that combines beautiful, inspirational photographs with information and creative ideas. Then, schedule visits with several florists who are in your price range. Ask questions. Write them out if necessary. Begin by learning what flowers will be available at the appropriate time of year, as well as the most popular styles today (romantic, country, traditional, European, tropical), and at what cost.

In other words, choose to make flowers a project. While you're doing that, perhaps your bridegroom, or mother, or even a friend might want to research wedding music. What type? Who is available? At what cost?

Planning ahead also saves time. Avoid two meetings with the same wedding vendors by getting organized before you meet them the first time. When you visit a florist, be ready to listen to her best ideas and to show her clippings from a magazine that show the style of bouquet you want, and possibly even photographs of the kinds of flowers and the style you want in centerpieces or decor. Give her a swatch of fabric you are using – that day – and avoid having to send it later. Be aware that flowers never match fabrics, but are intended to complement colors and styles. When you meet with musicians, have your questions ready and be prepared to hear their ideas for certain parts of the ceremony or reception.

Go to every meeting prepared to sign a contract, or give yourself a day or two, rather than weeks, to finalize your decision. Then stop listening to or taking advice from those who want to tell you about their (better) florist, their (more talented) band, their (more successful) way of doing things. Tell people (if they care) that you have a fabulous caterer, a wonderful florist, etc. Remind yourself that weddings aren't about competition.

Brides starting to plan their weddings may want to shop carefully for each and every detail. Unless you have unlimited time, don't do it. Those brides who become obsessive about every detail take the joy out of the process.

PARENTS AND WEDDING VENDORS

Another factor that can cause great complications, even for the most confident bride, is the constant involvement with others – family, friends, and wedding vendors – who all may have strong opinions about your marriage ceremony and celebration. Wedding logistics can be daunting and choices can be confusing. Everyone, from family members to servicepeople, may seem to have a stake in your decisions. Weddings are seldom like professional projects, with colleagues who already know each other and work as teams toward specific common goals. The complicated psychology of weddings means that expectations are sometimes in conflict, possibly within your family, between the bridegroom's family and your own, and perhaps between your fantasies and his expectations. Brides may need to remind themselves that the idea of "my perfect wedding" is impossibly romantic, and can be a surefire cause of stress

---

A Sophisticated Wedding

Marcia is a lovely young woman, a first-time bride marrying a man who had also never been married. She is a computer programmer of somewhat modest means who began planning her wedding knowing that "I can afford pizza for 200 or elegant food for about 75." While struggling to describe the feeling she wanted at her wedding, she came up with a name: Lauren Bacall. In other words, Marcia wanted a somewhat cool, sophisticated wedding, the kind she believed the actress might actually have planned for herself.

Keeping Bacall in mind throughout the planning was helpful. She stayed within her budget of $8,000 for 80 guests by having an elaborate cocktail buffet with both passed hors d'oeuvres and heartier dishes on tables. She rented two rooms of a simply and elegantly decorated suburban mansion with huge, high-ceilinged rooms, and a formal English garden. Instead of having an open bar, she served champagne, wine, and a variety of bottled waters.

Marcia wore a simple wedding gown with a draped top and a straight skirt—not a bead or bow in sight. Although she wore a headpiece and veil, she removed both at the reception. Her invitation was classical and elegant, although she purchased it through one of the less costly sample books. On it she specified "adults only."

As guests entered the church, organ music played. Later, at the reception, a string quartet played as guests entered, and continued playing during the reception. Marcia was not enthusiastic when her brother offered to sing an original song he planned to write for the wedding. But he sang and played the guitar, and it was the high point of the afternoon. Marcia later said it was witty and amusing and lighthearted, and she was glad she'd taken the risk. She laughed with slight self-mockery when she said, "Lauren Bacall would have loved my wedding."

---

and conflict if they are working with someone, a mother or florist or bandleader, for example, whose fantasy is different but just as powerful as their own.

Wedding vendors want your business. They may want to do things their way. You're willing to listen, but you need to tell them what you have in mind. They may speak in shorthand because of their familiarity with the subject. You are just learning the language. (And those who won't listen at all, who want to tell you how they always do weddings, don't deserve your business.)

How do you select the right vendors? As involved in the planning as you may be, you cannot run your own wedding day and should strive to hire servicepeople you trust and feel comfortable working with. Make sure that you not only trust their abilities, but that you like them. Although your caterer and florist don't have to become your new best friends, they're often professional women and men who will take a personal interest in your marriage celebration. Be sure they are people you'd feel at ease having with you on your wedding day. If you feel comfortable, ask the photographer how obvious he or she will be during the ceremony, where cameras will be set up, etc.

Style counts, too. A favorite photographer who shoots fashion and does an occasional wedding always wears funky Italian suits. Not everyone is comfortable with his urban, avant-garde look. You might prefer someone in more conventional black tie or a simple dark suit.

Parents may also have an internal wedding image, even though they've never articulated it, that is very clear and specific. They may tell you, down to the last item on the sweet table (dessert buffet), how everything should be. You may have other ideas.

For some grownup couples planning a wedding, parents are incredibly helpful. "I couldn't have done it without my mother," brides say over and over again. Samantha Appel tells how her mother did almost everything. "Our phone bills were extraordinary, but she enjoyed doing it, and I loved having her help. I came home a few days before the wedding and everything was done."

For other brides, mother-daughter conflicts become a painful source of frustration. You may need to remind yourself of your parents' emotional investment in the occasion. Weddings are revealing public occasions that tell the world about your taste, style, and financial status. Although few of us are immune to such pressures, weddings should not be held to demonstrate wealth.

The nature of the mother- and father-daughter bond will have made itself felt long before the wedding. Brides who are comfortable asking their mothers for advice will do the same now. Fathers who were always involved in their daughters' lives, whether that meant paying expenses through the years or keeping up with child support payments, will usually do what they have always done. But if the opposite is true, don't expect patterns to change.

The Best Thing About Our Wedding

"It was fun. We took out all the things that would have inhibited fun, such as parents' opinions and their power over us, and it was really, genuinely fun."

Sonya Reeves, 42, second-time bride.

COUPLES WHO WORK TOGETHER

If you and your bridegroom are planning your wedding as a couple, this will undoubtedly be the most complex project you have ever undertaken. One couple who had lived together and renovated a house said that planning their wedding, with the help of both families, was far more stressful than acting as their own contractors throughout the entire process of renovating their three-bedroom house.

Words of wisdom: Try to please each other. But don't be a martyr. Please yourself, too. Talk things over. Compromise. Be clear about what you want. Explain feelings patiently. Be kind. Forgive and forget.

I'm convinced that how couples handle wedding planning reflects how they will, or will not, live happily ever after. The woman who takes over all the details is probably admitting she'll be in charge of their domestic life. Some couples split the preliminary list of tasks right down the middle. If you are both working and busy, that makes sense. But keep in mind that the person who delegates must be happy with the choices the other person makes. Remember, too, that, with a few exceptions, bridegrooms are almost never as interested in as many of the details of the wedding as brides. On the other hand, I know many bridegrooms who liked being involved and wouldn't have done it any other way. The trend is definitely toward couples sharing the work.

REINVENTING THE FANTASY

There is no question that narrowing down choices is an excellent method of stress reduction. Choosing a style can free you from being the prisoner of others' pressures. Let's call this reinventing the fantasy. The woman who always wanted to be a May bride, and who envisions herself in the church she's attended since she was a child followed by a reception at her parents' country club, may be way ahead of the game if she decides to go ahead and carry out her lifetime fantasy.

But not all women either have such a dream or want to live with the fantasy they have. Brides today don't spring fully formed out of the ruffly, pink back bedroom of their parents' homes. They are often well

The Best Thing About Our Wedding

"We were married in one of the Ringling Brothers mansions in Sarasota because my parents live in Florida. It overlooked the Bay of Sarasota and was beautiful. We used three rooms and there was a lot of movement from room to room which kept people interested. We had 175 guests and that was just enough. We got around to talk to everyone, and it felt like a glamorous party. We hired a big band and chose a 1920s theme. I wore a perfectly simple flapper-style dress. In real life I like Armani, Calvin Klein, Go Silk clothes, and I wanted something similar. I did wear a long veil, which I also loved. I guess if there were one word to describe my memories, it would be glamor."

Nina Sanders, 24, first-time bride.

A Sexy Wedding

Jennifer wanted a "sexy" wedding, which not everyone understood. Even Jennifer didn't know exactly what she meant, although she had an instinct that her wedding could be both glamorous and sensuous.

She chose a beautiful downtown church for the early evening ceremony and a large space at the top of a downtown skyscraper, known for its excellent restaurant, as the reception site. The room's view was spectacular. At night the soft candlelight dramatically set off the lights from nearby tall buildings. The interior had cozy banquettes around the edge covered in plush navy-blue velvet.

Jennifer's dress was the kind only someone with her confidence and bearing could wear: a long slim gown topped by a full, beaded satin overskirt. At the church, Jennifer looked as demure as a debutante, albeit a sophisticated one. But when she literally stepped into the spotlight at the reception with her tall, handsome bridegroom, she looked glamorous. The overskirt had been removed, along with the gown's sleeves, the veil, and the long, white gloves she had worn for the ceremony. Jennifer held the bouquet at her side as an accessory and she wore a cluster of large, white flowers at the nape of her neck, which complemented her hair, now arranged in a classic French twist. She took everyone's breath away.

Jennifer proceeded to lead her guests in a set of dancing between each course of the dramatic, sophisticated dinner menu, a style of party this crowd had never seen. Jennifer and her bridegroom were good dancers. They were comfortable in the limelight.

Not everyone would have felt at ease in this setting. Some of Jennifer's mother's friends thought the wedding was in terrible taste. But Jennifer, at 29, is a successful cosmetics company executive and sometime model, and she thought it was her one day in the spotlight and didn't care what anyone else thought. Her husband, ten years older than Jennifer, is a successful American businessman who had lived in Paris for many years. He had been married before and he seemed slightly amused by his bride's choices. He loved the glamour, he said, adding that this was all very different from the simple, family-oriented French weddings he had grown accustomed to.

In private, Jennifer admitted to a few twinges of insecurity, to being unsure she could pull off her fantasy, and she asked several friends and her wedding consultant for advice and support on many decisions. But the day of her wedding, she looked as confident as a seasoned performer. Her natural theatricality found an outlet in her wedding.

traveled and have sophisticated ideas. Their notion of a typical wedding may have been replaced by a vacation experience where the bride and her fiancé sat on a terrace in the south of France and ate delicious food and drank superb local wine while in the company of laughing, happy people.

Sandra Carroll, a onetime San Francisco caterer who grew up in London, says, "I love American weddings. There are fewer stuffy people. They think, 'What is this marriage about? Joy? Family? Indoors or out?' They think about what makes them happiest and tell me they'd really like to have the wedding in Italy, outside, with dancing on the terrace. That's the vision. Now how can they have it in San Francisco on this budget? I love working with clients like that."

For some brides, having the entire world to choose from can be a problem. For the indecisive, wedding choices are made more complicated by the absence of rules. A friend in her seventies tells me that when she was a girl, weddings were simpler, and she thinks we may have lost something since then. "Everyone went from the church to the wedding breakfast and ate creamed chicken on toast," she says. "We thought it was grand. Petit fours and a silver coffee and tea service, that was elegance."

She says she will never forget how her wedding in New York in 1948 shocked her parents. They'd never seen so much shrimp in their lives, and a chef carving roast beef from a silver cart. Such extravagance! "I had changed and the traditional wedding breakfast no longer seemed so elegant. But what I can't stand is the weddings that are like theater productions. I'm invited not as a friend, but to be part of the audience. Things have gone too far."

CHAPTER TWO

Developing an Overview

You can have any kind of wedding you want. All it takes is forethought, planning, and the financial wherewithal to pay for your choices. Having an image that can be translated into an overview is as important as having a fat savings account or generous parents. Those who take time to conceive their ideal wedding before they make choices will have an easier time planning their marriage ceremonies and celebrations. The bride who knows and accepts her own personality will also have an easier time planning her wedding. "I knew I had to be in charge," many women say, not sounding a bit apologetic. "Therefore I did things, even when they were more time-consuming, that helped me maintain control." Another bride confided, "I know we're paying more at the University Club, but I trust the manager and know everything will be beautiful. And I won't have to worry or get very involved. I want to be the bride who sits down once, goes over the menu, and never thinks about it until the day of my wedding."

The reality of making wedding decisions, however, is that having so few rules and so many choices can be overwhelming. For example, I know a bride who began her wedding plans thinking she wanted an elegant, old-fashioned, somewhat cool feeling at her reception, and hired a string quartet. Later, she wished she had chosen music that was more exuberant and contemporary. But the site she had selected was inappropriate for dancing.

So before you even begin seeing sites or selecting a gown or other wedding goods, a good question to ask might be this: If I gave a beautiful party, where cost was relevant but the beauty of the celebration was even more important, what would I want? Only when the image—the feeling and atmosphere and type of wedding you really want—is in place should the first decisions be approached.

Marian did have a clear picture of her wedding before she began to make decisions. Unfortunately, she later decided it was a tired image that didn't feel right for who she was. This 32-year-old first-time bride ordered a traditional white wedding gown, low-cut with huge sleeves, a hundred tiny buttons down the back, and a long train to sweep after her as she walked down the aisle. The silk gown, heavily beaded on beautiful appliqued Alencon lace, was expensive and beautifully traditional. Instead of a veil, Marian chose a wide-brimmed hat. Originally, she envisioned a wedding in a formal garden, although she ended up being married in a hotel ballroom.

Two weeks before the wedding, Marian went into a state of panic, fearing she was too big, too old, too *something* to carry off her chosen image. "I'll look ridiculous. People will fall over laughing when I walk down the aisle." The part of her that had reached back into girlhood for the picture of herself as a Scarlett O'Hara bride was in conflict with the sharp-eyed businesswoman she is today. She survived her panic, stuck to her guns, and felt glamorous in her dress and hat. "I reminded myself that when you put on a wedding gown, you're wearing a costume," she said.

Marian later heard about a friend who bought a long, strapless white chiffon gown off the rack in the evening wear department of a major downtown store, and found a matching white scarf to drape around her shoulders during the ceremony. She was envious. "Why didn't I think of that?" she asked.

Setting Priorities

Before you begin making specific wedding plans, decide which components and choices on the following list are important to you. This checklist can help a bride or couple decide which elements should be priorities, which others are potential compromises, and which are not worth the time or energy.

- engagement and wedding rings that are distinctive and inscribed with a memorable message
- a glamorous wedding gown, with a twelve-foot train and a romantic veil, or something equally beautiful, but far less traditional

- a space for the wedding ceremony that is tied to family roots, ethnic or religious heritage, or the roots the couple will create
- wedding vows that express deeply spiritual or religious feelings, or vows that are unusual, reflect the couple's identities and personalities, or are suggestive of their culture, heritage, and family ties
- ceremony music that is contemplative and inspiring or exuberant and festive
- participation in the wedding ceremony by friends or family, or a ceremony with few participants
- wedding rituals such as the processional, or an absence of rituals in order to eliminate sentimentality
- a special space for the reception or celebration
- ambience: daytime or evening, dancing or conversation, indoors or out
- design and decor of ceremony and / or reception space
- style of reception music, whether for background or for dancing
- an abundance of champagne, wine, mineral water, or a selection of international beer
- an open bar to increase conviviality
- formal portraits or candid shots at the wedding and reception
- delicious, memorable food
- a beautiful wedding cake that also tastes great
- expressive, sentimental toasts by friends and family
- a warm, exuberant party with three generations dancing together or a cooler atmosphere with no children allowed

When we passed out this priority checklist, we told brides and couples to think also about the time involved in arranging each of these components. We encouraged them to identify the elements they simply loved, those that made their hearts beat faster. But we also cautioned against using this as a checklist for the wedding, saying that if they allowed themselves to obsess over making every detail perfect, they would not enjoy their own weddings.

First-stage decisions will establish the style and feeling of your wedding. Once they are made, an appropriate gown can be bought. Then, musicians can be hired, flowers can be ordered, and the details that make a wedding come alive can be put in place. Think of the first decisions as the foundation for every other decision. If you built a house, you would have your plans clear before you hired and instructed the carpenters or bought the mantelpiece or kitchen cabinets.

The guestlist. This determines the size and scale of the wedding. Whether the guestlist is predominantly the bridal couple's own friends, colleagues, and family or also includes extended family and parents' friends may be a major decision.

Site for wedding ceremony and celebration. Where your parents live, or in your new home city. City or country. Country club or art gallery. This is a major influence on the feeling and atmosphere at your wedding. Your guestlist may also be influenced by this choice, as will costs, and who pays. Parents, after all, may be more willing to pay or help pay for a wedding if it's being held in their area. As for the specific site, keep in mind that during the most popular wedding months, many ballrooms and halls are booked months, even a year, in advance. Also consider whether you want the ceremony and celebration to be held in separate locations or in one space and how this will influence your wedding. Remember too, the choice of food and beverage service may be locked into the wedding site.

The preliminary wedding budget. This is an approximation of how much you intend to spend on the entire wedding, as well as who will pay for what. Because food and beverage costs, with service, usually account for 50 to 60 percent of a wedding's total cost, you may want to start by getting a few preliminary estimates. Most hotels, catering halls, and caterers have wedding food service ideas and menus with prices.

The officiant. The individual who performs your wedding ceremony will often have his or her own ideas about the service. Since most weddings are held in churches, temples, or other houses of worship, the officiant is part of the choice of ceremony site. Many such sites are booked well in advance – a year is not uncommon. In other cases, where you prefer to hold the ceremony and reception in the same space, an officiant must be found who will conduct the kind of marriage service you want, and in the space you have chosen.

Time of year and time of day. This may be influenced by the clergyman or other officiant who will conduct the ceremony, which in turn will influence the kind of celebration you have. You also may have an idea firmly in mind: an evening dinner dance, an afternoon cocktail reception immediately following the service, a midday service and afternoon party, or a late morning ceremony and brief reception. Generally speaking, the earlier in the day, the shorter the party will be and thus the lower the cost.

THE GUESTLIST

The Best Thing About Our Wedding

"We both have a lot of creative people as friends, so instead of putting out the guest book before the ceremony, I had my godmother go around to tables and get everyone to write or draw in it. She has a lot of charm, and she waited at every table while people took their time. My famous writer friend started on the first page, and everyone took their cues from him. Some people wrote messages and others wrote silly stuff. There are also a couple of original drawings and cartoons. That book is priceless to us."

Maxine Woo, 34, second-time bride.

Guests help define a celebration. To start the process, bridal couples might get an estimated guestlist from both sides of the family, emphasizing that they haven't made up their minds but are thinking of several different kinds of weddings, ranging from big and exuberant to smaller and more personal. On the other hand, in order to establish control from the start, and if they have a clear image of who they want with them to celebrate their marriage, couples may prefer to set the number of guests and give a specific number to both sets of parents.

When developing a wedding guestlist, remember that all costs are figured per person. Additional guests may mean not just an additional cost for food and beverages, but more service, additional flowers and decor, a bigger musical group, and the longer use of a photographer.

Do you welcome the idea of your own and your bridegroom's parents' friends and of every aunt, uncle, and cousin from both sides of the families helping you celebrate? This traditional family wedding is what you may choose if you, your bridegroom, or either set of parents are members of a strong family, ethnic or religious community and want to stress continuity.

When couples marry, they may not have a clear picture of the kind of community within which they will be living. Parents, on the other hand, may have a fervent hope that sons and daughters will continue to be part of the religious or ethnic or professional community they were raised in, and thus encourage a traditional wedding in the mold that community knows and understands. This occurs most often among people who take special pride in their cultural heritage and prefer to resist assimilation into the American mainstream. At these weddings, parents introduce their daughter and son to their extended family of business and social friends.

One wedding that united two successful orthodox Jewish families brought over 600 guests, 300 each from the bride's and bridegroom's families and circles of friends, to one of the biggest ballrooms in downtown Chicago. The occasion was uncommon enough to be a topic of conversation. Although far from personal, it served the purpose of being a community event attended by everyone who knew both families. In today's social climate, it is not as common as it once was for brides and bridegrooms to find mates who share an attitude about the importance of belonging to the same ethnic and religious group. Even when both bride and bridegroom are Catholic or Protestant or Jewish, the question is, do they both come from close families who view friends and colleagues as part of an extended kinship network?

It is not just the less assimilated ethnic groups that encourage such weddings. The oldest American families, the patrician Anglo-Saxon Protestants with their clearly defined patterns of behavior, also have large, lavish weddings and for the same reasons. In the same way that debutante balls once introduced young people to "society," meaning to each other, such weddings introduce couples to their culture.

On the other hand, this kind of wedding can give some brides and bridegrooms, especially older brides and bridegrooms, or those who now live in cities and communities far from where they were raised, distinct feelings of discomfort. Many will resist the idea of a huge wedding that satisfies the community but bypasses their own needs. These couples may want a smaller, more intimate style of wedding.

Even those brides and bridegrooms who like big, extended-family weddings may envision celebrating marriage very differently, with 50 to 100 of their own friends and colleagues along with a few members of both families. Many weddings, of course, incorporate both ideas and are modified versions of the two distinct types of celebrations.

When thinking about a wedding guestlist, think in tiers. First, there are your immediate families of parents, siblings, grandparents, your own children. Next are members of your extended family such as aunts and uncles, cousins, nieces and nephews (if children are invited). Parents' close friends and neighbors form another tier. Their colleagues, employees, and employers are yet another tier. Your own friends are also grouped by the closeness of their relationship to you and by number: childhood friends with whom you are still in contact, high-school and college friends, social friends from a membership in an organization, volunteer group, or social club, and friends from work.

Generally speaking, if some aunts and uncles are invited, all should probably be on the guestlist. If some friends from work or your social life are included, for example, think of inviting everyone in a certain category, such as all the salespeople in your group, or all four executive assistants in the department, or all your pals from the small ski club you travel with every year. If the guestlist is very limited, you may want to tell one uninvited guest in such a group that you are having a small wedding and ask him or her to explain to anyone who might ask. Obviously, this is done to avoid hurt feelings and to prevent anyone from feeling excluded.

Beware of Bar Size and Bartender Service

When shopping for a wedding reception site, be especially conscious of the size of the bar, since the smaller the bar and the fewer the bartenders, the longer the line of guests waiting to be served. The result can be a logjam of thirsty, impatient guests. To avoid this, serve champagne and wine from trays to those waiting, or serve guests as they enter the reception. This also has an effect on cost: about two-thirds of those who accept a glass of champagne or wine won't bother to switch to mixed drinks.

If butler service is offered, say at a major hotel, this should not be a problem, since waiters take orders for mixed drinks. But be aware that serving more than 200 guests at the same time, especially if the staff is also doing a changeover in the main ballroom, may result in a short wait for drinks and hors d'oeuvres.

One bride included a fairly sizable group of family friends on her guestlist, two generations of neighbors who owned homes near her parents' lake house. She had grown up building sandcastles with this group and said she wanted them with her for this milestone. At the reception, group photographs were taken and sent as Christmas cards to these special friends.

SITE FOR CEREMONY AND RECEPTION

At the same time you're thinking about the guests you want at your wedding, think about whether you would prefer to be married in your home town or new home city. Would you like to be married in the countryside or in a sophisticated, urban environment or somewhere in between? Do you envision being married in a church or temple and going somewhere else for the reception? Or would you prefer to have the entire wedding in one place? All of these choices will strongly influence the feeling at your wedding, as well as its cost and who will pay for it. Parents may be more willing to pay for some part or even all of your wedding if it's being held where they live and they take part in the choices. Then too, the site, more than any other single choice, will determine the tone and attitude of your wedding.

There has never been a wider selection to choose from.

- your own home or apartment, or that of a family member or friend
- sumptuous private mansions
- gracious country clubs
- city-, county-, or town-maintained parks and clubhouses
- well-decorated catering halls known for excellent food
- high-ceilinged, elegant hotel ballrooms or smaller hotel spaces
- trendy restaurants
- backyard tents
- sophisticated gallery spaces and arts clubs
- country inns and small-town hotels and restaurants

Think also about whether you have access to a party room in a high-rise building or condo development, which can be decorated beautifully and may have an attractive view. Other spaces are suitable for parties: museums, atrium building lobbies (preferably with bathrooms and food service facilities nearby), outdoor dining halls and hilltops and meadows. And as one bride described it, under the perfect,

Going Home for the Wedding

Toni Manita, age 32, had lived in New York for nearly a decade. When she met a man from her hometown while they were both living in New York City, and they decided to be married, it was a pleasant surprise for both of their families in Cincinnati, Ohio. The families did not know each other, but they had ties nevertheless. The mothers had gone to the same high school, and they had friends in common. So Toni and her fiance had a choice: they could be married in New York and bring family and old friends to be with them, or they could go home for their wedding.

"When we started planning," Toni said, "I realized that if I got married in New York, I'd have to scout the church and reception site myself. I'd have to set up hotel reservations and transportation for guests and find a way to provide sitters for children too young to be at the wedding. On the other hand, we would have more of our new friends and the people we work with at the wedding. If we had it in Ohio I'd get planning and logistical help from my mother. My guests would be people who have known me since I was spitting up on my mother's shoulder. And more members of the family would be there. It would be a family wedding. The drawback was that I wouldn't have many of my friends or colleagues from New York."

They decided on the family wedding in Ohio, and it was a wonderful, warm occasion. Toni is now worried about managing the wedding party she and her new husband want to have for their New York friends. "I wish my mother were here to help," she says.

The Old Family Church

Janice is a Methodist who says that being married in her childhood church, where she is still a member, was one of the best things about her wedding. "I'd gone there all my life, and walking down that long aisle had special meaning to me. I love the choir, and got them to sing at my wedding. When they marched in singing we were up at the altar and it was incredibly beautiful. The pastor is an old family friend and someone very dear to me. I had to go home for my wedding even though it meant that a lot of our new friends couldn't be there with us. When I think of it, to this day it gives me chills. It didn't hold the same meaning for my husband, but I couldn't have been married anywhere else."

The Best Thing About Our Wedding

"We were married in upstate New York, at the home of friends in a really beautiful meadow where we set out Oriental rugs and quilts in a huge circle for people to sit on. Being married a three-hour drive out of the city meant that only the people who really cared about us made the trip. I knew that would be the case and so the guestlist self-selected itself."

Cathy Oberlin, 30, first-time bride.

What I Would Change About Our Wedding

"Once we decided to get married, we gave ourselves a month to plan everything and we invited 40 friends. I wish we'd invited more guests, rather than limiting our guest list. About 80 would have been perfect."

Betsy Miller, 34, first-time bride.

Wide Open Spaces

The size of the crowd attending the ceremony in your church or temple really shouldn't matter. But if you're afraid your small wedding will be dwarfed in the huge cathedral or vast temple of your choice, consider being married in the chapel, or in the choir space if it's up front and flanks the altar. Or instruct ushers to guide guests to the outside four to eight seats in as many pews or rows of seating as you specify, grouping family members and closest friends in the first few rows.

Even if the space feels empty, most brides and couples say that how this looks is not as important as their feelings about being married in a special place.

sacred grove of oak trees that she knows exists only in her dreams.

Weddings in hotels and private clubs with full catering services are unquestionably the easiest to plan. Tent and mansion weddings can have an extravagant feeling, given the right menu, food service, and florist or designer. The drawback of large spaces is that they can also feel the least intimate.

Remember that the range of styles between a small intimate space and a grand elaborate one is vast. Small spaces can be high-ceilinged with gilt pillars. Ballrooms can be large or small and simply designed, without a bit of gilt or a single beaux arts design element, or they can be as elaborate as a Middle Eastern bazaar. Until spaces are seen, it's hard to imagine the number of wedding sites available and their stylistic range, from the elegant to the casually informal, the polished to the rustic, from spaces that encourage exuberance to those that seem to foster a more restrained atmosphere.

The Boat Reception Destined for Rough Seas

It was a cool, gray day with gusty winds, and Lake Michigan looked more like the Pacific Ocean than one of the inland Great Lakes. When guests boarded the cruise ship anchored in the lake, they could feel the motion of the boat even in the protected harbor. The boat's captain approached the bride and her entourage and suggested they stay in the harbor for the wedding and reception. The lake was rough, and there might be some "discomfort" among guests. "Would it be safe out on the lake?" the bride wanted to know. "Absolutely," said the captain in his most reassuring voice. He explained that his concerns were more for the comfort of the wedding party and their guests and he added that food service might be a little more complicated given the rolling waves of the lake.

The bride and bridegroom decided they wanted to leave the harbor as planned. The caterer then entered the picture and strongly advised that they not leave the dock, explaining that food service would be much more difficult out on the water. "I didn't want to alarm them, but I was very specific about the potential for problems. They insisted we go out and so I said fine."

The caterer later explained that he would never, under any circumstances, allow that to happen again. "The minister was sick. The bridegroom spent most of the time hanging over the side of the boat, and about 20 or so of the guests were so sick they could hardly stand up. The worst came when we cut the cake. It started to slide, and we caught it, but in pieces. They got pictures before it all came apart, and we managed to serve it, but it looked awful. The one good thing was that they didn't serve much champagne or liquor and I cut their bar bill in half."

Since that time, the caterer adds, boat owners have made specific rules about when boats cannot leave the dock. Decisions are entirely in the hands of the captain, and people who rent the boat are told that this might happen. "Everytime I drive down Lake Shore Drive on a stormy day and see Lake Michigan looking like Victory at Sea, I remember that bridegroom hanging over the side of the boat."

A Small, Intimate Wedding

"I had lived in Chicago for too long to consider going home to Michigan to get married. My job, my friends, and my life are here. Also, I had changed since I left home, and didn't want to embarrass my family by having a wedding they thought was a little pretentious. My cousins are still being married in church with receptions in VFW halls and the church basement, and I didn't want to do that. We had a church wedding and reception in a restaurant. I watched every penny. In that, I am exactly like my mother. But I wanted elegant food and good wine and in that way my standards are no longer the small-town ideas I was raised with."

Mary Ella, 32-year-old first-time bride.

When visiting spaces, here are several factors to keep in mind:

- number of guests you plan to invite
- type of music and its variety of uses (background, listening, dancing)
- food service
- availability of facilities such as kitchens, bars, bathrooms, and usable adjacent spaces such as foyer, anteroom, or garden
- assistance the day of the wedding. (Hotel catering directors run everything, as do the banquet managers at some clubs, halls, and country inns.)
- flow of the event

Think about the sequence of your party. If you plan to have your receiving line at the reception, where is the most comfortable spot for it? If it promises to be long, can champagne or wine be served to guests while they wait in line to congratulate you? Do you want hors d'oeuvres served butler style in an adjacent room, or a buffet served in the main room? Do you want all activities to take place in one room, or should music for dancing be in one space and an adjacent room be reserved for quiet conversation? When you look at sites, make sure that bathroom facilities are adequate. Remember that at outdoor locations and outside some galleries, portable toilets can be erected. Immaculately clean, freshened up, and decorated with flowers, they can be attractive.

The scale and size of the space must be right for the feeling you want to create. Too many guests in a small space can seem uncomfortably crowded, but keep in mind a principle that event planners well know: To feel successful, a party has to have a few too many guests in a slightly undersized space. Nothing feels more adrift than a small group of guests in an oversized room or a few dancers on a huge dance floor.

One highly creative wedding held in the lobby of a contemporary downtown skyscraper worked well. The space was a six-story atrium and, when decorated and divided into a smaller space with folding screens, trees, and a truckload of plants, it looked dazzling. The plants were masses of colorful mums, and thus relatively inexpensive. The bride and bridegroom had twenty plants delivered to their home for planting, and the florist returned the rest to her shop, so only labor and rental costs were paid.

Lunch was served in a restaurant adjacent to the lobby and musicians played under an area with a dropped ceiling to absorb sound and avoid echoes in the hard-edged space. The wedding was beautiful in its unique surroundings, since lobbies in commercial buildings are built as sacred spaces, just as cathedrals were during the Renaissance. Many of these spaces are designed with painstaking care and use unusual and costly building materials in their construction.

Entering that glass and steel space to the sound of a taped Dean Martin singing "That's Amore" was breathtaking. "When the moon hits your eye like a big pizza pie" are the song's opening words, and guests were greeted with champagne and pieces of thin-crust, elegant, California-style pizza. Not everyone made the connection, but those who did got a good laugh and began to pay careful attention to the party's details, which included tiny figures of brides and bridegrooms all over the cake, in various positions that Aunt Fanny might not have approved.

Because the florist liked the bridal couple so much, she had taken pains to hang a big, foil-covered moon from one of the rafters. Although the couple didn't have to worry about paying for their wedding, money can't buy that sense of creativity and humor.

THE PRELIMINARY WEDDING BUDGET

Before establishing a wedding budget, brides and bridegrooms will want to think about who is paying for the wedding and, if appropriate, who is paying for which components.

First of all, be aware that the old rule, where the bride's parents paid for everything but the rings, the honeymoon, and the groom's dinner, is no longer rigidly followed. A traditional bride's family who can afford it may pay for the entire wedding. But American culture, more than others, is constantly evolving, and nowhere is change seen as clearly as in the constantly altering rules about who pays for which parts of the wedding. It's safe to say that unless your family is paying for everything and you are from a traditional culture and a family that knows and follows that community's rules to the letter, there will be no firm guidelines for you to follow.

If the bride and her fiance have lived together and supported themselves for years away from home, they may feel awkward expecting parents to pay for everything or, indeed, for anything at all. Many couples today do not take a penny of wedding funds from parents, especially if they're being married away from their home city. And second marriages can be a delicate subject if parents paid for a first wedding.

On the other hand, before making the decision to be completely independent, consider two factors: the probable cost of the wedding and parents' willingness and ability to help financially. It can be foolish not to accept assistance if it's needed, possibly as a gift. Even older brides and bridegrooms who have been self-supporting often accept funds their parents have earmarked for their weddings.

Let's assume, for the sake of discussion, that the bride and bridegroom must carefully consider costs and are hoping parents will offer to help pay for the wedding. Bridegrooms' families often underwrite an element of the wedding such as the band or flowers, or a photographer or videographer, or an open bar at the reception. They might offer to pay for their own guestlist.

Floating trial balloons might be more appropriate than asking whether they would consider sharing costs. Finances are delicate matters and families must be treated with both tact and dignity when it comes to wedding expenses. The best person to talk to parents may be their own son or daughter, although to avoid conflict, acting as a couple might be more appropriate. Think about the range of possibilities ahead of time and be sure you are in agreement as a couple. The bride's mother sometimes handles the negotiation of such matters, but occasionally the bride's and the bridegroom's fathers will meet or have a phone conversation and work out details. Two middle-class families may acknowledge that it is difficult for the bride's family to pay for every phase of the wedding, and the bridegroom's family may therefore offer to pick up some of the costs.

This entire notion, of course, might be unimportant if you're paying for your own wedding or if money is no object. But bear in mind that money and who pays for what almost always matter, even to the most affluent.

How Wedding Budgets Work

Here's how wedding budgets work: All costs in the final breakdown are figured per person. Thus, a $10,000 wedding for 100 costs about $100 per person. A $40,000 wedding for 400 would have approximately the same cost breakdown, that is, $100 per person.

The wedding gown and honeymoon are single costs and will not change according to the number of guests at the wedding. Some brides like to keep the cost of the gown and veil out of their budgets, thinking of them more as a personal (and private) cost. Bridegrooms who pay for the honeymoon may feel the same way about it.

The clergy member's fee, as well as that of the sexton, organist, other church musicians, and soloists, will also be finite costs. But the cost of flowers, linens, and decor grows with the guestlist, just as the amount of food and beverages increases with the number of guests.

Individual chapters in *Weddings for Grownups* are devoted to each wedding component, and savings techniques are described in each of these categories. But even before major decisions are made, recognize how wedding costs can be seen as percentages of the total amount spent. All percentages are approximate.

Food and beverage	50-60 percent

If you rent a place where you can bring in your own caterer, you'll pay for these areas: food (includes labor of preparation), liquor, service (waitstaff, bartenders, supervisor), equipment (glassware, dishes, linens, and other rentals).

Flowers	8-12 percent
Music	12-18 percent
Photography and videography	20-30 percent
Miscellaneous	10-15 percent

Miscellaneous costs can include wedding stationery such as invitations and postage, calligraphy, marriage license, officiant's fees, blood tests, gratuities on the wedding day, etc.

Expenses at the lower end of the price range add up to 100 percent. The higher percentages take into account a special interest. Those who spend a disproportionate amount of their wedding budget on an unusually good band or a symphonic-quality string quartet may want to economize in another area. One bride planned to spend $8,000 on her wedding, but fell in love with the process of choosing flowers and spent over $1,500 on fresh flowers and flowering plants (about 20 percent) that she later used at home and in the garden.

However the subject is handled, it is increasingly common for families to share wedding costs. We know of one wedding where the bride's mother casually asked the bridegroom's father, a successful architect but not a rich man, if he would pay for the wedding band. He consented without asking the cost, and when he found out that the band the bride and her mother had chosen cost over $10,000, he was angry. That amount represented the cost of an entire wedding to his family. He paid what he had agreed to pay, but he felt taken advantage of, and the relationship between the two families will never be warm. Needless to say, these families hold remarkably dissimilar attitudes about both money and weddings.

When a lavish wedding is important to the bridegroom's family, it is not uncommon for them to offer to pay for the entire occasion. In several instances where this was the case, the weddings went off without a hitch. But in one such situation, the bride never forgave her inlaws for insisting on paying for everything. This embarrassed her and her family, and made her feel like an outsider at her own wedding. She and her bridegroom would have been just as happy with the more modest celebration her parents could have afforded.

The potential for difficulty increases when there is a vast difference in social and financial stature between the bride's and bridegroom's families, and when the subject of financial ability becomes a source of embarrassment. His family may hate the taste level of the bride's family and what they can afford. Or her family thinks his family has more money than brains and resists doing what they want. There are about as many ways to be tactless about money as there are families, and we have heard some horror stories. However the subject is handled, it ought to allow both families to be dignified as well as candid about what they can or cannot afford.

The guideline to keep firmly in mind is that the couple must communicate clearly with each other for the rest of their lives, if their marriage is to succeed, and that there is no place for secrets or a sense of shame or embarrassment surrounding the financial underpinnings of the event that sets the marriage in motion. In order to prevent problems, one bride explained, "We decided to avoid all the fuss and take a flat amount from both families for the wedding, and supplemented it with our own savings."

Who Pays for What—a Historical Perspective

Etiquette is an ever-changing set of rules that can be useful in deciphering difficult situations. The negative side is that these rules sometimes ignore simple common sense. They also change through the years, as shown by these rules on who pays for which parts of the wedding.

In 1904, in *Good Manners for All Occasions,* author Margaret E. Sangster wrote: "The bridegroom's part in the expenses of the wedding day is limited to the clergyman's fee, the bride's flowers, and the carriage which bears him and his bride away. Every other expense is assumed by the family of the bride."

In postwar 1947 *Wedding Etiquette Complete,* by Marguerite Bentley, all that had changed: "The list of groom's wedding expenses includes the bachelor dinner, wedding ring, gift to the bride, bridal bouquet, mothers' corsages, boutonnieres, bride's going-away corsage, bridesmaids' bouquets, groomsmen's gifts, groomsmen's neckties, groomsmen's gloves, license fee, clergyman's fee, honeymoon."

"The bride's family," Bentley adds, "will carry the greater financial burden of the wedding and will pay all other expenses."

The 1964 *Emily Post's Etiquette* listed these bridegroom's expenses.

- The engagement ring—as handsome as he can afford.
- A wedding present to the bride—jewelry if he is able, always something for her to keep forever.
- His bachelor dinner—if he gives one.
- The bride's bouquet where local custom requires it, and in any case, a corsage for her to wear when they go away.
- The marriage license.
- A personal gift to his best man and to each of his ushers, and their hotel expenses unless they are invited to stay with neighbors or friends.

- Even if the entire outfit is rented, he gives his best man and each usher his wedding tie, collar, and gloves.
- He provides each of the above with a boutonniere, as well as his own and that of his father.
- The wedding ring.
- The clergyman's fee.
- From the moment the bride and groom start off on their wedding trip, all the expenditure becomes his.

Emily Post is equally explicit about the bride's family's expenses.

- The invitations to ceremony and reception, and the announcements.
- The services of a professional secretary. This expense may be omitted if the work is done by members or friends of the family.
- The service of a bridal consultant, if desired.
- The trousseau of the bride, consisting not only of her clothing but of her household linen as well.
- Floral decorations for church and reception, bouquets for the bride and bridesmaids, corsages for the bride's mother and grandmother, and a boutonniere for the father of the bride.
- Choir, soloists, and organist at church, and the fee to the sexton.
- Orchestra at reception.
- Automobiles for the bridal party from the house to the church and from there to the reception.
- The refreshments, whether the most elaborate sit-down meal or the simplest afternoon tea.
- The wedding cake and possibly boxes of cake (usually fruitcake) to be given to the guests.
- Champagne and / or other beverages.
- The bride's presents to her bridesmaids.
- Hotel accommodations for bride's attendants if they cannot stay with relatives, friends, or neighbors.
- A wedding present to the bride, often her flat silver or "good" china.
- Photographs taken of the bride in her wedding dress and candid pictures taken the day of the wedding. If a bridesmaid or usher or guest wishes to have a wedding photograph, she or he may properly order and *pay for* [Post's emphasis] a print from the photographer.
- Awnings, tent for outdoor reception, and carpet for church aisle if desired.
- The bride herself gives a wedding present or a wedding ring, or both, to the groom, if she wants to.

Before accepting wedding funds, recognize that whoever pays may feel entitled to help in the planning process or believe they have the right to influence decisions. Therefore, consider if an offer to pay will mean an attempt to influence your choices.

If you and your mother, or even future mother-in-law, have the same taste and style, it's probably fine to accept her offer of help, assuming you're willing to negotiate for what is important to you and to compromise on areas of lesser importance. Of course, even when parents pay for every last petit four, they may go out of their way to do what pleases both bride and bridegroom.

The Cost of an Average Wedding

According to a *Bride's Magazine* 1991 poll of readers, "Love and Marriage in the 1990's," the cost of an average wedding was over $16,000, which includes all ceremony and reception costs for an average of 202 guests.

In 1986, the average age of all brides (first and multiple marriages combined) was 28.6, of grooms 31.2. In 1990 the median age of first-time brides was 23.9 and of bridegrooms 26.1.

Practically all, 94 percent, of the respondents to the survey had formal weddings and 87 percent were performed in a church, synagogue, or chapel. Saturday (84 percent) was by far the most popular day of the week for weddings. More ceremonies took place in the afternoon (62 percent) than in the evening (26 percent) or morning (12 percent). The average number of attendants, in addition to the male and female honor attendants, was four bridesmaids and four groomsmen or ushers. Nearly 60 percent had children in the wedding party, and of that percentage, 23 percent had girls only, 13 percent boys only, and 64 percent both.

The average amount *Bride's Magazine* readers spent on honeymoons was $3,200, and 99 percent took a honeymoon with the average length of nine days.

THE OFFICIANT

One of the first contacts to make in planning a wedding may be with the person you hope will officiate at your wedding. If you are a lifetime member of a small church, this will not present a problem. But if you're living in a new city or are not a member of any religious congregation, or if you hope to find a judge or an ecumenically spirited member of the clergy to perform the ceremony, this may take both research and time.

Clergy of all faiths are used to performing marriage rites, and often have their own ideas, customs, and even rules about how the ceremony should be handled. Judges are another category of officiant, and although most are not allowed to be paid to perform weddings, some will accept a donation to a favorite charity in lieu of payment. Unless you or your family knows a judge, don't assume you'll be able to engage one to perform the ceremony. They are in constant demand and often guard their time commitments. Justices of the peace and specially appointed wedding commissioners perform marriage ceremonies in some states, and a few will come to your site.

Keep in mind that religious customs may dictate not just the time of day for the wedding but the time of year. Catholics are discouraged from marrying during Lent. Jews are seldom married around the High Holy Days. And no one is married on Easter or Passover. However, religious rules in general have relaxed over the past decades. Catholics, for example, no longer must be married at a Nuptial High Mass, and most parishes go out of their way to accommodate weddings, handling them with great care and seriousness.

Whether to include mentions of a deity in the ceremony may be a question. Many couples decide, for personal reasons, to forgo the faith of their fathers and mothers and it is important to confront this issue early in the planning stages. Whatever the affiliation of the officiant of choice, remember that there are only four weekends in the most popular wedding months of the year, and many ministers, priests, rabbis, and judges are booked for weddings far in advance. Do not, if this is an important or a sensitive choice, leave this until last.

MIXED-RELIGION MARRIAGES

There is an emphasis on tolerance throughout our culture today, although one still hears of grandparents sitting at a wedding with tears

---

Toasting Goblets

Both the Christian Chalice and the Jewish Kiddush cup are the original inspiration for wedding goblets that are used during the marriage service or reception at both Christian and Jewish weddings, and are then used on important occasions in the couple's life. Kiddush cups are a formal part of most Jewish weddings, and are often intended for use during family religious ceremonies. Wedding goblets can be designed in the taste and style of the bridal couple. Depending on the quality, such goblets can become an instant family heirloom. Toasting goblets may be monogrammed with the couple's initials.

Breakfast, Brunch, Lunch, Tea, Cocktails, or Dinner?

The cost and length of time for the reception are intricately connected, and they vary according to the type of guests you will have at your wedding. A small group of rather quiet people at a simple party leaves sooner than a large group at a wedding that features a series of orchestrated events. That's obvious. Refreshments and the type of service also will influence the length of time for the reception, and the amount of drinks served and food eaten, and thus the relative cost. Champagne and wine can be served for toasts or throughout the celebration at all types of wedding receptions, ranging from late morning to evening.

The *wedding breakfast* is called by this name in some parts of the country, but is really lunch, served immediately after a morning wedding ceremony. Of all weddings, this probably involves the shortest amount of time, from the beginning of the ceremony to the end of the reception.

The *wedding brunch* combines breakfast and lunch foods, and follows a late morning or midday wedding ceremony. This could be a buffet with morning-style beverages (juices and juices with champagne or wine), and is more elegant than breakfast, possibly with a chef making omelets or crepes. For a comparison, ▸

streaming down their faces because of a mixed marriage, or of family members refusing to attend such a wedding. My feeling about such situations is that those who feel very strongly that your marriage is misguided or unthinkable have no business attending if they can't keep their feelings to themselves. In this case, invite friends and those family members who either approve of your match or are tactful enough to behave decently.

In the Catholic church, once known for rigid rules about mixed marriages, not only are other religious ceremonies recognized as legal today, but weddings with one Catholic may now be held in the tradition of the non-Catholic. That is, a Catholic can be married by a rabbi, or by a minister in a church of another denomination.

Each Protestant denomination has its own rules, and within that framework each clergy member has his or her own policy about intermarriage. Call the minister of your choice for a church policy statement on intermarriage, but remember not to accept the cleric's attitude as decisive. The umbrella organization, bishop's group, or national head of the church may have a different opinion. If you want a religious ceremony, a minister who is tolerant on the subject may conduct your marriage ceremony, even though you and your bridegroom are not members of that church or congregation. Unitarian ministers are often willing to conduct mixed-religion marriage ceremonies for those who are not welcome in their own churches.

There is no uniform rule about intermarriage between a Jew and a non-Jew, other than it is strongly discouraged within orthodoxy and is tolerated among reform Jews. Because of the high percentage of such marriages taking place today, there is more tolerance than there once was. A reform rabbi can often be located to perform a mixed ceremony. Some will work with a priest or minister, but will usually insist on being the actual clergy member who pronounces the marriage vows.

Many interfaith marriage ceremonies today are conducted by two clerics. Tolerance rather than competition must be the spirit in order for this to work, because in every case one member of the clergy is the actual officiant who pronounces the vows and takes care of the legalities and paperwork.

In the case of mixed-faith and second marriages, a phone call to the synagogue or church where you and your fiancé are members may be just the beginning. Do not assume you can instantly find someone to perform your mixed-religion wedding ceremony. With luck, and in a big city with more members of the clergy to choose from, this may be true. But if you have few contacts within the religious or judicial community, allow time for what is viewed as a serious and delicate matter.

TIME OF YEAR AND TIME OF DAY

If you've always envisioned yourself as a June bride married at a morning religious service followed by a traditional wedding breakfast right out of Emily Post, which is actually lunch, then that's what you should have. But weddings today take place year-round and at every time of day and evening.

September and October rival May and June as popular wedding months. Thanksgiving weekend, with both Friday and Saturday evenings available for weddings, is a festive time to be married and an equally good time to celebrate an anniversary. Christmas and New Year's are dazzling times for weddings. April, when spring is in the air, is another good wedding month. And weddings during three-day weekend holidays such as Memorial Day, the Fourth of July, and Labor Day convey a relaxed spirit for a gala celebration, possibly held out-of-doors. If you have your heart set on a Valentine's Day wedding, with sentimental flowers and equally romantic sentiments, and if flowers are important to you, talk to a florist since most cannot handle the Valentine's Day rush as well as an event on the busiest day of their year.

You have to be a risk-taker to consider holding a wedding outdoors anytime, or in the snowy, winter months in northern climates. But winter weddings will not be in competition with dozens of other occasions for sites and services, although official, charity-oriented social calendars are busier then. Remember, too, that there are religious restrictions about holding weddings on certain holidays and during some periods of the year.

When thinking about the time of year, also consider colors and which flowers are popular and plentiful during specific seasons. If you dislike bright red poinsettias (as I do), you may not want a Christmas wedding in a church, since the flower is ubiquitous then. August and September, when flowers are at their peak and also less costly to buy, are glorious months for garden weddings. You may not want summery pastels in the coldest seasons of the year, or deep, wintry tones in the summer, but be aware of exceptions. Now that everyone, including attendants, wears black to weddings, black linen can look crisp in the summer, and white can be elegant around winter holidays when everyone expects Christmas razzle-dazzle.

The time of day you choose for your wedding is a key factor in

think of the elegant brunches served in hotels and fine restaurants.

The *wedding lunch* is held after a midday or early afternoon ceremony. Think of light dinner food rather than any kind of lunch menu. Luncheon weddings usually last for two to three hours, including the ceremony.

The *cocktail party reception* follows a late afternoon wedding and is distinguished by a more limited menu than dinner. It might be a buffet with entrees or simply finger food and drinks.

The *wedding tea* follows an afternoon wedding. It might feature typical English tea food (not high tea, which is a light supper) such as sandwiches and desserts, with both coffee and tea.

The *dinner party* is the longest and most expensive wedding reception style and follows a late afternoon or early evening wedding. Guests frequently attend a ceremony that begins between 5 and 7 P.M. and go immediately to the reception, often spending until late evening with the bridal party and guests. Plan on a minimum of four hours from the beginning of the ceremony until the end of the reception.

determining the atmosphere and feeling at the ceremony and celebration. This may be (but is not always) dictated by the hour of the wedding service and the customs of your church or synagogue. This choice,

Boogie All Night Long

The most exuberant dance parties are held after dinner. Daytime dancing is more restrained, probably because people drink less in the daylight and thus retain inhibitions. It's no accident that the liveliest daytime dances are held in ballrooms or other spaces without natural light. A tea dance with light jazz or rock and pop music is relaxed. If you envision a set or two of spirited cut-loose dancing at your wedding, you're probably thinking about a dinner dance, with the lights turned down low.

Hold That Spirit

At one time, and still in some churches, weddings had to be held early in the day. If the choice was to wait until evening for a dinner-dance reception, it was difficult, if not impossible, to retain the excitement and high spirits throughout the day.

The trend now is toward weddings where the reception immediately follows the ceremony. There is nothing more festive than going right from the wedding ceremony to the party with guests you have chosen to help you celebrate. In one Episcopalian wedding, the bridal couple held their receiving line in the aisle of the church and went directly from there to the home reception, and thus never lost the excitement level they had felt at the altar.

Jewish weddings are frequently held in one location, with the ceremony and celebration in the same room. The space is set for the ceremony with chairs in rows, then is reset for the meal service while guests are in a cocktail reception. The changeover, as hotels call it, can be done in less than an hour.

For couples who want to be married in a location that holds special meaning for them, such as the family synagogue or church, cars must be arranged to carry the wedding party from one location to the next. This could be the time for a carriage ride, or for the use of rented vintage cars or a reliable limousine service. One bride hired a violinist ("a fiddler" she called him) and a flutist to lead the entire wedding party and all their guests from the church to the reception site a few blocks away. In its urban setting, this parade stopped onlookers in their tracks and became one of the most memorable parts of the wedding.

in turn, will influence the food service and thus the type of party you choose to celebrate the marriage.

Morning weddings followed by brunch and midday services with lunch after the ceremony are growing in popularity, especially with those couples who say they don't always like spending an entire evening at others weddings and so don't want that kind of wedding themselves. Tea parties and cocktail buffets can be held in the late afternoon or early evening, whereas the dinner dance is always scheduled for a long evening.

As a general rule of thumb, the longer guests are expected to stay, the more permanent and comfortable the seating must be. Today, there are as many exceptions as there are rules, and guests often like to wander at parties, mingle with other guests at other tables, and not stay as close to their tablemates as they would with assigned seating. If there are many guests on the list who won't know other guests, however, you can assume they'll want specific seats. Before deciding on the seating style, analyze the guestlist. And remember, no system will please everyone.

Before settling on a final date, you may want to choose two or even three potential dates as long as a year in advance if you're hoping to book one of your area's most popular ballrooms or wedding sites.

CHAPTER THREE

Wedding Rituals, Traditions, and Symbols

Wedding rituals and traditions range from the slightly ridiculous to the near sacred in their reflection of humanity's age-old need for pageantry to mark significant occasions. Because of massive social changes in our culture, today's brides and bridegrooms often feel that many of the rituals, especially those attached to wedding goods such as the traditional blue garter or silver-plated toasting goblets with the couple's new monogram on them, seem antiquated, silly, or unsophisticated.

Rituals, traditions and symbols that might be sweet and innocent to one bride can appear childish or passe to another. No one wants to take part in ceremonies that seem artificial or strained. I have seen mature, sophisticated brides throw their bouquets to waiting crowds of their laughing, happy women friends. I've also seen women refuse to gather for this tradition, which they thought made them look foolish. This is entirely a matter of individual taste and style. I would never forgo cutting a traditional, multitiered wedding cake and my husband and I gently feeding a piece to each other, because of what it represents. But I would never use matching monogrammed wine goblets for toasts, and I might pass on a traditional processional. You may feel just the opposite.

It's safe to say that every American bride today will alter at least some wedding rituals or relinquish a few of the most recognizable wedding symbols, rather than accept the idea that she must have a ceremony and reception that follows a single, predetermined structure.

THE ORDER OF EVENTS

Before you decide which traditions, rituals, and symbols you like and which you prefer to exclude from your wedding, think of them in two categories: those that are part of the ceremony and those that are attached to the reception. Here is the order of events in traditional wedding ceremonies and receptions that have become ritualized in the Judeo-Christian culture that has shaped our customs. It's wise to remember that individual clergy members often have specific ideas about wedding procedures where they officiate, and may specify a processional and order of service. At the reception, the same is often true, but less compulsory, of band leaders, wedding consultants, and catering managers.

The traditional ceremony

- Guests are ushered to pews or to a less formal arrangement of chairs.
- Wedding music – the prelude – is played.
- Grandparents and other honored guests are ushered down the aisle just before the main part of the processional begins.
- Parents of the bridegroom and the mother of the bride are ushered down the aisle. In Jewish weddings and increasing numbers of Christian weddings, parents are part of the processional, and each set walks down the aisle, one with their daughter, the bride, between them, and the other with their son, the bridegroom.
- After a pause, the music selected for the processional begins.
- The officiant, if he or she is entering alone, enters the sanctuary.
- Attendants take their turns in the processional: bridesmaids and groomsmen first (and usually arranged according to height), honor attendants last so they are close to the bride and bridegroom. Attendants can walk singly or in pairs. If the women walk alone, groomsmen may enter the sanctuary with the bridegroom and officiant. Flower girl(s) and ring bearer(s) immediately precede the bride.
- The bride walks down the aisle, accompanied by her father or between her father and mother.
- Wedding vows are exchanged according to the customs of the couple and the officiant.
- Rings are exchanged, or the bridegroom gives the bride a ring.
- Special wedding prayers, readings, music, or songs are part of the ceremony, with family members or friends participating.
- Accompanied by recessional music, the married couple comes back down the aisle followed by attendants and family members.

Tossing the Bouquet

Tradition says that whoever catches the bride's bouquet will be the next woman to marry. There are as many attitudes about this small ceremony as there are bridesmaids. One contemporary woman in her early thirties says she doesn't take any chances: she bribes all the other women in the crowd at weddings not to compete with her when the bride tosses her bouquet. "I need all the help I can get," she says, making no effort to cover her tracks as she high-jumps for the bouquet. Some brides, of course, cooperate with a sister, friend, or even their divorced mother and make sure the toss goes their way. There are crowds of women too sophisticated for such a ceremony, and brides frequently omit this ritual. But if the bridesmaids want to emulate Michael Jordan high jumps, or friends guarantee to make this fun, it can be a lively wedding ritual, even though it's reminiscent of the days when catching a husband was every young woman's major life focus.

Generally, this small ceremony takes place just before the bride and bridegroom leave their reception, with a friend or the maid of honor gathering the eligible women guests into a crowd for the bride. Often, the bandleader or deejay will announce the impending ceremony.

- A receiving line is held as guests leave the church, temple, or other ceremony site.

The traditional reception

- A receiving line is held at the beginning of the reception, if not at the ceremony site.
- The wedding couple is introduced at the reception by the band leader or master of ceremonies as, for example, "Mr. and Mrs. James Jones," or "Sally and Jim Jones," or "Sally Smith and Jim Jones." (This is customary in some ethnic groups but is unheard of in others who think the receiving line is adequate introduction.)
- Wedding toasts are offered, beginning with one given by the best man, then the bride's father, then family and friends (or friends and family, since the order is seldom organized), and possibly the bride and bridegroom toast each other.
- Wedding food is served.
- The wedding couple's first dance takes place.
- The wedding cake is cut by the bride and groom, and after they have fed each other the first slice it is removed to the kitchen to be cut and served.
- The bridegroom removes the bride's garter.
- The bride tosses her bouquet to single women attendants and guests.
- The bride and bridegroom change into their going-away clothes (if they're going on their honeymoon from the wedding).
- Rice, birdseed, or flower petals are tossed as the bridal couple leaves for their honeymoon.

It's important during the early phases of planning a wedding to understand the difference between rituals and traditions with genuine meaning, and the procedures that bring order to ceremonial behavior. Wedding rituals are established ceremonial acts and behaviors performed in a set manner. Rituals are linked to the substance of an occasion and often grow out of traditions. They may be codes of behavior that regulate social conduct (such as "you must have a receiving line in order to meet everyone"), define the wedding ceremony and celebration, and help make them memorable. Traditions are long-established ways of thinking and behaving that are handed down from generation to generation, often by word of mouth. They are strongly tied to the beliefs of those practicing them and are important symbols of the customs they represent.

A procedure, on the other hand, is the sequence of actions and

The Send-off

It was once customary to shower the couple with rice as they left the wedding reception for the honeymoon. Most churches, synagogues, hotels, and halls no longer allow this practice, since they say it is difficult to clean up, attracts rodents, and is unhealthy for birds to eat. Instead, they encourage the bridal couple's friends to shower them with birdseed or flower petals.

Guests often cheer as they toss the birdseed or petals, a tradition based on frightening off evil spirits with noise while also guaranteeing the couple's fertility by showering them with something symbolic of fecundity. In France, wheat is thrown at the couple. In Greece, the bridal couple flees through a shower of dates and nuts.

If the couple intends to be the last to leave their reception and still wants the shower of birdseed, care must be taken to hold this traditional ceremony earlier, possibly when they leave the wedding ceremony. Some brides provide guests with small packages of birdseed wrapped in fine net and tied with a ribbon, or present each guest with a satin rose filled with seed and placed in a basket (sold by mail from ads in the backs of bridal magazines). Someone should be put in charge of getting these into the hands of guests at the proper time and also of making sure that the photographer is standing by and that the couple exits at the proper time.

Grownup couples may forgo this ceremony, unless it can be handled in a somewhat impromptu way by a thoughtful friend or attendant. Often too, they are the last to leave their wedding receptions, and so the practice is allowed to go by the wayside in lieu of the couple staying longer at the party.

---

instructions followed at a wedding, including the details that make the event work. Once you have decided to have a receiving line, for example, you will then decide who will stand in it and in which order, the procedure. Orchestra leaders, disc jockeys, and other wedding service providers often want their procedures to become your rituals.
A bandleader may say, for example, "I always introduce couples as Mr. and Mrs. Jones as they enter the ballroom." You may have decided to do away with the entire tradition of being introduced via microphone, and especially may not want to be announced as Mr. and Mrs. Anything. Don't let others control either the rituals or their procedural uses.

When weddings drive brides or their mothers crazy, the reason is nearly always because the details of the rituals – the procedures – are allowed to become too important. Wise couples will decide which traditions and rituals they want included in their weddings, and then avoid getting overly involved in the procedures that shape them.

ATTENDANTS

Family members and close friends have always played a role in weddings. It is customary, for example, for the sister closest in age to the bride to be her maid or matron of honor. Emily Post suggests in her etiquette book that if the bride has no sister, a cousin be invited, or the bride's closest friend. Brides and bridegrooms usually have between two and ten attendants. The best man is often the bridegroom's brother closest in age if there is more than one, or a cousin or close friend. Occasionally, a bridegroom will choose his father to be his best man.

Although at one time selecting attendants wasn't done any other way, having a matching set of female and male attendants is not necessary today. In several instances where brides had a number of close female friends they wanted to be in their wedding, and the bridegroom didn't have nine or ten close male friends, the women stood on both sides of the altar, flanking the couple and the groomsmen. Although there are exceptions, the reality is that men often don't have as many close friends as women. Choosing a matching number of attendants should not be a major problem. This is a marriage ceremony and celebration, not the passenger list for Noah's Ark.

Children in the Wedding

Children are invited to have a role in the wedding for several reasons: they are charming and introduce a note of sweetness and naturalness to the proceedings and just as important, the invitation honors a little sister or brother, niece or nephew, or special friend's child, as well as the child's parents.

Flower girls and ring bearers are usually between the ages of three and seven or eight. Before the age of three, children are notoriously unreliable, although some two-year-olds can be trusted to walk down an aisle with a familiar bridesmaid or with his or her mother or parents. If you decide to include children in your wedding, the only possible attitude to take is that whatever happens will be fine. That way, having a flower girl walk down the aisle between her smiling parents at the last minute because she is frightened is not a tragedy. Or witnessing the ring bearer stop and talk to a friend is not upsetting. Still, even at three or four or older, an especially high-spirited or difficult-to-control child can be an inappropriate choice for flower girl or ring bearer if the bride feels she must have a certain level of decorum at her wedding.

Remember too that young children may not be attentive during a long ceremony, but may be able to sit with their parents in a front row.

Older than eight, boys and girls are junior bridesmaids or junior ushers. In the processional, the flower girl and ring bearer immediately precede the bride, while junior bridesmaids and ushers take their place with other attendants, often according to their height. The flower girl carries some form of flowers, possibly a basket of petals to scatter in the aisle. The ring bearer carries a small white cushion with the wedding ring or rings pinned to it, or with inexpensive gold- or silver-colored rings attached. If the real rings are used, they should be pinned to the cushion just before the ring bearer starts his walk down the aisle, and removed by the best man in time for the ceremony. Does the gender of these roles ever change, with the flower girl carrying a cushion with the rings on it? Although I haven't heard of it, why not?

All children are dressed in finery similar to what is worn by other attendants. The flower girl might wear a more simply styled dress than the bridesmaids, but in a fabric and color that are complementary to theirs. The ring bearer may forgo a suit or black-tie ensemble and wear short pants and knee-high stockings in black and white or all white. He may substitute a looser tie for the small, neatly tied black bowties that men wear. He may also wear a somewhat old-fashioned white shirt that buttons down the back with short pants and no jacket. Tiny, tailored suits that match those of the groomsmen are not very sophisticated. Children should not look like miniature adults.

More than almost any other area of the wedding, this can be a minefield. Parents of young children are frequently eager for them to be part of a family member's or close friend's wedding, and can be hurt if they are not invited. Offering a rational explanation, such as, "we've decided not to have children in our wedding because of their unpredictability," may be the most tactful reason to offer since almost no logic that is linked to a child's personality or behavior will be accepted. Tread carefully.

What is changing is the gender choice of honor attendants. Couples today may choose to have a best man and best woman. In several cases the best man was the bridegroom's sister, called the best woman, and the maid of honor was the bride's brother, who was called her best man. Parents can be asked to be honor attendants, as can the more traditional sister or best friend. Do you have two sisters who are close in age and to whom you are equally close? Make them both honor attendants, rather than designate one as maid of honor and the other as bridesmaid.

The other factor that is changing in wedding attendants is that brides often choose not to have them wear matching dresses, in pastels, with big bows and puffed sleeves, or carry identical bouquets. Gail Ragni had three college roommates coming from all over the country to her Boston wedding. She told them to buy dresses they loved, to the knee or below, in a jewel-like tone, but not red. As it turned out, they each wore a silk dress. One was purple, one was green, and one was a deep blue, which Gail thought was just fine. The colors of the flowers in their bouquets tied together the three different dress colors. "The logistics of getting them into matching dresses seemed difficult, and silly," Gail says. "This way, they wore beautiful dresses they could really wear again, and they looked great."

Another bride told each of her bridesmaids to buy a great short black cocktail dress – not too bare – and to wear it with quiet jewelry. "And they looked contemporary, like they were going to a party where they would have fun, not dressed up like Barbie dolls," she said.

Traditionally, all attendants are responsible for paying for their wedding garb, although the bride chooses what they will wear, either specifically or generally as the brides did above. The bridegroom's attendants will nearly always wear outfits identical to that worn by the bridegroom, unless they wear dark suits instead of formal wear, when black, dark gray, or navy suits are appropriate.

Many couples think of attendants as a tradition that is both warm and reassuring. As one bride in her forties who had all nine members of her women's group as bridesmaids, wearing rented 1950s prom dresses, said, "I wanted all my best friends there with me that night. Who wouldn't?"

Wedding rituals and the individuals who populate them are adapted to a couple's personality and style today, because both the traditions and the reasons behind them are being challenged. Some brides and bridegrooms forgo the idea of attendants altogether. "It's one of those traditions that doesn't make sense to me. I've been a bridesmaid and know how women feel about it. We all complain about the expense and the travel and everything that goes into participating. It's not out of lack of friendship, it's just much ado about nothing – really the only thing bridesmaids do is walk down the aisle. And what's the point?"

Another bride and bridegroom tell how they watched a younger sister get married three months before their wedding and vowed to do things differently in every possible way.

"She asked me, 'Who is giving you away?' And I said, 'Nobody.

Why would anyone give me away?'" says the bride, who is from Virginia and married a man from Pennsylvania. "It was important for her to do everything by the book. 'A year from your wedding date, you make reservations and then you follow a checklist. Six months before you do this,' and on and on. There was not a step she left out. And what confirmed for us that we were on the right track was watching how awful it was for her to go through all her planning. People never stop to think, 'Is this important? *We* are the ones getting married and is this important

---

The World's Best Maid of Honor

The best maid of honor I have ever witnessed was the college roommate of an exceptionally nervous bride. "What I tried to do was to see things through her eyes, and because I know her so well, I knew what would make her nervous. It's hard to remember the minutiae I got involved in. I remember checking with each bridesmaid that she had all the things she needed, and knew where she should be so no one got lost. I took messages to the groomsmen when they arrived. I was glad to be of help. I really love this friend."

After the wedding, this woman in her late twenties, a student of psychology, explained that she has been maid of honor to two close friends, both of whom had complicated family histories and a lot of stress on their wedding day.

"My one friend's mother and father were divorced and her sisters had an argument with the bridegroom a month before. The mother was an alcoholic and her new husband was not friendly with the bride or bridegroom. I remember taking my friend for a walk between the time she was dressed and the time of her wedding and telling her how gorgeous she looked, which was true, and how this was her day and to focus on herself and John, her bridegroom, and on having a wonderful time. At one point, I had the bride doing relaxation exercises and deep breathing to calm her down. While she was having her hair fixed, I told her to imagine she was relaxing on the beach where we'd both been last year."

The woman says that being part of her friends' bridal parties has made her think seriously about weddings in general. Her advice is, "Don't have expectations of a storybook wedding. That way you can enjoy the day and relax. Try not to please everyone else. You can't do it. And throw away the three-ring binder [filled with notes and information]."

As for her own wedding, she says with a laugh, "I want an incredibly casual wedding, which I think is the best way to keep it stress-free. I'll have immediate family and friends, and I'll serve finger sandwiches and champagne and that's it. I'm not kidding."

What Attendants Pay For.
What the Bride Pays For.

Unless a bride has deep pockets and *offers* to pay, attendants buy their own wedding garb, whether it's a dress or gown for the woman and rented formalwear for the men, and travel to and from the wedding, as well as a gift for the bridal couple. Generally, the bride is responsible for her attendant's lodging, the bridegroom for his, which can range from a deluxe hotel suite to a friend's spare bedroom. The bride pays for all attendants' flowers.

Why I Would Have Fewer Attendants

Bonnie Rodriguez had what she describes as a perfect, traditional wedding, complicated by only one factor. "My husband has about a thousand friends and so we each had six attendants. Making the arrangements with that many attendants gets to be cumbersome. When you called one, you had to call all twelve, which is a lot of phone calls to make for every detail. It felt like we were accommodating them, that we did it to appease others. I wish we'd been a little more selfish and discriminating. They could have participated in another way."

to *us?*' I wanted to think about what's behind the traditions."

The history behind the maid of honor, best man, and other honor attendants might be comparable to that of a lady-in-waiting or equerry to a queen or king. Generals have staff assistants to help with the details of their lives. Similarly, brides and bridegrooms do not carry shopping bags or folders overflowing with papers on their important day.

The role of the honor attendants (or the bride's mother or a paid wedding consultant) is to help the bride and bridegroom have a wedding day free from worry over details, although attendants should not be put in complete charge of managing the logistics if the wedding is a complicated occasion. This role is not quite that of a maid or valet, even though the female title actually has the word *maid* in it. The maid or matron of honor and best man are also there to help the bride and bridegroom feel less nervous than they might be if they were alone, as well as to help them get ready and to run errands, if necessary. At elaborate formal weddings, being the bride and bridegroom can be a complicated logistical process. Someone, perhaps the bride's mother, may need to be in charge of the attendants themselves, making sure they are where they are supposed to be and are on time.

Etiquette books once contained long recitations of the best man's duties, though they were vague about the responsibilities of the bride's honor attendant. "Your best man is rightly named," Marguerite Bentley told the bridegroom in her 1947 *Wedding Etiquette Complete,* "for he will be all things to you on your wedding day. Her lengthy description of the best man's duties includes ensuring that the groom's bags are packed, guarding the marriage license until it is given to the clergy member, serving as the toastmaster and timekeeper at the reception, and making travel arrangements for the couple's honeymoon.

She wrote, "As the organ plays the "Bridal Chorus " from *Lohengrin,* he will walk with you to the door leading into the church, and before you know it, you and he will be standing at the chancel gazing up the aisle–waiting for your bride. Mechanically you will take off your gloves, which your best man will waft from your hands and, at the auspicious moment, he will have the ring ready."

"[Before leaving the reception], he will escort you to the room where you are to change your clothes, help you to dress perhaps, and he will give you the key to your hotel room so that you will not have to stop at the desk in the hotel for it, confetti falling from unsuspected places on your person. All in all, he will play a perfect role on a perfect day."

By 1964, Emily Post had not revised this list much, other than to suggest that the best man check to see that the bridegroom "has not packed ski clothes for Bermuda or a tennis racquet for a winter vacation in Canada." She adds that he sits on the bride's right at the bridal table (still a good rule to follow), and that it is his responsibility to make the first toast to the bride and groom.

Much of this has changed. Today's best man and maid of honor often do not expect to perform more than a few helpful tasks on the day of the wedding. They are, after all, *honor* attendants.

In reality, there are many small tasks that both bride and bridegroom will want to delegate to someone else on the day of the wedding. These are often handled by a paid wedding consultant or a representative of the hotel, hall, or club where the reception is held. The person who assumes this role must be comfortable taking charge and supervising servicepeople such as the florist, bandleader, etc. He or she also oversees a rough timetable and leaves everyone else to enjoy the occasion and not worry about logistics.

I have never seen a best man help with many of the duties described above. Perhaps we have become a more casual culture and feel uncomfortable asking for that kind of assistance, or perhaps wedding attendants prefer to be more footloose and less obligated. Nevertheless, best men are expected to do the following on the day of the wedding.

- Spend time with the bridegroom, driving him to the wedding site if he needs transportation, and, if necessary, driving the newly married couple to their destination.
- Take care of the marriage license and wedding ring or rings.
- Make the first toast at the reception.

If you feel comfortable asking the best man to perform other duties, do so. Occasionally, a bridegroom asks his best man to take charge of gifts brought to the reception, or to remove extra liquor or champagne the couple has bought and paid for (with the caterer's permission), but beyond that, a best man is seldom expected to do much.

THE PROCESSIONAL

One of the most eagerly awaited parts of the wedding is the processional, that stately walk down the aisle when the bride is preceded by her attendants and accompanied by her father, parents, and, sometimes, her bridegroom. Guests are in their places. The music has been playing, but now changes from the prelude to the composition carefully chosen for the processional. There is a feeling of anticipation. Guests rise and vie for a good look at the bridal party and the bride.

This symbolic walk into the arms of the bridegroom can be seen in several ways, as simply the procedure that gets everyone to the altar for the ceremony or as an important ritual marking the passage of the bride from her old life into her new one. More practically, the processional gives the bride, bridegroom, and their closest friends and family members a position in the spotlight.

Still, not everyone wants a wedding processional right out of an etiquette book, or as prescribed by the clergy member officiant. Weddings may be less formal today and are often held in locations that are not built around a long aisle to walk down. Contemporary women may not want to be "given away" by anyone. In Jewish weddings, a point is made of the bride not being anyone's to give, and she is accompanied down the aisle by both parents, as is the bridegroom. This emphasizes the importance of family, but without the sexist overtones. Many Christian brides are adopting this ritual, which seems appropriate for today's women.

Natalie Trevino said the traditional walk down the long aisle of her church seemed comically unsuitable to her. "We'd been living together

---

Instructions for Ushers

Ushers are groomsmen chosen by the bridegroom to escort guests to their seats at the wedding service. An usher offers his right arm to each woman in a party as it arrives. If the rear of the church or temple is crowded with arriving guests, he offers his arm to the oldest woman in the group and takes the entire group, by saying "follow us please." Under ordinary circumstances, an usher escorts every woman guest, and the men and children who may accompany her, down the aisle. He asks if she and her party prefer to sit on the bride's or the bridegroom's side, which are left and right in Christian ceremonies, and right and left in Jewish services. Ushers do not offer their arm to men, unless the guest is old and in need of assistance. If reserved cards or "within-the-ribbon" cards are used, guests must tell the usher they are to be seated in their special, designated spots. Ushers do not ask, which would imply that some guests were more special than others to those without such reserved seating.

Can ushers be women? Of course.

---

for years and walking down that aisle looking at my bridegroom with stars in my eyes seemed overly dramatic and too theatrical, not like us," she said. Instead of using a musically orchestrated march to introduce them to their guests, she and the groom came out together from a door at one side of the altar. Both sets of parents and the groom's young children, rather than identically dressed attendants, preceded them in the short processional.

Another bride, a young lawyer being married for the first time, said she thought there ought to be a procedure like the one used by the justices of the United States Supreme Court, who enter the courtroom from behind a curtained area. "They wear their long robes and they walk in together. It's very dignified and impressive. Suddenly they're just there," she said. "I wanted to do something like that at my wedding." She and her husband walked down the aisle together, arms linked, to traditional processional music, but played up-tempo to accompany their brisk pace. They were preceded by both sets of parents and two attendants, who also walked in arm and arm.

A Jewish bride, in a culture where the bride and bridegroom usually walk down the aisle between their parents, walked down with her father only, since she could not envision herself between her long-divorced parents. A Catholic bride, offended by the idea of having her father "give me away to my bridegroom," walked down the aisle between both parents, who each gave her a symbolic goodbye kiss at the altar.

A bride in her thirties marrying a pediatrician, a first marriage for both, invited a dozen of her friends' children to lead her down the wide, curving stairway in the upstate New York mansion where she was being married. "They wore their best clothes, but nothing matched. At the last minute, we passed out flowers," she recalls. "It was thought through, but also spontaneous. I told them ahead of time I wanted them to have some role in the wedding, but didn't give any details. They were all thrilled. Everyone loved it. Especially me." Yet another bride in her thirties, being married for the second time but having her first real wedding, said she would not even consider giving up the traditional walk down the aisle on her father's arm. "I want things exactly the way I've envisioned them. I know I'm not my father's to give, but I love the image of us walking down that aisle together."

Then there are the couples who couldn't resist including their dogs in their processionals. In each of the three cases I know of, the dog wore flowers. Twice, they wore wreaths around their necks, and in one, Coco, a chocolate Labrador retriever, carried flowers in her mouth. Being accompanied in that momentous walk down the aisle by the family pet, or having the flower girl or ringbearer bring it on a leash will surely be seen as either spontaneous and charming or completely tasteless.

The Best Thing About Our Wedding

"We put a lot of care into the Episcopal service and I loved that. Our four grown children all had a role. They did readings that we chose especially for each of them, and that made it warm and loving."

JoAnne Maroni, 46, second-time bride.

WEDDING READINGS

An increasingly common way for a couple to demonstrate their personalities and values is through the choice of readings (in addition to the regular service and exchange of vows conducted by the officiant) during the wedding ceremony and reception. A secular ceremony can become somewhat religious in feeling, or a highly religious ceremony can have a more temporal tone. Most ministers, priests, rabbis, judges, and other officiants allow appropriate verses or readings to be read by special friends or family members at designated times during the service. A favorite clergy member or friend could also be asked to say a blessing before the meal or food service, or to perform a short reading before, during, or after dinner. Friends may get together and write a witty but meaningful poem that is read as entertainment during the reception.

Readings usually fall into these categories.

- scriptural readings about love, marriage, and the nature of joy and happiness
- classical selections of poetry or prose with similar themes contemporary poetry or prose psychological insights or philosophical ruminations about the nature of the marriage bond
- original poetry or prose written by the couple, the bride or bridegroom, a family member or a close friend

---

Render Unto Caesar...

Janie Rosen, a lawyer in her forties, said that when she heard about Israeli weddings where guests gather casually and stand on the *bimah* (the raised platform in the synagogue, called the sanctuary and altar in Christianity), she began to develop a feeling for the spontaneity and closeness she wanted for her second wedding. "I had a sense that ritual is substance," she said, "but that the details shouldn't be allowed to become overly important."

For this bride a certain artlessness was important. "When I heard someone say that weddings are not opera productions, with weeks of rehearsals and a staff of professionals behind the scenes, it made sense. It also explained why a lot of today's weddings feel so wrong.

There's such an emphasis on perfection that the couple gets exhausted and all the juice—the life and the genuine feeling—are squeezed out of them.

"I had this feeling that we ought to render unto Caesar the things that are Caesar's, and unto God.... What I mean is that the part of the ceremony that is religious ought to be. And that because weddings are festive occasions, there ought to be a grand party with all the people in your lives. For me, getting married was a communal event, as well as something that involved the two of us. You don't just marry each other. I don't think very young couples understand this, but you are marrying each other as part of your community. This time I wanted to have the wedding in a synagogue, because that's where our communal and religious bonds are. But then I wanted to go somewhere fabulous and really have the best party I could possibly give."

Janie originally made a joke out of her second wedding. "Right after my divorce, I said if I ever get married again, it will be in Soldier's Field [where the Chicago Bears play], and I'll fill the stands. And we'll have the huge lighted billboard on Lake Shore Drive with our names on it."

That same bravado was evident in Janie's choices for her second wedding. She did not want bridesmaids or attendants. Her own and her husband's children, however, were significantly involved in the ceremony. Janie's daughter wrote a poem about her mother and her mother's new husband that brought down the house at the reception.

After a private and somewhat ceremonial signing of the marriage contract in the rabbi's study, the bride and bridegroom walked arm and arm and beaming into the sanctuary of the synagogue. The public part of their day started off on that note and it was unforgettable. "You could almost feel how happy they were," said a guest.

During the ceremony, they drank out of the same wine goblet (called the chalice in Christianity and the Kiddush Cup in Judaism), a special cup the rabbi had encouraged them to buy for all the family ceremonies of their lives. Although Janie and her husband are not highly sentimental, their wedding Kiddush Cup nevertheless has a place of honor in their home.

The Reverend Gene H. Heglund, pastor of St. Timothy's Lutheran Church in Columbia Heights, Minnesota, says he has not found many biblical verses over the years that seem just right as readings for the marriage ceremony. "The one place in Scripture where Christ went to a wedding is in John, where he turned water into wine at Canaan in Galilee." And that's a wonderful metaphor for how God's love overflows to us, he says. His suggestions for scriptural readings include Jeremiah

29: 11-13, about hopes for the future; Jeremiah 32: 38-41, about establishing a relationship with God; Colossians 3:12-15, Paul's description of how Christians should live, especially within a marriage relationship; and 1 Corinthians 13: 1-7, about the nature of love and goodness. When choosing readings it is wise to remember that many scriptural verses on love and marriage, according to Rev. Heglund, are "unbearably chauvinistic" and thus inappropriate for today's weddings.

The Reverend Charles Carter III of St. Paul's Episcopal Church in Chestnut Hill, Pennsylvania, says he encourages brides and bridegrooms to read the appropriate lessons from his church's Book of Common Prayer and to make appropriate choices of meaningful Scripture from the book that contains every Episcopalian service, including the marriage ceremony. "Each of the readings on the list says something about marriage and how the church, through the centuries, has developed its understanding of marriage and human relationships."

St. Mary's in Lake Forest, Illinois, and many other Catholic churches recommend a booklet published by the Ave Maria Press of Notre Dame, Indiana, *Together for Life,* by the Reverend Joseph M. Champlin, which contains close to 100 pages of scriptural selections and commentaries inspired by interviews with married couples. Authorized readings, prayers, prefaces, and blessings are included. It is a thought-provoking look at wedding commitments and vows.

During the Jewish ceremony, the attitude about readings is entirely controlled by the individual rabbi. Among the most commonly read scriptural verses are The Song of Songs, from the Book of Solomon. Because the liturgy of the Jewish wedding ceremony is relatively brief, anything too long can feel stagy and overwhelming. A rabbi often reads or chants the seven marriage blessings. It may be appropriate to ask an honored guest to read them, or for the bridal couple to read them in Hebrew and in English.

As for classical poetry selections on love and marriage, many are taken from Kahlil Gibran's *The Prophet,* William Shakespeare's Sonnet 116, and the writings of Elizabeth Barrett Browning and Robert Browning, William Keats, and Lao Tsu. Contemporary prose and poetry readings might be selected from Robert Frost, e e cummings, Gian Carlo Menotti, Margaret Mead, Anne Morrow Lindbergh, Pearl S. Buck, or John Updike. Dictionaries of quotations can give you an idea of the huge volume of material available on the subject of love, happiness, and marriage. *The Oxford Dictionary of Quotations* is especially comprehensive and helpful. Feminist quotations are grouped in specific books of quotes by and about women.

One friend said that if she had it to do all over again, she'd have a friend read the lyrics of a favorite song. Admitting that she once would have found this highly unorthodox, she says, "I'd have the lyrics of a great Bruce Springsteen love song read during the ceremony. It's so poetic, so beautiful and very contemporary." Her choice is "If I Should Fall Behind," from Springsteen's *Lucky Town* album.

Not every couple wants something unusual read at their wedding. When a magazine editor with literary tastes and a good memory was asked to read at the wedding of two friends, she recalled and suggested three passages she had read years earlier. Each said something about the nature of love and romance in marriage: in James Joyce's *The Dead,* where the character Gabriel thinks in very romantic and loving terms about his wife, his relationship, and his marriage; in Walker Percy's *The Second Coming,* where Alison ponders on the mutual salvation she and her partner have found in a new relationship; in Gabriel Garcia Marquez's *A Hundred Years of Solitude,* where an especially sensuous scene shows a man and a woman's attraction for each other. The bridegroom thought they were too eccentric for his church wedding and suggested Elizabeth Barrett Browning's "How Do I Love Thee?" from her *Sonnets from the Portuguese.* The friend recalls, "At the time I wished I could have left off the first line, which has become sort of trite, but when I actually read it I remembered how beautiful it was. It made them happy so it was fine."

The only way to find something original for your wedding is to write a piece of prose or poetry yourself, or to ask a friend to create something special for the occasion. Professional writer friends may love to be asked to do such a task, though most are well aware of the time commitment involved in the research and writing. The subjects most often reflected on are the nature of love, friendship, family, joy and happiness, and community and continuity, and the importance of these in every marriage. On a more psychological level the importance of forgiveness, understanding, and a willingness to compromise are good topics.

One of the best original poems I've ever heard at a wedding was read during the service, and it reflected with earnestness and conviction on the well-matched man and woman being wed, with biblical verses used to support points. It was written and read by the aunt of the bride, who is a religious scholar and who knew which verses emphasized her points.

A final precaution: Before asking a friend to write original prose or poetry, ask yourself whether you can be gracious and approving if you do not like the results. Original poetry is fraught with the peril of sounding hopelessly amateur or overly sentimental.

THE RECEIVING LINE

Receiving lines can take as long as an hour or even more, if the bride, bridegroom, and their families have friends who want to stop and chat. If it's a small wedding, little time may be spent formally greeting guests and accepting their congratulations. The receiving line should never be a huge chore. If you think it might be, you may want to rethink the underlying premise of your wedding and its guestlist.

Traditionally, receiving lines included mothers of the couple, the bride and groom, and the bride's attendants. No one else. Today, the couple's fathers are nearly always included. The mother of the bride is first in the line, which is set up close to the door at the reception, so that guests pass through the line as they enter. The bride's mother greets guests and introduces them to her husband. He introduces them to the bride, she to the bridegroom, he to his own parents and on to the attendants. Guests unknown to the bride's mother introduce themselves to her.

The number of individuals in your receiving line is one factor in its duration. Ten bridesmaids and a maid of honor mean more hands to shake, more cheeks to kiss, more greetings to offer. Receiving lines for 200 guests can take as little as 20 to 30 minutes, or approximately 6 to 9 seconds per guest. They can also take as long as an hour, which means guests spend approximately a minute and a half offering congratulations and chatting.

Catering and banquet managers know that some weddings, including those of certain ethnic, religious, and even professional groups, have receiving lines that are slower than others because the guests stop and chat at length, and, perhaps, are less intimidated by formal occasions. Also influencing the nature of the receiving line are the personalities of the bride, bridegroom, and their families. Outgoing, relaxed, and talkative couples spend longer with each guest than quieter, more reserved individuals, who take less time.

Some receiving lines follow immediately after the ceremony. In one case I know of, in the aisle of the church the bride and bridegroom stopped, embraced, and were immediately surrounded by friends. Some popular, big city churches schedule weddings tightly during the busiest wedding months of the year, which is something to keep in mind. If you have your receiving line at the reception, you will want to leave the ceremony site as soon as possible so that an informal receiving line does not

The Princess Tradition

The old rule of etiquette was firm about how guests could not leave the wedding until the bride and bridegroom left. This was, and sometimes still is, true of honored guests at formal occasions. The guest of honor must leave first.

Stories abound about parties where guests were dying to leave but had to stay until Princess Margaret or Princess Anne made her departure. Whereas that might work in Great Britain, such a custom would be impossible in the United States. Guests would be inconvenienced. In America, at least half the guests would leave early just to show their independence.

The major reason for the "bride-and-bridegroom-leave-first" rule was more than social convention. It had to do with *The Wedding Night.* Brides and bridegrooms used to stay at their receptions for a fairly brief period of time, because, as the story went, they were exhausted by their wedding and were eager to get on with the other main event of the day, their first sexual encounter. They left early. Guests could then go home. Everyone was happy.

But grownups plan weddings where they can have a wonderful time rather than be so exhausted they can barely make it through the day. As for their wedding night, maybe they'll have one, ▸

form. Be aware that right after the marriage ceremony, wherever the bride and bridegroom stop, however briefly, guests will begin to form a line to offer their best wishes to the newlyweds.

Several brides and bridegrooms I know decided against having a receiving line because of family conflicts and other potentially difficult situations. In one instance, an announcement was made from the altar that no receiving line would be held, and that the bride and bridegroom would greet their guests all evening. In another case, the bridal couple intended to make a special effort to greet guests at their reception, rather than standing in line with their parents and stepparents. Whereas it might have felt right for them, many guests never met the couple, who never got to each table to say hello.

maybe they won't. Chances are they already have.

So the picture of the bridal couple waving goodbye to guests as they climb into their rented limousine, she in a special ensemble complete with corsage, he in a suit and tie, may have given way to the couple who spends every possible minute visiting with their guests or dancing the night away. Today's bridal couple often departs for their honeymoon, if there is one, a day or two after the wedding.

OLD, NEW, BORROWED, AND LIVELY

If your ethnic background or culture is important to you, you may want to make it an important part of your wedding. An engaged woman who was born in Ireland stood next to me at a Jewish wedding as we clapped to a set of lively dancing with music by a klezmer band. She wished out loud that she could have a Jewish wedding. "Why not have an Irish wedding?" I asked. She felt uncomfortable with the way Americans interpreted all things Irish, she explained. "I hate anything with shamrocks." "But why not hire an Irish band? Or have some authentic Irish poetry read in the form of toasts?" I suggested. She liked those ideas, which she felt were more genuinely traditional than what she viewed as the false, overstated sentimentality expressed on St. Patrick's Day.

There are Italian brides who wouldn't think they were married if they didn't do the tarantella at their weddings. Others think it is too hokey. These attitudes are attached, I believe, to the bride's confidence as well as to how assimilated and proud of its heritage the family is. An Irish bride (who had a French name and German forebears as well) and a Jewish bridegroom were proud of the Irish band they had discovered at a street fair and engaged for their wedding. To them, Irish music meant exuberant, lively, unconventional songs played with spirit and sentiment. Their band was a huge hit with guests.

Whether grownups want to use any or all of their own customs, or borrow wedding traditions from other cultures, it is wise to remember that all wedding behavior flows from these streams: the ceremony that unites the bride and bridegroom in marriage, the religions and cultures in which the bride and bridegroom were raised or the one to which they now belong, and their taste and style. Some traditions feel appropriate for the contemporary bridal couple and thus fit better into grownup weddings. For couples with deep or shared roots, traditions linked to a long religious or cultural history often feel mandatory.

There are ways to incorporate tradition with sophistication. When Maggie Cerchevsky, 29, married Tom Dalrymple, 31, she was the last of her 50-some cousins in a big Polish-Catholic family to be married. Every member of her family had been married in the neighborhood parish church with a catering hall reception to follow. An artist and photographer who no longer lives in the neighborhood, Maggie is proud of her Polish heritage and wanted to express it, but in a way that was more connected to her life now, in other words, in a sophisticated, artistic style.

Although the couple is not religious, they both wanted to be married in a church, preferably one close to home where they would feel comfortable as members after their marriage. They also wanted the reception to follow the ceremony, without the long break so common in neighborhood weddings where the service is in the morning and the reception some hours later.

Me Tarzan, You Jane

Brides who grew up in a culture where every wedding included the garter ceremony, complete with an orchestral drum roll as the bridegroom fondled the bride's leg and removed her lacy blue garter—or, worse, dragged it down her leg with his teeth!—can easily see this as a leftover from an era when the "Me Tarzan, You Jane" mentality was the norm. They may not think twice about excising it from their wedding reception. Others may find it an amusing and harmless part of the evening's entertainment.

First, they found a beautiful church in the city where they live. Because Maggie is an artist and Tom an architect, aesthetics were important to them and they made no apologies about their search for a church with historic and design significance. They located a beautifully decorated, upscale eastern European restaurant known for excellent food and they worked out a special wedding menu with the catering director. Rather than hiring a polka band that could play other music, Maggie and Tom hired a small elegant band with a jazzy sound, and she got a tape of spirited polka music so that everyone could dance the traditional Polish dance. And her tall floral crown was the kind of headpiece that only an artist of her confidence and poise could wear.

Maggie knew that during the reception her mother would tie a white satin apron around her waist, and that dangling from that apron would be tiny baby-bottles and other symbols of domestic productivity. She didn't want to tell her the custom no longer fit who she was. To diffuse the situation, Maggie's partner in their graphic arts and photography business followed up the traditional Polish apron dance with another announcement. "To ensure another kind of productivity, I want to give Maggie *this* symbolic apron." Accompanied by laughter, Maggie's matron of honor tied a black photographer's apron over her friend's gown. Attached to the apron were symbols of the work they shared: tiny cameras and painter's tools and bright yellow boxes of film. The guests loved this new twist on an ethnic tradition. And Maggie felt that the two aprons accurately portrayed what she wanted her life to be.

Another couple, in a second marriage for both that took place in their city apartment, asked the owner of his favorite restaurant to cater the party, and the fact that it was Greek food had nothing to do with their own ethnic backgrounds. "We love Greek food and it's that simple," said the bridegroom.

Adopting the best-known and most symbolic act of the Jewish wedding, Betsy Nolan and Robert Kunze were married in San Francisco, and although neither of them is Jewish, they stepped on and broke a glass when the wedding was over. The audience, a mixture of East Coast and West Coast friends and family – the couple has homes on both coasts – called "mazeltov." There are generations of interpretations about the breaking of the glass, each explanation slightly different from the one before. Generally, rabbis say this should introduce two ideas: one of celebration dating back to when glasses were broken to symbolize levity, and another serving as a solemn reminder to everyone present that although weddings symbolize hope, the world is filled with destruction. Betsy and Robert liked introducing these ideas into their ceremony.

Many customs that have become highly traditional in some cultures are unfamiliar to those outside the culture. Some of these customs center around the amount of food served. An abundant display of food and a lavish sweet table may feel appropriate to one group, but may be regarded as a wasteful and vulgar display to others. What looks like a plentiful offering of food to one group may appear penurious and skimpy to another. Limousines, gifts of money, bringing gifts to the reception, and groom's cakes are a few examples of customs that are expected at some weddings and unheard of by other brides and bride-

The Wedding Food Fight

The cake-cutting ceremony is intended to be a loving symbol of the feeding and nurturing the newly married couple will do for the rest of their lives, rather than an out-of-place version of a food fight. There is nothing quite so juvenile as the bride and bridegroom feeding each other their first piece of cake and smearing it on each other or smashing it into each other's faces. One couple who decided against feeding each other the first piece of cake admits it is because they had seen it done tastelessly so many times that even knowing the real meaning couldn't encourage them to do it right. For them, this custom had been ruined.

grooms. Remind yourself that no one way is correct. The mixing of ethnic and cultural groups in the United States should encourage a familiarity with many customs and thus a generosity of spirit about other styles.

GIFTS

Some controversy often surrounds the giving and accepting of gifts today. The long-ago English custom where the lord of the manor displayed gifts the day after the wedding may be the origin of certain modern customs. For some people it is perfectly normal to display gifts at the home of the bride's parents or to open gifts with family and close friends the day after the wedding. If, however, this causes unwanted familial competition, perhaps it should be avoided.

It is considered normal, by some wedding guests, to give, for example, antique silver pieces or unusual art objects to the bride and

---

Wedding Favors

The bride who has attended weddings where some small favor is always given to guests may want to follow this custom. She may decide to give away two pieces of fancy chocolate in a beautiful small box for guests to take home. Or she may choose to give away the same sugar-coated almonds tied in small net bundles that she's received at many weddings.

One bride, raised by an Italian father and Jewish mother, had three beautiful small dishes of candy on each table at her wedding dinner. Baci, which means "kisses" in Italian, are the chocolate-covered hazelnuts that the bride loves. These and chocolate truffles were in one dish, traditional white Jordan almonds were in another, and a sugar-coated nut confection, a long-time family favorite prepared by her brother, was in the third.

A New England bride always loved getting small gifts at weddings and decided to devote time and attention to this detail for her own wedding. She and her husband, who had met many years earlier in art school, had a sketch done of the two of them waving from a sailboat. The design was then transferred onto 100 plates, which the couple put into small pizza boxes they had hand-painted. Each was then shrink-wrapped. "We wanted to send guests home with something to remember our wedding by," said the bride.

"Commemorative plates? That sounds suspiciously like souvenir mugs to me," said another bride. "With their own pictures on them? Sort of like the dishtowels with Princess Diana and Prince Charles on them? I think that's the height of narcissism," said yet another.

---

bridegroom, no matter what the couple's taste may be. The idea behind this custom is that the gift giver's style is what matters and the young couple must be flexible enough to accept what is given. Some brides, of course, don't think twice about returning such gifts. In families where family silver and elegant dishes are handed down over generations, such gifts seem more appropriate. In families where the bride is hoping to put together eight place settings of sterling silver flatware, such a gift might be unwelcome or even considered thoughtless. To older brides and bridegrooms who have already furnished their homes, it can be wasteful to receive another toaster or silver that doesn't go with anything they have.

Our Favorite Wedding Gift

"My aunt, whom I lived with when I was in college, gave me an antique wedding dress from her collection as a shower gift. Then, as a wedding gift, she gave us an antique brass bed. I still have both and wouldn't part with either of them for the world."

LouAnne Hansen, 28, first-time bride.

"A pair of hand-made canoe paddles with our names carved in them. We love the outdoors and that was such a perfect, thoughtful gift, from a group of friends who paid a mutual friend from college to make them. They took him months of work and are a real labor of love."

Megan Greeley, 25, first-time bride.

Because of the potential for unsuitable gifts, most brides register at department and specialty stores, listing gift items they would like to have so that wedding guests can give them something useful. Although I find this somewhat impersonal, it does serve a function, often helping young couples get silver flatware and china sets they might not otherwise be able to afford. As a young woman, though, I watched brides register and end up with partial sets of everything, without the funds to complete their sets, which seemed wasteful. And I recently heard a young bride complain about having to register for gifts at a store in an upscale suburban village shop that did not at all reflect her own or the bridegroom's taste, because her future mother-in-law thought many of the guests from their side of the family wouldn't know how else to choose a gift for the young couple. The bride then returned everything, chose a few suitable gifts to keep, and still had a hefty store-credit that the couple uses to send gifts to the bridegroom's friends and family members when they register at this same shop.

Another bride, marrying for the second time and having lived with the bridegroom for some years, complained after the wedding that they received odd gifts, and decided it was because guests didn't know what to give them. "We had everything in our home, and didn't need silver candlesticks that I would never use," she said, wishing she had registered for gifts, or that they had specified a charity for donations in their honor.

Still another grownup couple specified on their invitation "no gifts please" and made sure that both sets of parents told their friends they really meant it. Most of their own friends took them at their word, although they got a few unusual gifts, including theater tickets, a Sunday brunch gift certificate, and a crystal vase filled with flowers that was delivered when they returned from their honeymoon.

Guests continue to bring gifts to weddings (except in cultures where everyone gives money, and gifts are seldom given) – no matter how many times Ann Landers advises them not to in her columns and no matter how many upscale (and snotty) florists refuse to decorate gift tables – and they should not be made to feel they've committed a horrid faux pas. In cases where close friends and family members stop by the couple's house before the wedding, it seems entirely appropriate. And although money is not given as a gift in some cultures, guests who hand an envelope to the bride or bridegroom with a check or cash inside should not be made to feel vulgar or foolish. I know of one bridegroom, who, while standing in his receiving line, was handed an envelope. "What is this? " his bride overheard him ask no one in particular. The guest, who heard his question, leaned over and whispered tactfully, "It's my gift to you."

At weddings where cash or checks are common gifts, brides and bridegrooms often appoint someone to watch over such gifts, keeping them all together and in a safe place. In some cultures it is common for the bride to wear a white satin and lace-trimmed bag while dancing. When guests give her or the bridegroom their envelopes she places them in the bag. Somehow, no matter how traditional this may be in some groups, it strikes me as a not-very-grownup custom for the sophisticated bride and bridegroom.

TRADITION OR UNBREAKABLE RULE?

The decision whether or not to take part in wedding customs that feel like unbreakable rules to parents, but not to the bride and bridegroom, may go back to the central questions: Whose wedding is this? Who is planning and paying for it? And how is the occasion viewed by everyone involved? Not everyone, after all, wants a daughter or son to have anything but a highly traditional wedding with rituals well known to everyone in the family and community.

Ellen Russell, the mother of a bride, explains that since the bride was in California and the bridegroom in Washington, D.C., the main planning of the wedding fell to her. "I wanted everything to please them, but at a certain point had to say, 'trust me,' and they did," she says. "They weren't here to make decisions. In the end, they made one rule. They didn't want our friends who didn't know them at the wedding. This was not to be business entertaining, or a payback party. If the guests didn't know the bride or the bridegroom, they couldn't be on the list. And I completely understood that."

The mother of another bride confides that since she and her husband paid for her daughter's wedding, they intended for it to reflect who they are. "I'm not going to any more weddings in meadows where I have to walk a mile and sit in the hot sun for an hour," she said vehemently. "If parents invite their friends to their children's weddings, they ought to be damned sure it's something they want to be included in, not some circus," she adds.

On the other hand, it is common to hear brides say they allowed their first weddings, if they were quite young when they married, to be "for my parents" or "for my mother," and their second for themselves. Alice Rayner admits she had a band she didn't like and a wedding consultant she couldn't stand. "I couldn't fight my parents," she says simply.

Not that every wedding with a grownup bride and bridegroom is the tasteful expression of the couple's most private values or style. Newspaper stories and guests tell of an expensive wedding in an exclusive suburb of a big eastern city as "pure show biz," with its horse-drawn carriages, a bridegroom who rode in on a black stallion, the rental of an entire club for a whole weekend, an elaborate schedule of events where attendance was mandatory for guests, expensive silver gifts for everyone in attendance, and generally overstated, tasteless exaggeration of wedding customs.

Still, what one couple considers a "circus" might be seen as spontaneous and lively by another. Most brides and bridegrooms feel that some wedding customs and traditions just won't work for them. They may not be able to articulate why, but they are sure about their feelings. However, before casting aside traditional wedding rituals in favor of entirely new ones, it's wise to think about the origins and roots of customs. As brides and bridegrooms explore their historical and philosophical beliefs, they begin to decide whether or not to include certain conventions, or how to tailor them to their styles.

CHAPTER FOUR

Invitations: What to Write and What to Write It On

Except for those who want formal wedding invitations, which have remained much the same over the years, change is in the air. Even formal styles are not as rigidly formulaic as they used to be, and there are many more of what used to be called informal wedding invitations, in enough variations to make an etiquette writer's head spin.

Because the invitation is the first thing guests see, many couples choose to make it a strong indication of the wedding's style. Beyond how invitations look, many couples invite guests in their own names today. Other copy changes have occurred because of divorce and remarriage.

As recently as the postwar years, an etiquette book's wedding invitation advice sounds stilted, if not positively archaic. *The Wedding Etiquette Complete,* by Marguerite Bentley, published in 1947, reads: "The engraved invitation's forms are essentially rigid. There is no more formal occasion than a wedding, and the invitations and announcements for such an occasion follow an undeviating formality. Simulated engraving and printing are not suitable and should never be used.

"All wedding invitations and announcements are engraved on the first page of a double sheet of paper.

"If the family of the bride has a coat of arms it may be plainly embossed at the top of the first page."

After cautioning that this family emblem must never be used in color, and warning that no other marking or device at the top of the wedding invitation has the same endorsement of good taste, the author writes, "I strongly advise against using lovers' knots and initials or monograms." Without taking a breath or explaining why, she adds that "it is also well to remember that a woman renounces the right to use her family's coat of arms when she marries. She takes her husband's name and his heraldic emblem. . . . "

Ignoring the advice about the heraldic emblem, this may still be one area where an unconventional bride or couple chooses to follow the rules for the appearance and addressing of very traditional wedding invitations. On the other hand, if you are an informal person, you may scoff at a few of the rules' finer points, such as never including children's names on the outer envelope, or sending separate invitations to anyone over 16, even if the son or daughter is still living at home.

The best rule for invitations: Use your common sense.

What would work best in your personal life will be the most natural expression of who you are, and this should influence your choice of wedding and invitation style. If you might have a formal New Year's Eve party with guests in black tie and cocktail dresses, and would send fairly formal invitations, you won't consider doing anything different for your wedding. If, on the other hand, you are more the "help-me-with-the-buffet" kind of hostess, that attitude may well influence your choice of wedding and the invitation style as well.

Here's a list of actual information that must be conveyed in every invitation:

- who
- what (ceremony and/or reception)
- when
- where (never assume people know the address)
- what kind of food service and entertainment (meal? cocktails or champagne buffet? dancing?)
- map
- response

Concerning the language used on wedding invitations, again, surprisingly little has changed except that divorce and remarriage have added footnotes to the once highly stylized form. And whether or not the bridegroom's parents contribute toward the cost of the wedding, their names are often included on today's invitations. As for design, wonderfully creative and witty invitations can be used to invite guests to weddings. Many couples look for a way—either subtle or direct—to tell guests "there will be something unusual and different about this wedding."

INVITATION STYLES

Here are some of the best invitations I've seen.

Traditional

For the traditional invitation, nothing surpasses an oversized, formal invitation engraved in simple script type on creamy white, high rag-content paper, with a tissue. The tissue, although not needed to keep the engraving from smudging, adds to the dignity and formality of the stationery. This invitation came with a separate reception card, which once was intended to invite guests to the reception. Today, the reception card is seldom necessary, since wedding ceremony guests are generally invited to the reception as well. A matching response card was also included. The entire invitation was contained in inner and outer envelopes. It was beautifully addressed, although not in calligraphy. This kind of invitation, in impeccable traditional taste, could just as easily have come from the White House or Buckingham Palace.

The cost of formal invitations depends on several factors, including the quality of the paper and the service and taste level of the seller. The elegant jewelry store that embosses its name on the envelope flap charges for its high-quality service and for the genuinely helpful guidance its wedding consultants provide. These salespeople take their business seriously and know how to phrase invitation copy formally and appropriately in unusual situations.

Some stationery stores sell goods at a discount, even those lines of invitations they sell through sample books. Other than from the individual jewelry store lines, the highest-quality invitations come from Crane's (who supplies Tiffany and Co., for example, with a personalized line of beautiful stationery) and Buening's, and they are seldom if ever sold at a discount.

If you're on a budget, even the least expensive wedding stationery books have one or two lines of traditional invitations that are attractive, though the paper is not the highest quality. Reading any of these sample stationery books will give you ideas about copy. The text, however, is often a little souped up for my taste. I don't think it's sophisticated to invite guests to "share in the joy of our love," for example. Depending on the quality of the paper, size and amount of type, and use of engraved or raised type, expect to pay from $1 to $10 per person for the traditional formal invitation.

Less Traditional

These invitations usually use traditional elements in two of these three elements: paper, type, and copy. They often look completely traditional but have unusual, contemporary, and informal copy.

- An elegant, simple invitation with script printing, but in white, on oversized, folded pink paper. The reception invitation, as it frequently is

When to Mail Invitations

Generally, invitations should be mailed three to four weeks before the wedding. Exceptions are when a large number of out-of-town guests are invited, when international mail systems are used, and when the wedding is scheduled for a busy holiday weekend when advance planning may be necessary. Under these circumstances, add from two to four weeks to the mailing schedule.

today, was included on the wedding invitation. It came with a response card, a tissue, and double envelopes.

Much Less Traditional

These are by far the most fun to receive, but the margin that separates them from bad taste is narrow. They require professional design and carefully written copy. Wit, with style, can be appropriate, but no jokes please. All of this is why professional artists, designers, and writers often design them for their own weddings. Amateurs beware.

- A newsman's wedding with a series of comic-strip cartoons of the bride and the bridegroom, speaking in cartoon bubbles: In the first bubble, the bride says, "Church." The groom says, "Temple." Then, in a bubble of agreement, they say, "Our place." In the next strip, she says, "Immediate family." He says, "Everybody." Next, they say together, "Special Friends." After his, hers, and theirs comments about dress that end with her wearing cream rather than white, the invitation opens and inside begins "After exhaustive planning . . . " and continues with copy where the bride and bridegroom invite guests to their informal, lively home wedding.
- An invitation in the form of a Mobius strip, with an explanation of its creation and engineering by German mathematician August F. Mobius – "a continuous surface formed by twisting one end of a rectangular strip through 180 degrees . . . " – which fits the contemporary definition of marriage as something continuous and lasting that takes effort.
- An Anglo-American wedding with a trifolded invitation. The first sheet, with a small U.S. flag and a U.K. flag printed in full color at the bottom, says in dark blue ink, "On July 4, 1776, the United States declared its independence from Great Britain." Inside the invitation, the flags have moved closer together, and the text reads, "A new era of Anglo American relations is about to begin," and gives some logistics of the invitation. By the final page, the two flags have merged into a small heart shape that combines the Stars and Stripes and the Union Jack. If awards for graphics and design were given for wedding invitations, this one to the wedding of an advertising agency head and a retailing executive would take first prize. The red, white, and blue theme was carried through the Independence Day weekend wedding.
- An oversized heavy, cream-colored card, embossed with a double rule about a half inch from the edge, printed in dark green, with reception copy as part of the invitation. It came in a single envelope, with a response card.
- An invitation on heavy, white, handmade, imported paper (especially beautiful handmade papers come from Japan and Mexico), with a tissue of semisheer paper with gold and silver flecks. This was tradition-

ally printed, included a response card and return envelope, and was enclosed in inner and outer envelopes.

- An invitation to the reception only, on a medium-sized, pale blue card, which began, "Come celebrate our marriage" and continued with the logistical details. The few guests invited to the very small ceremony that preceded the party were asked by telephone. A more formal invitation to the wedding itself could have been printed on an even smaller card and included in the invitation.
- A 1950 photograph, *Kiss by the Hotel de Ville, Paris,* by Robert Doisneau, with discreetly worded, straightforward copy inside the bifold card, where the bride and bridegroom do the inviting.
- An art deco style card, printed in black, with a border of black and gold art deco motifs around the edge. This invitation used type reminiscent of art deco design and contained traditional language. The deco theme for the wedding was first revealed to guests in the invitation.
- An invitation that begins "Married three weeks and still in love. Please join us to celebrate." The copy continues with details of the reception, on a traditional card with type that is often used in wedding invitations.
- A beautifully designed invitation with an artist-drawn, abstract flower on the front, done in deep pink from a silkscreen, with copy in matching ink inside. Traditional copy, traditional type.
- A traditionally sized and printed invitation with a small handcolored photograph of the bride and bridegroom carefully centered and glued onto its cover, with fairly traditional copy and printing inside. This was a photographer bride's wedding.

The Corner Card Shop

One bride, who spent over $20,000 on an elegant small wedding, allocated less than one percent on her invitations from "the corner card shop." "I was surprised at how many sample books they carried and how nice and reasonably priced they were," she admits.

Stationery, office supply, and card shops generally have books of sample invitations, and although most specialize in overdecorated invitations with flowers and rainbows and ribbons, they all have simple, discreet invitations as well. These are priced very competitively and can often be printed (not engraved) within a week or less.

Every one of these invitations was exquisitely designed and carried the mark of a professional graphics designer or artist. Except for the Mobius strip, they were in traditional shapes, and something about every one of them said "wedding."

The cost of invitations, from highly traditional to extremely creative, can vary as much as party invitations. Expect to spend from $1 to $10 per invitation depending on the cost of the graphic artist, the paper, and the printing.

Allow plenty of time for the choice and delivery of every kind of invitation, from traditional to custom designed. I have had party invitations designed by a graphic artist friend in the mail within a week. But if she had been unusually busy, more time would have been necessary. One bride tells how she ordered her traditional invitations from a book in a stationery shop and had her entire order within a week. More unusual invitations that involve gluing and pasting of layers of paper take longer. January is not too early to order custom invitations for a summer wedding, since stationers get backed up before the busiest wedding months. Finding a designer who shares your taste and can work within your budget, of course, can take even longer.

Tasteless wedding invitations, decorated with rainbows, entwined rings, flowers, and the like, have always been available. But there are now overdecorated invitations on the market that can cost as much as $25 per guest and are often in terrible taste. How do you rationalize a

---

Detailsdetailsdetails

Details count. The right stamp, carefully placed on the envelopes, gives a neat appearance to an important invitation. Attractive handwriting is a must. Some sense of the proprieties looks sophisticated. On the other hand, hours and hours of time can be spent getting every detail just right, and busy brides and couples may not want to spend time in this way. Here are some details brides and couples enjoyed using with their invitations, as well as some tips about designing, ordering, and addressing invitations.

- When you pick up your invitations, make sure you have one assembled correctly. Traditional invitations have an unsealed inner envelope and a slightly larger outer one. The invitation should be inserted in its inner envelope and placed in the outer envelope so that the names are face up when it is opened. Cards and other enclosures should be on top of the invitation. Names of guests and children, if they are to be invited, are written on the inner envelope, while the appropriate name (your own or your parents) and return address are on the outer envelope.
- The old rule is that you should not abbreviate titles such as Dr. and such words as Street and Avenue on wedding invitation copy but could use shortened versions of state and country names. Use your judgment.

- When addressing an invitation to a couple living together but not married, use her full name first, on one line, then his full name.
- Two doctors ought to be invited as follows: "The Doctors Karen and James Gantner." Two PhDs would be invited in the same way.
- One bride sealed envelopes with sealing wax and used a fleur-de-lis stamp tied into her French country wedding theme.
- There are attractive, whimsical, hand-carved rubber stamps that can add a note of style to less formal invitations.
- Computer calligraphy is either a very good idea or total fakery, depending on your attitude toward fancy handwriting. It is slightly less costly than the real thing and looks uniformly neat and tidy.
- If you make your own invitations, be sure to produce extras, just as you would if you were having them printed. Whoever addresses the envelopes always makes a few mistakes.
- Allow plenty of time for addressing envelopes from a reasonably organized list of guests' names. The less orderly the list and the greater the haste, the more likelihood of errors, and the more time you'll need.
- You can always special-order extra envelopes, unless they're custom-designed. Most orders include some extras.
- Don't assemble your guestlist in your head or on the backs of envelopes, or expect to take it right off your Rolodex. Copying from your Rolodex, on the other hand, can be an effective use of time, and the list can double as your thank-you note list.
- If you're especially busy, clerical work such as organizing your list from your address book or Rolodex can be done by a part-time secretary hired for the occasion from an agency. Don't underestimate the amount of time involved in addressing invitations.

huge three-dimensional paper rose with a lace ruff behind it on an oversized moire card with the invitation printed on yet another kind of paper and mounted at a 90-degree angle? This invitation must be mailed in a padded envelope or a box. Wanting to stand out from the crowd and show you can afford it is not the best motivation for choosing an invitation. Lace-edged outer envelopes strike me as not grownup at all, and wide colored stripes in foil to match the color motif of the wedding just aren't elegant. Glass invitations with the copy etched into them? I don't want your wedding keepsake in my china cabinet (even if I had one), but at the same time I am too frugal to throw it away, so it might hang around and annoy me for months. The tendency toward the unique and unusual can be taken too far. There are more sophisticated ways to be individualistic.

Engraving and Thermography

Engraving is a traditional printing technique that results in raised print and an indented line on the reverse side of the paper.

Thermography is raised printing that is shinier than engraving, is a great deal less costly, and leaves no indent in the paper. Don't use thermography thinking guests will be fooled into thinking it's engraving. It's a different printing technique entirely and worthy of consideration on its own. As for offset lithography, commonly used for personal and business stationery, it is less costly than either engraving or thermography and is entirely appropriate for wedding invitations.

The Corner Print Shop

Whether the corner print shop is a well-known franchise or an independently owned neighborhood printer, it may offer savings on invitations if they are printed on paper stock the shop carries. Most shops have several appropriate typefaces, and some have complete desktop publishing programs that save you labor costs. Almost none will do engraving, except through the invitation books they carry and from which they order.

If you want a fairly simple invitation, you may be able to save as much as half the total cost by dealing with this kind of printer. Remember, though, that the local printer is not an expert at anything but printing. Do not look here for design or language advice. Many of these printers also carry standard invitation and stationery books. Some offer discounts.

INVITATION COPY

The trend is to be fairly explicit: If the reception is a country dinner and dance, that is made clear. If it is black tie, or black tie optional, that, too, is spelled out. One of my favorites said, "Please share in the joy of our wedding and wedding dance. (Bring a side dish for a country buffet)."

For the most part, the traditional invitation should still use fairly elegant, simple language, the more straightforward the better.

Mr. and Mrs. Eric Harteenian
request the honor *(or honour)* of your presence
at the marriage of their daughter
Jennifer Caryn
to
Mr. William Warren Grathwol
Saturday, the twentieth of October
Nineteen hundred ninety four
at six o'clock
The Arts Club
6200 West Hubbard Road
Tranquility, Texas

Often, today's bridegrooms like to include their parents in the invitation, especially if expenses are shared. In that case it would read as follows:

Mr. and Mrs. Albert Johnson
request the honor *(or honour)* of your presence
at the marriage of their daughter
Arnetta Louise
to
Mr. Thomas Aaron Golding
son of Mr. and Mrs. Harvey Golding
Saturday, the twentieth of October
Nineteen hundred ninety four
at seven o'clock
The Sunrise Club
1412 Michigan Avenue
Happiness, Florida

Because of divorce and remarriage, and because couples themselves like to do the inviting, a fair number of deviations from this form are now necessary. If both parents, now remarried, are inviting guests, the mother's name (with or without her husband's, which should depend on their relationship with her daughter, as in "Mrs. John Henry" or "Mr. and Mrs. John Henry") should be first. If your father is remarried and your mother is deceased, you may want to indicate that you are his daughter, as in "Mr. and Mrs. Murray Johnston request the honour of your presence at the wedding of his daughter," etc. In the case of divorced parents who prefer to issue their own invitations to their own guests, invitations with his or her name only can be printed and sent to the respective lists.

When both parents are remarried, and the bride is on friendly terms with her stepfather and stepmother, invitation copy should read as follows:

Mr. and Mrs. James Loiseau *(mother and stepfather)**
and
Mr. and Mrs. Arthur Cohn *(father and stepmother)**
request the honor of your presence
at the marriage of their daughter
Susan Elizabeth
to
Mr. James O'Neill Reardon III
son of Mr. and Mrs. James Reardon II
Sunday, the twentieth of May
Nineteen hundred ninety six
at six o'clock
At The Saddle and Cycle Club
137 Fairmont Avenue
Highland Park, Arizona

In the case of divorced parents who wish to issue separate invitations, without their new mates or if they are not remarried, the copy should read as follows for the father:

Mr. Harold Bremmer
requests the honor of your presence
at the marriage of his daughter
Eliza Beth
to
Mr. Richard Marchow
son of Mr. and Mrs. Robert Bergazyn
Saturday, the Fourth of June
Nineteen hundred ninety seven
at four o'clock
At Prince of Peace Lutheran Church
Smith and Cullen streets
Pascal, New Mexico

The mother's version uses both her maiden and married names:

Mrs. Janet Smith Aulinsky
requests the honor of your presence
at the marriage of her daughter
Eliza Beth
to
Mr. Richard Marchow
son of Mr. and Mrs. Robert Bennett
Saturday, the Fourth of June
Nineteen hundred ninety seven
at four o'clock
At Prince of Peace Lutheran Church
Smith and Cullen streets
Pascal, New Mexico

If the bride's mother is deceased and her father is remarried, then the invitation copy should read as follows.

Mr. and Mrs. Arthur Cohn *(father and stepmother)**
request the honor of your presence
at the marriage of his daughter
Mary Virginia
to
Mr. Ronald Barry Bergazyn
son of Mr. and Mrs. Elias Bergazyn
Saturday, the Fourth of June
Nineteen hundred ninety seven
at five o'clock
At Temple Beth El
1224 Rockaway Avenue
Woodmere, New York

*Of course, the information in italics is not to be included in the invitation copy—it is there to indicate to the reader that the bride's mother should precede the bride's father in the copy.

There are several trends among grownup brides and bridegrooms that are expressed in the invitation copy they use. Many of today's couples prefer to invite guests in their own names, rather than having parents issue invitations. This is determined by many factors, including whether the location of the wedding is in their new home city or in the place where the bride was raised, whether or not they are paying for the wedding or even sharing costs, and the couple's feelings about tradition. When the couple issues the invitation, the copy should read something like the following:

Moira Anne Garfield and Darrell Mohammed
request the honour of your presence
or invite you to dance at our/their wedding
or invite you to share the happiness
at our wedding
etc.

If the reception invitation is included in the main body of the invitation, it can read, after the body of the invitation, as follows:

Dinner and dancing after the ceremony at
The Pine Tree Inn
13500 Meadowbrook Road
Thoughtful, Oregon
or
Cocktail reception to follow the ceremony
or
Reception at eight o'clock
The Arts Club
etc.

Another trend in weddings that can be indicated on the invitation is specifying that guests not send gifts. When older brides and bridegrooms have fully furnished homes, they often prefer that guests contribute to a favorite charity in their names, or that they simply forgo the wedding-gift custom.

As one bridegroom put it, "We'd been [living] together for years and I didn't want people to think they had to send us a crystal vase or a piece of silver as a wedding gift. That's for young couples who are starting out with nothing." In the lower left hand corner of their formal invitation, they specified, "No gifts, please." Another couple said "Your present is your presence" on their casual invitation.

Some grownup couples prefer that children not be brought to their reception. If they believe that some guests will bring their sons or daughters, and they are too young to enjoy the reception or will be in the way, they specify that children are not included in the invitation. Ordinarily, writing "Mr. and Mrs. Jones" without their children's names on the inner envelope was enough, but not everyone is aware of the subtleties of etiquette. We know one couple who wrote, in the lower lefthand corner of their formal invitation, "No children, please." Were their guests offended? They don't know or care, they say.

Type Styles

The choice of type and the rather formal-looking typesetting are what convey a sense of formality or say "this is a wedding." Script and Gothic type styles are longtime wedding favorites. Never mix type styles or sizes. Simplicity is elegance in wedding invitations.

ENCLOSURES AND EXTRAS

Maps

For formal weddings where directions or a map must be included, the map is customarily printed on a card of the same paper stock. Occasionally, maps are done in a whimsical style. Be sure to include directions for guests arriving from a variety of starting points such as the airport, from the south as well as the north, etc. Some churches and hotels have preprinted direction cards. Make sure they are concise as well as accurate.

Pew Cards

The old-fashioned pew card, with a number that told guests in which pew they would be seated, was sent to guests who then whispered the number or showed the card to ushers who then seated them in the preferred seats near the front of the wedding ceremony site. Often, "within the ribbon" cards were issued to family members or honored guests, and these indicated they were to be seated "within the ribbon" that was stretched across the front rows to keep others from sitting there.

These cards were given to guests to guarantee good seating, and although they may still be used for the most formal weddings, I have never seen one. On the other hand, they could be a good idea. What does seem unnecessary is the trend of serving hors d'oeuvres or champagne in a room adjacent to where the wedding will take place, opening the doors at the last minute, and letting guests scramble to whatever seats they can find, without benefit of ushers or any other assistance. Informality can be just as confusing as the old rules based on class consciousness. Brides and bridegrooms may want to have some kind of seating procedure, though they need not return to pew cards or the "within the ribbon" designation.

Sending Wedding Announcements

To announce your marriage to friends or family members who were not at the wedding, an announcement similar in style to what the bride either used or might have used on her invitation is sent. Announcements do not require a gift as a response and are never sent to anyone who attended the wedding. The variations in language correspond to the variations used in an invitation. The most standard wording is as follows:

Mr. and Mrs. John Smith
announce the marriage of their daughter
Susanne
to
Harvey Spaulding
Saturday, the twenty-first of June
One thousand nine hundred and ninety five
Portland, Oregon

Response Cards

This is a good way to keep track of responses. Just saying RSVP on invitations, even with an accompanying address or phone number, will probably not work. Allow one to two weeks between the time you receive final responses and the date when you must let caterers know the exact number of guests. Response cards are enclosed in a separate envelope, printed with the bride's address so she can get a final count of guests. You may still need to telephone some guests, especially those of college age. Although the tendency of guests not to respond to invitations seems rude, I think it's more that people are impatient with unnecessary formality, and often are unsure exactly how to respond. (Do I need a certain kind of stationery? What wording should be used?)

Response cards are usually stamped, for your guests' convenience, and read as follows:

Please respond before (date)

M ____

Number of Persons______________

Why the *M* at the beginning of the second line? It's the first letter of *Mr., Mrs., Miss,* and *Ms.,* and indicates that you should write "Mr. and Mrs. Robert Bergazyn" or "Miss Eve Bergazyn will be pleased to attend," rather than the less formal "Carroll and Bob." I sometimes break with form, cross out the *M,* and write "Carroll and Bob can't wait" or "Carroll and Bob are looking forward to being with you," if, of course, that's true.

Thank-You Notes

The trick for writing thank-you notes is not to leave them until you have a huge number that need to be done, and you are feeling overwhelmed and guilty. A hint: Make them personal and thoughtful. It's more work, but at least it makes the job interesting.

Addressing Envelopes

Addressing is done somewhat formally, with formal titles and names written out, although state abbreviations may be used. Women's names precede men's names: "Molly Jonson and Peter Painter." Traditionally, the formal "Mr. and Mrs. John Callahan" is used.

The inner envelope is left unsealed, and the guests names are written again, using their titles and last names. If children under 16 are invited, their names can be used on the inner envelope only, not the outer envelope. The traditional rule is that children over 16 and still living at home are sent separate invitations. It's a rule I would consider breaking.

Be sure to have your invitation weighed. If they are overweight, the post office will return them for additional postage. That means reordering and readdressing envelopes unless you don't mind sending them stamped "returned for insufficient postage" by the post office.

If you don't have a return address printed on the back envelope flap of the outer envelope, be sure to write it out, or you may never know if the invitation was undeliverable, since it will not be returned.

Calligraphy

There are those who wouldn't consider sending a wedding invitation without having it addressed in calligraphy. I am not one of them. To me, calligraphy smacks slightly of gilding the lily for the young fairy-princess bride. For those who can't live without it, be forewarned: Order invitations early and allow plenty of time for calligraphy. Make sure, too, that you have reserved the time of a calligrapher whose style you prefer, and who has a reputation for not making too many mistakes. Costs range from $1 per invitation to about $4, for a special job with enclosures.

ORGANIZING RESPONSES

I suggest two boxes (keep your stationery boxes if you have them) for acceptances and regrets, and a master list that includes name, address, whether the guest has accepted or declined, number of guests accepting, and local phone numbers. If necessary, leave a blank space so you can make notes: "both architects, friends of John's family," or "driving in from Pittsburgh, need a babysitter at the hotel," or "coming to rehearsal dinner." This can also be a good way to keep track of gifts received and thank-you notes sent.

STATIONERY

Programs

Especially in the case of religious or culturally mixed marriages, where many of the wedding guests will be unfamiliar with the rituals included in the ceremony, wedding programs can be useful. When new elements have been carefully developed and added to the ceremony, programs that describe these additions can also be welcome reading. Examples: A bride and bridegroom that spend time lining up unusual music might want to tell guests about their choices. An Episcopalian-Jewish couple might want to tell guests about the meaning of the symbolism in their ceremony conducted by a priest and a rabbi.

Programs often include the time and date of the wedding along with other specific details such as types of prayers, music, and processionals, and names of those in the wedding party, honored guests, clergy member, and soloists. To avoid looking commercial ("and special thanks to a fine florist"), they do not contain the names of wedding service providers. Some have a special greeting or a carefully written paragraph or two on the history of the type of religious service or perhaps translations of prayers that are offered in a language other than English.

One of the most beautiful programs I've seen was a handwritten scroll listing the wedding time and date, the participants, and a schedule of events the day of the wedding. Printed in script, it was rolled and tied in beautiful, double-edged, dark green ribbon that matched the

Formal vs. Informal

What *is* the difference between a formal and informal wedding? Most etiquette books carefully refrain from defining the differences, using words such as large and elaborate or small and simple, rather than formal and informal, except in defining what the bride and bridegroom wear.

In the past, the large, formal wedding was held in the evening or daytime, and both men and women wore full dress regalia appropriate to the time of day. For the bride, that meant a gown with a train that fit her surroundings, with, for example, a cathedral-length train in a large church, temple or hotel ballroom, and a less elaborate gown in a smaller space. For evening, a man wore what was called "full dress," which included a tail coat, stiffly starched white shirt, wing collar, white bow tie, white waistcoat and white evening gloves. For a formal daytime wedding, the men in the wedding party wore silk hats with cutaway coats, or hombergs with black sack coats. This wedding was followed by a formal reception, which included a formally served meal and, often, dancing. Invitations were formal, which meant discreet and written exactly as the book recommended. The receiving line was set up according to the book (mothers only, no fathers).

Outside of circles where protocol is still carefully observed, formal weddings are less common than they once were. When weddings are referred to as formal, a certain elaborate quality is what is meant, along with contemporary formal dress for the wedding party, which usually means black tie for men and a long gown for the bride.

Informal is every other kind of wedding, and the trend, though it may be towards elaborate style in weddings, is toward the more casual and personal occasion.

Must You Invite Friends' Escorts and Dates?

If friends are engaged and if you know their future mate or are looking forward to meeting them, and if they are willing to travel from out of town to attend your wedding, you may want to invite them both. However, it is never mandatory to invite an escort or date for each single friend on your guestlist. You may want to mention that cost is a consideration, but most polite wedding guests will not expect to be invited as a twosome.

wedding's color scheme. Another program included the menu and names of wines served at a party that featured special choices in both areas, and it too was appreciated by guests who like to have details about what they are eating and drinking.

Programs are often delivered to guests by ushers or children, or can be placed on chairs or in pews. Printing costs decrease with volume. Be sure to have enough printed, and to appoint someone to pick up extras.

Other Stationery

You might want to order with your invitations the stationery you'll use in your married life. The old-fashioned way of viewing this was that since the woman was in charge of such details as thank-you notes, her married name ought to grace her stationery, as in "Mrs. Tom Johnson." Some women continue to use their husband's names, but other women often buy less formal stationery with their first name and married last name, or they continue to use their own names. Thus, Mary Johnson calls herself just that, or perhaps Mary Smith-Johnson. Couples often have both names, either first names only, as in "Mary and Tom," or with their last name or names, "Mary and Tom Johnson" or "Tom and Mary Smith Johnson," printed on note-style stationery. In any case, many couples, whether they have ours or his-and-hers names, will write thank-you notes for wedding gifts on a simple card or small stationery that is in a style similar to their invitations and is ordered at the same time.

Some brides wouldn't think of having a party without cocktail napkins stamped with their names. Some also like giving out books of matches and table cards that pick up a motif from the invitation and are ordered at the same time. This is entirely a matter of choice.

TRAVEL INFORMATION FOR GUESTS

Some brides and bridegrooms send packets of tourist information to guests who may be spending time in the area for the first and perhaps last time. A bride planning her wedding for her country home in upstate New York sent lists of antique shops, a map of the area, and a list of visitors' attractions suitable for children and adults. A bride being married in Chicago, where she had lived for many years, sent her eastern family and friends a booklet listing tourist attractions, a list of the couple's favorite restaurants, and a list of hotels with rates and locations.

Another thoughtful bride sent a New York public transportation map, a copy of a map of the downtown area where her wedding was taking place, and a list of common attractions and their hours of operation to her family and friends in Ohio. "If they could squeeze in a visit to the Statue of Liberty, I wanted to help them do it," she said. She also compiled a weekend schedule of luncheons, rehearsal dinner, photo sessions, and how bridesmaids and groomsmen should get around the city by car pool or taxi.

CHAPTER FIVE

The Wedding Gown and Other Ideas

A fairly clear image most brides have of their weddings is related to feeling absolutely beautiful. For many women this comes alive with the choice of a wedding gown, which they consider the most important and delicious decision of the entire planning process. Whether the wedding gown is highly traditional or entirely unconventional, no other symbol is as closely linked to both self-expression and the style or theme of the wedding. The wedding gown and the headpiece and veil are important symbolic garments, often the most carefully chosen ensemble a woman will wear in her entire lifetime.

When women talk about what they wore to be married in, they explain how and why they made their decisions with a vocabulary that is related as much to philosophy as it is to fashion. Favorite anecdotes are pulled out, dusted off, and told with renewed enthusiasm. Their voices change and their eyes light up. More than any other part of the wedding, the choice of apparel reflects who brides are and "what this wedding is all about."

STYLES OF GOWNS AND ACCESSORIES

To a certain extent, brides fall into categories when it comes to the philosophy and reasoning behind their choice of wedding gowns.

One group of women sees the wedding dress as a costume, a unique feature of the marriage ceremony and a more elaborate dress than any they have ever worn before or will have the opportunity to wear again. The traditional wedding gown is a ball gown with bridal features. When most women think of a wedding dress, they envision beading, embroidery, lace, a train, petticoats, and a full skirt with layers of fabric, or a slim gown with a mermaid bottom or overskirt—or several of these features (but not all of them), combined.

This traditional gown is usually worn with a headpiece and veil, white shoes, classically styled fine jewelry, and possibly gloves. As her major accessory, the bride carries a bouquet of flowers. If you have any doubt that this is a costume and ought to be seen as just that, ask when else in your life you will ever have the opportunity to wear a fabulous white (or off-white or pastel) gown with a veil, white gloves (indoors), and elegant white or pastel dyed-to-match shoes? How many lace or tulle or beaded dresses will you own? How many opportunities will you have to buy the perfect beaded bag, antique or new, that becomes an heirloom the minute you use it for your wedding? A traditional gown with accessories is something many women crave, and it can be adapted by a bride of any age and any level of sophistication. There is a wide range in even the most traditional wedding gowns, from synthetic ruffles and frills to elegantly designed silk.

Another group of bride-consumers wants a wedding dress closer in feeling to what they normally wear for special occasions. Even though the older, professional woman who wears suits and dresses every day sees her wedding attire in a somewhat lavish way, her interpretation may be less traditional than the full-skirted ball gown. A lawyer chose an ecru, all-sequin dress and she felt great in it. Similarly, a long slim dress in pale apricot silk and lace with an off-the-shoulders bodice and long sleeves takes the bridal image and gives it a contemporary twist. If she can afford it, the bride in this category might commission her favorite designer to create a special afternoon or evening wedding dress for her.

The third group of brides wants a wedding dress they can wear again and they mean it. Although brides rarely do wear the dresses they were married in on other occasions, that doesn't negate the validity of the "wear-again" sentiment. Saying you want a dress you can wear again is another way of saying you don't want it to look exclusively bridal. That you could wear the gown again is comforting and gives you a definition of how you want your dress to look and feel.

Why don't brides wear even fairly simple, nonbridal wedding dresses again? Some do, of course. Even dresses bought with another use in mind are often worn just once because they never seem quite appropriate for other occasions in a woman's life: once they've been worn for a marriage, they seem too significant for any lesser occasion.

The tea-length pastel Victorian lace or finely pleated and tucked

The Wedding Shoe Store

Some stores stand out from the crowd because of the comprehensiveness of their unique merchandise. Peter Fox in New York City is one of those shops, with a stock totally devoted to wedding shoes. The perfect lace-up boots for vintage Victorian cotton, the right heels for the 1920s dance dress, dozens of contemporary shoes that perfectly accessorize every wedding gown—all can be found at Peter Fox.

batiste vintage dress might be perfect for an elaborate garden or tea party. But how many formal teas or garden parties are American women invited to these days? On the other hand, the simple designer silk suit in off-white, worn with a black picture hat and black gloves, might actually be worn again, without the hat and gloves.

"The wedding dress is so incredibly significant, it takes a lot of time and thought. I'm embarrassed to admit this, but I bought two dresses before I got the right one. I'm an incredibly cheap person, a real tightwad, but the fact that I paid $750 – wholesale! – for my dress didn't faze me. It was hard to find a dress without frills that felt right for my wedding. I bought it thinking I didn't care if I never wore it again. I'm only going to get married one time. I might have been the oldest living first-time bride, but my dress was going to be perfect."

Betsy, 47, a first-time bride, who wore a Joan Vass off-white tea-length "petal dress" that the designer made especially for her. On her head, she wore a witty, chic wire crown created by Maria Vella of Bomarzo in San Francisco. Cost: $750 wholesale for dress, $100 for crown.

"I'd always envisioned myself wearing a very traditional, beautiful wedding gown. When I turned 30, I tried to give up that fantasy. But when I tried on the dress I ended up buying, it felt perfect. The dress is so important, I allowed myself time to shop to get exactly what I wanted. That dress made me feel gorgeous. And once I had my dress, everything else fell into place."

Ellen, 32, first-time bride, who wore a pure white, name-designer, silk taffeta gown with a re-embroidered and beaded lace bodice and a skirt constructed of two lavishly gathered poufs. The natural flower wreath she wore on her head held in place a tulle veil with a twenty-foot train that her maid of honor cut off after the marriage ceremony. Cost: $3,400 for gown and veil, a package price from the bridal shop.

"I had a sense that this dress was very meaningful and was excited about buying it. But I hated myself in white. So I made a real mind leap and had a dress made in apricot silk charmeuse and a beautiful reembroidered matching lace. The color made it nontraditional, but the fabric made it a wedding gown. It had a lace top that went past my hips and a swingy sort

What Do Women Want?

"Brides today are very smart. They come in knowing what they want and there is very little fluff or feathers about it. Sophisticated brides want dramatic looks, what I think of as the Audrey Hepburn style.

"Less is best, but it has to have a dramatic impact to it. A drop-dead look where the dress is fairly unadorned and the eye is brought right to the bride's face is what many women want. By sophisticated, I mean a smooth, clean line without a lot of breaks to it. Some beading, but not very much. As sure as I say that, brides will come in and want lots of beading. In this business, the more you know, the less you know. I thought when I got into this end of retailing that I had a great eye for the kind of dress women wanted, but I found I was often wrong. Wedding dresses are a matter of style, but also of fantasy. I tell brides not to judge dresses by hanger appeal, but to try them on. Ballgown-style dresses look very different on than off.

"Trains seem to scare older brides. I think they make them feel like Barbie Dolls all dressed up. But gowns can be ordered in a sweep length that just touches the floor or just brushes the top of the shoe. And I know that some brides buy dresses, especially at sample sales, and have the trains cut off."

Brenda Hendrickson, bridal salon manager, I. Magnin

of trumpet skirt with a modified train. The satin was cut on the bias so it fell beautifully and was very sophisticated. The wedding was in the fall so I carried deep-toned autumn flowers. I didn't want anything in my hair, but my hairdresser talked me into weaving a few flowers into a French braid."

Josie, 25, first-time bride. Cost: $1,400.

When Kitty Murphy first saw the white strapless chiffon dress hanging in the evening wear section of a department store, she says, "I thought it would be perfect for my wedding. You have to wear something that makes you feel gorgeous. But I also wanted a dress that felt like it belonged in an important ritual. This dress was made of beautiful silk chiffon and looked sort of straight even though the skirt had yards of fabric in it. The strapless top was gathered and the whole thing was beautifully detailed."

Kitty, 27, first-time bride. Cost: $500 for dress, $60 for matching scarf for her shoulders during the ceremony part of her side-yard urban wedding.

"She said, 'Why invest $2,400 in a dress I'll never wear again,'" a bridegroom said with pride about his wife's choice of a nonbridal gown. The bride interjected, "I looked at dresses in a traditional bridal salon. The good thing about that is seeing these really gorgeous, elaborate dresses with prices to match, so when you look at normal clothes the prices look reasonable. I chose an ecru chiffon dress, ankle-length and slim and beaded with bugle beads, an updated version of a 1920s dress. It was not a costume, but evocative of that era and very classic and chic at the same time."

Madeline, 35, second-time bride married to first-time bridegroom, 34. After much forethought, the bride went bareheaded. Cost: $1,200.

"My brother loves antiques and has collected some tiaras. He offered to loan me one. I took my favorite along when I was looking for a dress. It was an antique yellow gold with a lot of stones, so it needed an unusual dress. I finally bought a runway dress in off-white silk shantung with a train and applique and embroidery in shades of pink and blue and green. I saw it in a fashion show and it was a showstopper. The salon told me they couldn't get the dress. I didn't believe them until I saw it on the cover of a European bridal magazine and called the showroom and they said they weren't cutting the dress because of the labor costs involved in producing it. So I ran back to the bridal salon and bought the sample and had it altered to fit. Then my father changed the stones in the tiara to match the gown."

Janet, 26, first-time bride. Cost: $2,800 for gown.

When comedian Jenna Kahn got married, she says, "I was intent on buying something I could wear again, because I always dress up onstage. So I got this fabulous art-deco style suit with a straight, floor-length skirt," she says, "and had a pillbox hat made to match with a long veil in back and a little detachable veil in front. I always tell the audience that this is my wedding dress, that I'm the only living bride who actually did buy a wedding dress she wears again. They laugh. It was perfect for our art deco wedding. When we did a tango as our first dance, it was perfect."

Jenna, 34, first-time bride. Cost: $1,200 for suit, $100 for custom-made hat.

"We wanted to spend a total of $6,000 on everything at our wedding for 100. I don't like showy, expensive weddings because it seems to me that the bride and bridegroom get lost in them, that they're more for the parents. I wanted to wear something that said who I am, and found a beautiful, brocade-weave white wool jacket and had a matching white, tea-length chiffon skirt and top made. A friend insisted on sewing them and made that her wedding gift. I bought a $6 headband and my hairdresser put flowers on it."

Julia, 32, first-time bride. Total cost: under $500.

"I've never considered myself a traditional woman. But when I got pregnant and we had about a month to plan our wedding, I had to decide instantly whether I should wear a wedding gown or not. I wanted to, really wanted to, but thought maybe it was in such terrible taste that I'd feel stupid. My mother and a friend in the wedding business convinced me to wear what I wanted, and I found a beautiful white dress that rustled when I walked and I loved it. What I hadn't counted on was the change in my figure. My stomach was flat, but my breasts were huge. I filled out that dress and then some."

Anneke, 27, first-time bride. Cost: $700 for sample gown bought on sale and altered within a week.

"I knew the feeling I wanted from the first minute we chose the site for our wedding reception, which was a fabulously simple downtown arts club. I wanted a designer dress or suit, and found a white suit with black polka dots that was short and chic," says Mariellen, married in a bishop's study with the reception to follow in a private club. When she wears the suit again, and she is convinced she will, she'll forgo the dramatic black cartwheel hat and black midarm length black gloves she wore at her wedding. Mariellen insisted on not carrying flowers. "This was not a frou-frou ensemble, and flowers would have been a dumb accessory," she says.

Mariellen, age 34, second-time bride. Cost: About $1,500 for the ensemble.

The History of the Wedding Gown

Just a century ago, French and English lower-middle-class women who could afford it were married and buried in the same black silk dress, probably the best dress they would own in their lifetimes. Black was a formal color saved for wearing on special occasions such as family christenings and others' weddings.

Until Queen Victoria was married in 1840, royal brides were dressed in cloth made of silver. Although today we hardly consider Queen Victoria modern, she was regarded as quite contemporary for her era and wore white as a way of symbolizing a return to simplicity.

Not until this century did middle-class American brides begin to buy what we now think of as a traditional wedding gown—something designed to be worn only at the wedding. Even so, during the first decades of this century, many women continued to be married in their best dress or suit, just as they had for centuries before.

"I loved my outdoor wedding on a hillside at a friend's country house. I could finally use my collection of antique quilts on guests' tables and I wanted a dress that matched that feeling. After shopping for several months, I found a long, pale-blue-and-white-checked gingham dress with smocking around the hips. My only accessory was my bouquet, loose-tied summer flowers in vivid colors. What made the dress even more special was that my mother had worn a pale blue dress when she was married in the 1930s."

Molly Wendt, 40, second-time bride. Cost: $400 on sale.

"I love working on weddings, with brides who are confident and want to do things their own personal ways. I'll never forget a bride who had no idea at all about what she should wear or even where to hold her wedding. She said, 'I hate traditional things, and can't imagine myself in one of those huge wedding gowns.' So I took her shopping. We went to Comme des Garcons and bought a strapless tube dress. It was uncompromisingly contemporary and so everything in her wedding took its cue from that dress. It was an eggshell matte jersey and she was slim and it was just gorgeous—perfect for her. We did flowers in every shade of white with lots of branches and greens. The entire style of the wedding grew out of that choice."

Maria Vella, Bomarzo, San Francisco

JOIN THE SEARCH

Women who love clothes especially enjoy deciding what to wear to be married in, and choices have never been greater. In the past, wedding etiquette governed every decision, and those gracious but firm stipulations were meant to be followed. They told the bride what to wear at what time of day, for the precise degree of formality of her wedding, and for her state of grace and matrimony. *Good Manners for All Occasions,* by Margaret E. Sangster, published in 1904, minces no words: "Everything for the first time bride must be white...a hat is not to be worn with this [wedding] dress. At her second marriage a lady wears pearl gray or lavender, not white, and is very unostentatiously dressed." For the bride who was afraid of looking foolish or of making a mistake, such a formula might have been welcome.

Quality, Workmanship, and Fabric

Quality of design, fabric, and workmanship defines the wedding gown. The most elegant fabrics in the world are created for special-occasion dresses such as this. Satin, taffeta, tulle, mousseline, organdy, dotted swiss, silk in all its variations—charmeuse, four-ply, chiffon, organza, shantung, crepe, lace—are the kinds of fabrics used in wedding gowns. As for polyester satin or taffeta, don't sneer. Some is almost indistinguishable from silk and is often beautifully made into dresses that are much less costly than the real thing.

Workmanship counts. In the least costly gowns, beading and applique are glued to the fabric. In the more costly gowns, decorations are hand sewn. If you want your gown to become an heirloom, make sure it will withstand years of storage without disintegrating. Glue hardens and discolors. Two kinds of fabric used together in a dress can age differently.

As for "heirloom dry cleaning and storage," it is nothing more than placing the gown in a sealed box with the promise of being "airtight." Be forewarned: No cardboard box will be airtight enough to protect a gown from discoloring. Store your wedding gown, after having it cleaned, in a plastic bag that is sealed at the top and bottom, inside a box if that will make storage easier. No storage or special cleaning process exists that will guarantee the dress will retain its original shade of white. Most fabrics darken with age.

Today, the boundaries of individual style prescribe what brides wear at their weddings. "I always wear pants," says one bride, wondering whether she should adapt her style to her wedding, perhaps by wearing a custom-designed pantsuit in heavy, white, four-ply silk with a lace camisole underneath. Or should she forgo her normal garb and choose something tailored but in keeping with how she likes to see herself. There is no correct answer.

Another bride may want a Victorian-style gown because that's the source of the old-fashioned, romantic wedding fantasy she wants to emphasize throughout her wedding. Or she may want to wear something very different from what she normally wears, to emphasize the importance of this special occasion.

Whether a woman wants to spend $500, $1,500, $3,000, $5,000, or even $10,000 on a wedding gown, there is an entire industry ready to help. "Women change when they put on a wedding gown," says a bridal consultant in a small, exclusive bridal gown salon, echoing a sentiment I hear again and again. "It's my job to help them live out their dream." If this seems inappropriate for grownup brides, remind yourself that elaborate ball gowns are purchased with the same forethought and pleasure as wedding gowns. Costume parties, too, never go out of fashion, for the simple reason that people like to dress up in clothes they would not ordinarily wear.

What I Would Change About Our Wedding

"In the first store we went to during a shopping day in New York City, I found a perfectly simple, off-white silk dress by Jessica McClintock that had beautiful lace at the neck. I thought it was perfect but wanted to shop a little more. Later that day, we went back to get it and it was gone. The store called every one of its branches and the closest they could come was a size ten. I'm a size six, so it would have been too big in every way. I settled for another dress that was okay, but nothing like that first dress. I'm still mad that I didn't recognize perfection when I saw it."

Joan Malkow, 36, first-time bride.

As for the role the bride's age should play, the only limits are your personal wedding dream and your sense of good taste. For every two or three brides who want to dress up like Cinderella, there is one who does not. And yes, the bride of a certain age, no matter how slim and beautiful she may be, looks slightly ridiculous in a full-dress wedding gown. Before you make a final choice or decide to shop for one kind of wedding gown, consider just how narcissistic and fairy-princess-like you want to look. The image of the traditional bride is demure, young, graceful, pure. If you feel you deviate from that dreamy image, you may choose to reflect in your style of dress the kind of woman you actually are. Today's weddings, after all, do not pick up where fairy tales left off.

On the other hand, perhaps you don't care if you look slightly puerile – or don't think you do! – and want your wedding to be as close to a State Occasion as possible. Then go all out for the costume look in wedding gowns. Be comfortable knowing that your choice is based on an interesting theory: wearing the traditional wedding gown is an attempt to transport yourself outside of time and the vagaries of fashion. Just as we think of weddings as part of time eternal, we choose gowns that differ from day-to-day clothing as our way of being linked to something ageless.

One bride tells why she ended up dressing up far more than she thought she would. She describes a childhood ballerina fantasy and how it influenced her choice of wedding dress: "When I was 13, I thought, 'Well, I'll never be a ballerina,' and it was really disappointing. So when I found this dress that was a copy of a 1920s dress but had a real ballerina feeling to it, I thought I had one small moment to reclaim that fantasy. I bought that dress and loved every minute of wearing it."

As for common sense and good taste, no one wants to be caught on a sweltering hot day in a long-sleeved, heavy satin dress, or on a blustery winter day in a simple cotton Victorian garden dress. Cathedrals call for big, important dresses, in the same way that grand music from pipe organs or musical ensembles feels at home in churches. However, huge dresses with long trains look overstated in the simple church in the vale. Most women have an innate grasp of the qualities that distinguish one kind of wedding gown from another – formal from informal, charming and ingenuous from polished and sophisticated, glamorous from elegant.

And there is simply no universal rule of what is and what is not in good or bad taste. Even if there were, why assume that someone who dresses like a Las Vegas show girl would want to tone down her style for her wedding?

Most wedding gown saleswomen, called consultants, can tell you whether a cathedral-length train is or is not appropriate for your wedding's time of day, and they may even have a chart to prove it. If you care, listen carefully. Then rely on your own instincts and make your own decision. At one of the most charming outdoor weddings I've attended, the bride wore a 20-foot tulle train that was part of her veil, which breaks every rule in many books for what to wear to an afternoon wedding. Yet the effect was beautiful, and the bride didn't care about following old-fashioned rules of etiquette.

Generally speaking, your dress should be at least as dressy as what guests will choose to wear to your wedding. I've heard several stories, one told on herself by a bride who had decided to wear a white suit and then felt slightly annoyed when guests were more dressed up than she was. One guest was even mistaken for the bride! The guest wore her own informal wedding dress, a lace afternoon dress that was as appropriate for evening as it had been to be married in. The real bride, wise enough not to be annoyed at her guest, realized that she was a little underdressed.

At one time, the rule was never to wear either black or white to a

---

Bridal Gown Fabrics

Although there are no hard and fast rules about which fabrics should be used in which seasons, comfort and common sense dictate that a heavy satin or velvet gown could be uncomfortable on a hot summer day, and an antique batiste and lace dress would look odd during the coldest winter months. But these rules don't take the tropical southern states' climate into effect, and so these are simply guidelines.

Spring and Summer. Cotton, lawn, batiste, organdy, organza, dotted swiss, silk, lace.

Fall and Winter. Satin, velvet, taffeta, crepe, raw silk, moire, chiffon, velveteen.

Veiling fabrics. Tulle, Russian veiling, net, lace.

Laces. Venetian, alencon, chantilly, lyons, re-embroidered, point d'esprit.

Sewing a Gown and Veil

If you have a mother, friend, or dressmaker with excellent design talents and sewing skills, or you are an expert seamstress, having a custom-sewn wedding gown and headpiece or veil is an excellent way to save. Expect to have at least four, and possibly more, fittings. Remember also that patterns for wedding gowns are available from most major pattern companies.

According to one bride and the mother of a bride who made elaborate wedding gowns, sewing a traditional wedding gown is a time-consuming undertaking. "Don't do it unless you have hours and hours of time to devote to the project," says Susan Hollis, the mother of a bride. "It isn't something everyone should do. Wedding dresses often require tailoring skills, because the lining and interfacing are what give body and shape to the design. What's inside a gown is as important as what's on the outside."

Susan's sister, another expert seamstress, made wedding dresses for her daughter's first and second weddings. "The first time, we made it into a project and visited the local historical society to do research on nineteenth-century American wedding gowns. That made it really interesting, and the dress was gorgeous, with authentic details." ▸

wedding. The rule is now obsolete. At sophisticated urban weddings, more than half of the women guests may be wearing chic black dresses. White is still the choice, however, for first- and second-time brides, though women marrying for the second time often opt for ivory or cream-colored afternoon dresses. Whatever color you want to be married in can be appropriate. Chinese women wear red, the color of celebration. What is important is considering the reasons for wearing what you wear, and knowing why they are significant to you. A bride tells a story about a friend: "She walked into a bridal shop and saw this fabulous bridesmaid's dress with a black velvet top and a flowing white chiffon skirt. And she thought that the ruckus it would cause in her own and her bridegroom's family would make it not worth wearing." With a less conventional family, it might not have been a problem.

Differing points of view about what to wear can cause more conflict than any other part of the wedding. Barbara Lucas still hasn't gotten over the fit her mother had when she saw the vintage dress she wanted to use as her wedding gown. Aware that this might happen, she had chosen another alternative. "I didn't want to wear a dress to please her, but hated the idea of embarrassing her in front of her friends by wearing something she hated," Barbara says. "The dress was beautiful, cut on the bias in white satin from the thirties and in perfect condition. But it was backless and sort of sexy, and I thought she might have a fit

Bridal Gown and Veil Vocabulary

These are some frequently used design options in wedding gowns. Bishop, dolman, fitted, leg-o-mutton, cap, or oversized puffed sleeves. Bouffant, layered, mermaid-style, trumpet, gored, overskirted, swagged skirts. Sweetheart, bateau, cowl necklines. Embroidered, re-embroidered, appliqued, beaded fabrics. Seed pearls, crystals, sequins, and other beads.

Trains and Veils

Although the old rule was that the longest train was worn only at the most formal wedding, that no longer holds true. A charming tulle veil and train may be worn in the morning or afternoon, and many brides choose to be married wearing no train or veil at all. From longest to shortest, here are descriptive words for trains: cathedral, chapel, sweep. For veils: long, full-length, hemline-length, shoulder- or fingertip-length.

because it didn't look very bridal. My sister and I hid behind the nearest rack of clothes when she saw me in that dress, because she practically had a seizure she was so upset. But I had a less radical dress ready for her, and she didn't mind that one so much. I still think if I'd tried on the first one with a veil, she might not have been so shocked. "

It's wise to remember that the most mature individuals are not always those who insist on doing what they want, all the time and no matter what, but those who are willing to see other points of view, take them into consideration, and compromise before making a decision they know they will feel comfortable defending.

HEAD COVERINGS

To retain a sacred, ritualistic feeling at ceremonies, attention is paid to head coverings. In every culture around the world and throughout history, women and men have donned special clothing and have covered their heads as a sign of respect before entering houses of worship. Until recently, Catholic, Jewish, and some Protestant women and men always covered their heads in churches or temples. Many still do.

The veil, part of religious symbolism, is also a centuries-old symbol that many brides especially love because of its beauty and its essential "bridalness." In Genesis, Rebekah covered herself with a veil out of modesty when she first met her husband-to-be. The tradition of lifting the veil during the ceremony dates back to the Old Testament story of Jacob marrying Leah instead of Rachel, the woman he loved, because he did not see through the heavy veil during the ceremony.

The veil-as-symbol is precisely what some women resist. They may not like its historical associations or that purdah, still used by Muslim and Hindu women to cover themselves, is linked to women's repression.

On the other hand, bridal veils are so beautiful and different from what most women wear in their day-to-day lives that even the feminist bride may want to wear one of these wedding symbols. Today, though, the use of a veil is most often based on fashion or custom rather than on any set rules. "There is no ecclesiastical or church regulation about head coverings in church today," according to a Roman Catholic priest in Chicago. Whereas churches have individual traditions, it is generally considered the bride's right to decide whether or not to wear something on her head. If you are being married in a house of worship, check with your clergy member about customs and rules.

Veils and headpieces are far easier sewing projects than gowns. The simplest veils consist of gathered tulle anchored to headpieces. Creative amateur seamstresses will have no difficulty with even fairly complicated veils, if they're willing to experiment. If you have a well-developed eye for fashion, you may be able to forgo trying on veils with your wedding dress. If you are not sure, try headpieces and veils on for style and scale before you attempt to design your own, or find a dressmaker to make one.

Even low-priced fabric stores often have extensive lines of headpieces. Fabric boutiques carry higher-quality bridal fabric and headpieces, and all types of fabric stores carry tulle veiling.

Set Your Wedding Gown Delivery Date Early

Wedding gown manufacturers seldom deliver wedding gowns before the date specified on your order. If the shop where you buy your gown doesn't suggest using a date somewhat earlier than your actual wedding date, insist on it so you can avoid paying for high-priced, last-minute alterations, or worse yet, not having your gown in time.

If you wear a headpiece and veil, choices have never been more varied or aesthetically pleasing, from the simplest headbands to elaborate hats, to yards and yards of the sheerest tulle attached to flowered or jeweled headpieces. Bridal salons often custom-design headpieces with a variety of veils and can offer advice about what type of veil should be worn with which dress.

Individual preference and fashion trends are the strongest influences for those women who choose not to wear a bridal veil. Other than an occasional headband or barrette, women today seldom wear hats, veils, or hair decorations. People often understand symbols without being able to articulate the reasons behind them, and, not surprisingly, more brides and attendants than ever before go bareheaded today, forgoing head coverings once worn for reasons they no longer advocate, such as an extreme of modesty. The woman who says "I never wear anything in my hair and think it would make me feel uncomfortable to do something so out of character at my wedding" may either wear nothing at all on her head or choose a simple flower-decorated barrette, comb, or headband that accessorizes her dress. A single fresh flower, antique silk rose, or simple ribbon-decorated hair accessory might feel right for this bride.

Many brides say they wore something in their hair as a peacemaking gesture to those around them rather than out of personal preference. Others resist the pressure. A bridal consultant observes that "brides put off the decision until last and then they feel stuck and don't know what to do, so they end up wearing something they don't like. In the old days, when everyone wore hats, women knew what they liked to wear and what they looked good in. And they also used to wear fancy hairdos for special occasions more than they do now."

On the other hand, the woman who sees herself in a veil should not sacrifice her fantasy. There is no doubt that the wearing of a headpiece or a crown is tied to the regal feeling a bride traditionally wanted on her wedding day. People behave differently when they are dressed in elegant clothes, and a head covering such as a veil, hat, or headpiece adds to a formal look.

Unabashed Sentiment

Sentimental about your mother's gown even though you don't want to wear it? Have a small piece of lace or her bridal handkerchief sewn into your own gown. Some day, her gown may be discarded. But you will have a piece of it, along with a photograph, to show your daughter or granddaughter.

WEDDING ACCESSORIES

Ideally, your daughter or granddaughter will someday treasure your wedding finery. In the meantime, choosing accessories is a wonderful way of investing the occasion with another layer of meaning. That the accessories are the best you can afford, within the range of your taste and budget, is what counts.

An embroidered lace and linen handkerchief, a white satin evening bag, beautiful 1920s-style shoes, graceful, lace-to-the-ankle Victorian-style boots, the elegant jewelry you wear – these could become objects of sentiment, perfect for a daughter, niece, or good friend to borrow or own. A vintage or unusual new evening bag to hold your lipstick, tissues,

---

My Mother's Wedding Shoes

One of my earliest memories is of my parents' wedding photograph, a sepia-toned picture of my mother and her sister alongside my father and his twin brother. I still have that photograph, in a notable position as part of an arrangement of family pictures that spans five generations. My mother wore a pale grayish pink suit of a beautiful-quality wool, my father a tweed suit.

But what I remember best are my mother's shoes. I remember them as if I held them in my hands yesterday, although I last saw them when I was five. We moved then, from an apartment to a postwar suburban house with small closets, and my efficient mother must have discarded her wedding shoes rather than move them, a decision I regret. They were of a closely worked, multicolored fabric of palest pink, yellow, and blue, like a bargello weave but with the colors closer together, almost like finely embroidered or crocheted stripes.

The feeling I get when I think about those shoes is of childlike awe. They were probably the most expensive shoes my mother ever owned, and I can imagine her excitement when she found them—the perfect wedding shoes. Her attitude when she showed them to me said "these are *very special* shoes." They were off-limits in the elaborate dress-up games we played where her cast-off clothes and shoes were fair game. They were, I still think, the most beautiful shoes I have ever seen. If I were ever to see a pair like them, I would buy them in an instant, out of some visceral need to re-create that moment in my mother's foreshortened life: wartime, 1942, at her marriage to my father in the study of the Basilica of St. Mary's in Minneapolis, Minnesota. In a pink wool suit and the most beautiful shoes in the world.

The Best Thing About Our Wedding

"Looking gorgeous for the first (and maybe last) time in my life! I found that the dress and flowers really set the tone for the wedding and a lot of plans and ideas fell into place once they had been decided upon. My advice: don't compromise on your dress or your rings. The first you'll remember the rest of your life; the last you wear for the rest of your life.

Lori Greenwood, 25, first-time bride.

What I Would Change About Our Wedding

"I wish I'd worn a longer veil with a train on it, rather than having a train on my wedding gown. I knew before my wedding that bustling the gown never really works because the fabric is so heavy and my bustle came down about ten times while I was dancing. If I'd had the train on the veil, I would have had it cut off to the middle of my back and would have kept it on during the whole reception."

Priscilla Hennessy, 29, first-time bride.

and keys might be just the item to have and to hold. If you love shoes, make them an interesting and unusual accompaniment to your dress. As for jewelry, most brides, even glamorous ones, choose something discreet, either real or the best costume jewelry they can afford.

How do you find unusual wedding accessories? Some department stores specialize in collections of beautiful bags, hair decorations, and other accessories that don't look obviously bridal. Boutiques and vintage clothing stores may have just the shawl or handbag you're looking for. And, of course, bridal gown salons often show designer collections of bridal jewelry, bags, and other exquisitely designed accessories.

Wedding Lingerie and the Trousseau

Beautiful lingerie is an unmistakable part of the bridal ensemble. Everything new from the skin out should be the best you can afford, whether that means a lacy merry widow bra that gives you a smooth line under your dress or the perfect lace bra and garter belt with sheer stockings or panty hose in the perfect pale tint. In an era of fitness and jogging bras, it can be a pleasure to buy fragile and beautiful lingerie.

Chances are that purchasing your lingerie will be nowhere near as "thrilling" as Marguerite Bentley wrote about in her *Wedding Etiquette Complete* in 1947: "Assembling your lingerie trousseau can be a thrilling task, because the items you will buy are so dainty and beautiful. Here is your chance to indulge your fondest wishes, but you must use your head as well as your heart in the selections of the pretty things you like best and will need most in your new life." Bentley's comprehensive list of almost 75 items included "best," "second best," and tailored sets of matching slips, negligees, nightgowns or pajamas, bedjackets, and step-ins or short, close-fitting panties of glove silk. Also on the list were some "miscellaneous suggestions":

Tailored crepe robe, quilted robe, or woolen housecoat for winter, 1 negligee of the soft, dainty type, tea or hostess gown, 2-3 pairs of mules or bedroom slippers, 2 daytime girdles or foundation garments, 2 sport girdles, 1 evening girdle, 2 evening slips, 6 daytime brassieres, and 3 evening brassieres. The list concluded with 12 to 18 pairs of stockings and suggested that monograms are rather nice and that brides should have them embroidered if they can afford it.

Why so much? Margaret E. Sangster explained the reasoning behind the trousseau in her 1904 book, *Good Manners for All Occasions*. "The bride's outfit when she leaves her father's house is very complete, because she will not any longer send her bills to her father or ask him for money to buy clothes. From the moment she becomes a wife her good man must pay her expenses whatever they are. The young wife naturally desires to defer the period when her husband must be asked to purchase things for her—wearing apparel particularly."

She adds, "I have seen brides so worn, so pale, so 'tuckered out' by the sewing of weary weeks, that they went like wan ghosts to the altar; they had used up nervous tissue so shamefully that they were unfit to enter on marriage. But...women...no longer prepare for a wedding as if they were about to emigrate to a wild region beyond the reach of shops."

Needless to say, times have changed, and lingerie shops for the quick, impulsive purchase of something beautiful are everywhere. About half of what's on Bentley's 1947 list is nowhere to be found in the Victoria's Secret catalog, and no one I know under the age of 60 has ever owned a bedjacket.

Ask friends. Check the Yellow Pages. Look at the ads throughout bridal magazines, including those small ads for boutiques and specialized services in the back pages. You may not have known that most major department stores have a handkerchief counter where handmade Swiss cotton hankies edged in lace are sold. Only your self-image and confidence and your pocketbook need limit your choices.

WEDDING MAKEUP

Grownup women don't need magazine cosmetic dot charts to show them how to apply eye shadow and blush for their weddings. On the other hand, your wedding day may be a fairly long day in the spotlight, with photographs being taken from early morning until late at night, and you will want to look your best. You may prefer to have your makeup done by a professional. But keep in mind that you won't want to look markedly different on your wedding day from the way you do the rest of the time. "An actress friend offered to do my makeup," says one bride, "and so I had her do it a few weeks before. My eyebrows looked awful the first time, but we worked on it and she did a fabulous job. I needed more makeup for pictures, but didn't want to look as if I had been made up for the stage."

You may want to use a slightly heavier hand for the day of your wedding than you would for normal daytime or evening wear. But this is not the time to attempt unusual or special effects, unless they've been tried well in advance, other than slightly more dramatic and carefully applied foundation, eye makeup, and lip and cheek color. Brides generally think of appropriate cosmetics colors as soft and romantic. A woman who usually wears dramatic makeup, however, will not want to alter her normal look by forgoing her bright red lipstick or theatrical eye makeup.

BRIDES' HEAD COVERINGS

Brides often have strong ideas about what to wear on their heads. This sampling of opinions shows the wide range of appropriate head coverings.

> "I didn't want to wear anything on my head. I have very short hair and everything I tried on looked dumb even though my mother thought they looked great. So I put my foot down and said no. And the day of the wedding it was fine. I loved the way my dress looked without a veil and was glad I stuck to my guns."
>
> **Julie, 32, first-time bride.**

> "I feel as though maybe I shouldn't have worn even a short veil since it was my second marriage. But I loved the idea of my husband-to-be lifting the veil during the ceremony and so I had one made that was very short all around and detachable. I anchored it to a beaded headband that I wore at the reception and it looked and felt good with my dress."
>
> **Priscilla, 28, second-time bride.**

> "I loved my veil and wouldn't have considered not wearing one. I only wish I'd followed my instincts and made it even longer."
>
> **Deborah, 28, first-time bride whose hairdresser designed and made her a 20-foot tulle veil anchored to rolled fabric roses made to match her wedding gown.**

> "It was bad enough that I was wearing a white dress at 47, but then I had to wonder what to wear in my hair and that was an even more difficult decision. When a friend gave me a party in the studio of another friend who is a florist, we all tried on these crowns they had on display, laughing and admiring them. So I picked out the one I liked most and had them incorporate into it my father's Masonic pin and a necklace my mother wore on her wedding day. They were married in 1940 and were poor, but there were these little pewter animals on the necklace and it looked great at the back of the crown. It was very, very special to me. I still display my wedding crown on an antique wooden head on my dressing table."
>
> **Betsy, 47, first-time bride.**

"I'm like my mother. I like to know what's right, and then decide what to do. Etiquette books say 'no veil for a second-time bride.' I thought, well, that's fine. So I wore a headpiece with veiling in back, just no veil over my face. My mother made the headband, which came under my bangs on my forehead, out of lace that matched my dress. And then there was a big pouf in back, and veiling that hung down over the backless part of my dress. It was perfect. As for all the rules, I didn't feel that this was my second wedding. I felt as if it were my real wedding, the one that counts."

Melissa, 29, second-time bride.

CHAPTER SIX

The Look: Decor and Flowers

Beautiful surroundings and decorations are part of most brides' wedding fantasies. Some brides envision themselves carrying an outstanding bouquet of flowers. Others have an image of making flowers an important part of their overall wedding style and they often find working with a florist an especially satisfying part of planning a wedding.

"Flowers make you feel good, which is why so many cultures have worn them throughout history," says Maria Vella, co-owner of Bomarzo, a creative florist in San Francisco. Beth Tarrant, a painter and graduate of the Art Institute of Chicago who owns Anna Held Florists, says, "Nothing makes you feel more special than surrounding yourself with the aroma and beauty of fresh flowers." Beth tells a story about her five-year-old niece. "You're like the good fairy who sprinkles pixie dust and makes everything look beautiful," said the flower girl at a family wedding after witnessing her aunt set up the flowers.

Before you begin making appointments with florists, consider these three basic elements of party planning.

To create memorable parties, many professional planners establish a theme that then influences their choice of food and decor. Because this is a wedding, you don't need more than a subtle decorative idea or theme: a spring garden or an Italian vineyard. The bride who draped the ballroom ceiling with acres of blue cheesecloth and hung stars from it seems to me to be reaching for overstatement. The wedding *is* the essential theme.

Consider the atmosphere and flow of the party you want to create. Do you want guests to move around and chat or to remain seated, moving only back and forth to the dance floor? This will be influenced by the decision whether to have elaborate buffets set up throughout the room or traditional food service.

Remember to think big when it comes to room decor, and small when it comes to details such as your wedding bouquet and cake decorations. Even weddings for 50 guests must be held in fairly good-sized rooms, and big ballrooms need a lot of work to transform their personalities. Colorful table linens with abundant centerpieces on risers can establish a distinctive feeling the minute you enter a room. Black linens, candlelight, and mirrors, with tropical, exotic floral centerpieces at the center of each table, create a sophisticated look. Pastel tablecloths draped with yards of white tulle and sweet-smelling, country-style flowers create a romantic feeling.

The late John Calori, formerly head of I. Magnin's display department in San Francisco, in business for himself as an event designer, was known for his great taste and style. "You need to think about the overall effect for a big party, which is what weddings are," he explained. "A room with huge windows that are pitch-black at night and which overlook the San Francisco Bay is beautiful, whereas the same room during the day might not work at all. When brides say to me, 'Well, we could bring in trees,' I tell them to find a place that doesn't need such major work if they're on a budget.

I might suggest using two huge urns of branches and flowers right where people enter a room to create a startling and memorable effect," John said. "Then, you can go with more greens and fewer flowers in the centerpieces because you've already made your statement." As for flowers and flower costs, he recommended that brides find out when the flowers they love are in season. It sounds so basic, he said, "but if you want lilacs and peonies, don't think of being married anytime other than spring."

The best wedding he helped create? The last one, John said, laughing. "I worked with a caterer and we set up a seafood buffet with fresh oysters being shucked and huge clamshells filled with shrimp

Bridal Bouquets

Because this may be the only bouquet they will ever carry, most brides want wedding flowers that are unusually beautiful. There should be no unpleasant surprises when a bride opens her flower box just before the wedding begins. Inside that box, she should find flowers that make her feel happy just looking at them, flowers that she will be proud to carry down the aisle (assuming there is one for her to walk down), that will look lovely in the photographs, and that she'll have a pleasant memory of for the rest of her life.

The bride's flowers should complement the style of her gown or dress, as well as her personality and the style or design theme of the wedding. Wedding bouquets can be described by shape and by the style of flowers.

Cascade. Like a waterfall or cascade in a river, this bouquet flows downward and may have a blossom or two suspended below the bouquet by its own stem or on a ribbon. This is the most common and traditional shape for bridal bouquets, worn with full-skirted or elaborate ball gown-style wedding dresses.

Presentation Bouquet. Think of the roses carried by Miss America along her left arm as she waves with her right. This can be as simple or as elaborate as your own and your florist's ingenuity can con- ▸

around a rock waterfall with circulating water. We created little vignettes like a meadow, and an Italianesque food station with terra-cotta and huge sunflowers, and it was visually very exciting. Each scene fit the food. That made it unusual and fun."

DIFFERENT APPROACHES

Scott Johnson, a bridegroom in his thirties, is still amazed by how much he learned about the wedding business while he and his fiancée were planning their wedding. He and Eileen Marriner are lawyers and they approached their marriage ceremony as they would a work project, creating a time line for the tasks that needed to be done. "The difference was," Scott says, "that this had our own happy deadline."

"When I started, I knew absolutely nothing about flowers. But to me there's no such thing as an ignorant question, and so I learned a lot," says the bridegroom. Eileen still isn't sure what kind of flowers they had at the wedding. But they loved the sophisticated combination of bright colors with jewel-toned flowers that they first used at their ceremony and then moved to the reception. "If you'd told me we would spend over $4,000 on flowers, I would have thought you were crazy. Now, I think they were worth every penny," she says.

Scott and Eileen are Protestants of different denominations who decided they wanted their entire wedding in one location so guests could go from ceremony to cocktails to dinner without leaving. They chose an elegant, venerable Chicago hotel and found a Methodist minister who was willing to perform the ceremony there. "The rooms were all beautiful with high ceilings and molding, but they needed something to make them feel like a wedding was taking place there, since they didn't have the traditional beauty of a church," Scott says, explaining why they had chosen flowers to beautify their space.

They had a classic hotel wedding, complete with the changeover of the main room where both ceremony and reception were held. To define an aisle between the rows of upholstered chairs that hotels set up for wedding guests during the ceremony, they used centerpieces on risers. The colors they had chosen were rich, a palette that ranged from purple to blue to red, with lots of yellows and golds.

After the ceremony, the 150 guests went from the ballroom where the ceremony was held, to an adjacent room for a stand-up cocktail hour. During that time, the room was reset for dinner, and the aisle flowers were removed from their risers and transferred to the centers of the tables. Scott and Eileen spent a considerable additional amount of their decorating budget on special linens. The hotel could have supplied white or pastel tablecloths, but they chose burgundy moire table coverings with brighter red brocade napkins. During the one hour when guests were in the cocktail reception, the cake and cake table were also extravagantly decorated with flowers, carrying out the European millefleur theme (sizable bouquets of small to midsize flowers in a wide variety of colors) they had chosen for the entire wedding. Earlier, the walls had been swagged with thick garlands of greenery with fresh flowers at the point of each swag. The room was kept a little brighter than usual, so the deep colors in the flowers looked bright and lively rather than dark. "The effect was like something in an Old Master's painting," the bridegroom remembers. "People still talk about our flowers," says Eileen.

Outstanding Bouquets

Most bridal bouquets are not very memorable, except perhaps to the bride. These were distinctive enough to stand out, the kind of flowers that would gladden any heart.

- Two dozen of the palest peach tulips were arranged with white French, double-flowering lilacs in what the florist described as a combination of the loose-tied and presentation bouquet styles, stems showing, but constructed so the bouquet fit into the crook of the bride's arm. The strong lines of the tulips and the softer, more romantic quality of the lilacs made a wonderful combination.
- A wildflower bouquet carried by a bride at an informal city wedding with a country theme had loads of Queen Anne's lace, a few full-blown pink roses, and wild-looking garden flowers in blue, yellow, and white. This bride wanted flowers that moved. Although her bouquet looked completely unstructured, the florist spent hours taping and wiring some of the more fragile flowers so they wouldn't droop. But it looked unstructured, and yes, the flowers moved.
- Julie, married for the first time at 26 to a man who had been married before, carried what her husband still refers to as her "wand," a single cala lily wrapped in silk ribbon. The bride and bridegroom are both architects, and this understated style went with the very design-oriented, "less-is-more" motif of the entire wedding.
- Elena carried an extravagant, multicolored bouquet that weighed in at just under ten pounds. Several dozen of the palest peach roses and at least a hundred stems of wildflowers in every shade of rose and white were all carefully wired, taped, and arranged in a cascade-style bouquet.
- Susan Elizabeth carried an almost round, tightly arranged bunch of palest pink roses and peonies for an unexpectedly romantic bouquet that complemented a contemporary, simple silk dress. There were no greens, but dozens of thin silk ribbons in shades of pink, white, and off-white cascaded from the nosegay.

---

ceive, but should not be longer than what can fit comfortably, with some spillover, along the length of your lower arm.

Round Cluster Bouquet or Oversized Nosegay. This might have a ruff of lace or tulle behind it, and can be made of one type of flower or a mixture. A favorite is a tight round cluster of roses, or roses and peonies, with few other flowers and minimal greens.

Loose-Tied Bouquet. This is made up of a variety of flowers chosen to go with the gown and wedding style. They are arranged as if just picked from the garden and are tied with silk, double-edged ribbon, or a combination of ribbon and lace.

The Best Thing About Our Wedding

"It was the smallest of my weddings and very personal. It was in our apartment and the chandelier was decorated with about a hundred roses and everything looked beautiful. I hired the best caterer in New York and the food was great. When my father came to get me in the apartment next door where I was getting dressed, he didn't say much and I said to him, 'Dad, don't you think I look nice?' And he said, 'Honey, you always look nice when you're getting married.' That still makes me laugh."

Marjorie Roth, 35, third-time bride.

Floral cost breakdown: $2,250 for 15 table centerpieces; $1,000 for two urns filled with flowers at the ballroom entrance, later moved to the dance floor; $400 for an arrangement for the place-card table; $300 for decoration of the wedding cake and cake table with flowers and garlands; $500 for wall garlands. Total spent on flowers was $4,450. Linen rentals were an additional $650.

Not everyone spends that kind of money on wedding flowers. At the other end of the financial and design spectrum is Janet, a 24-year-old bride, her mother Anita, and the bridegroom's mother Sally, who decorated their church and the park district mansion where the reception was held for less than $400, which came to just a little more than $1.25 per guest. "I'd love to spend $4,000 on flowers, but couldn't possibly afford that," says Sally, who worked out most of the details of her son's wedding decor. As the head of her church's decorating committee, Sally is used to thinking on a big, though never lavish, design scale. The secret to the low cost? "We did it all ourselves," she said, "and I started buying things on sale even before I knew what I'd do with them."

The wedding was held in a suburban Lutheran church that had so much beautiful stained glass that Sally didn't think it needed many flowers. The park district clubhouse used for the reception was another story. Chosen for its reasonable cost and proximity to the church, it was not perfect. "It was beautiful, but the ballroom, with its stone fireplace, and dark beams and woodwork, felt cold. I wanted to soften and lighten it for our summer wedding," Sally explains.

The day before the wedding, Sally and her husband John went to the downtown farmer's market to buy whatever was fresh, plentiful, and inexpensive and also went with the pink and rose color scheme. They bought long-stemmed pink roses for $12 for two dozen, a bargain price that still amazes Sally. They also bought full, sweet-smelling herbal bouquets for table centerpieces. The bouquets were made up of flowering basil, oregano, and thyme, with flowers such as snapdragons and zinnias, at $4 each. Sally bought a few extra pink flowers and inserted them into the bouquets where she snipped off the bright zinnias.

The morning of the wedding, family members went to work, delivering the flowers and decorating supplies to the reception site. Sally had her tools, which included wire, flower and wire cutters, and a small stepladder. She and her crew mounted 16 precut pieces of tulle, 4 yards each, on 16 lighting sconces around the room. Each tulle pouf had trailing streamers and was decorated with silk greens and pink roses. "The sconces were high on the wall, or I would not have used such inexpensive

More than a Corsage

Corsages do not have universal appeal. Care should be taken to make sure the flowers for the mothers of the bride and bridegroom are appropriate and pleasing to them. A single flower pinned to a dress or onto an evening bag, or a small nosegay or cluster of flowers that can be carried, may be more appropriate than a conventional corsage.

Flowers for the Men

Boutonnieres are customary for the bridegroom and his attendants, ushers, and fathers, grandfathers, and honored guests. Expect to pay somewhere between $4 and $20 for each boutonniere, depending on the type of flowers used and the labor.

Boutonnieres need not match each other. In fact, it is often more interesting when they do not. The bridegroom's should be distinctive, similar in style to the flowers used throughout the wedding, or can duplicate a bloom in the bride's bouquet. Some brides like colorful boutonnieres; others prefer white. Boutonnieres should not be overly elaborate. Men do not wear peonies (unless, of course, this full-blown flower matches their gold chains and blow-dried hair), although I have seen small gardenia boutonnieres that looked glamorous and festive.

Roses, stephanotis, and small orchids are commonly used. Lilies of the valley were once traditional but are seldom seen today because of their fragility and limited availability.

silk flowers," she says. Wired to each sconce was the tulle, which resembled a bridal veil, two silk rose bushes, and a small branch or two from the birch tree in the bridegroom's backyard. The long-stemmed roses were used to designate special tables.

More than cost, there was a major expenditure of time on planning, purchasing, and decorating the reception site. "Some people might prefer hiring a florist to do everything but I loved decorating myself," Sally says. "I tried a couple of draped, swagged effects before I decided on the tulle poufs on the sconces and the swagging on the fireplace. Everyone thought they were great-looking and I thought it all worked."

The investment of time kept the floral costs modest. "I bought the silk bushes [the greens] on sale, two for $1, and the tulle was three yards for $1, for a total just under $100," says Sally. Flowering plants for the altar were rented for $4 each. Pews were decorated with large white bows that had been saved from another family wedding, dried

The Toss Bouquet

Some brides prefer to save their bouquets and purchase specially made toss bouquets of inexpensive flowers. Remember to keep the toss bouquet handy during the reception for the bouquet-toss ceremony.

Your own bouquet may become a memento. The toss bouquet will almost always be misplaced within a few minutes after it is caught. This may be the one place in your wedding when a simple bouquet of carnations and other inexpensive and common flowers is appropriate. Even if you're planning to have gorgeous, extravagant flowers, the toss bouquet is distinguished by not being worth much forethought or expense.

baby's breath from Sally's own garden, and white feather doves from a previous Christmas decoration. The plant rentals were $4 each and were delivered with the bride's flowers, which cost about $150 and included her attendants' bouquets, boutonnieres, and several corsages. Reception flowers from the farmer's market came to $110, for a total of about $360.

CHOOSE YOUR FLORIST WITH CARE

Most brides begin planning their weddings not knowing much about flowers. Mothers who have entertained a great deal or who, like Sally, know something about decorating, may be better prepared to work with florists. As one mother of a bride put it, "Let her pick her own flowers? She doesn't know a thing about them." In reality, because learning about flowers is often so satisfying, working with a florist can become a both interesting and enlightening part of planning a wedding.

Choosing the right kind of florist or floral designer, or making arrangements to do your flowers yourself, is clearly an important decision. There are all kinds of florists, and to a first-time flower shopper, the field can look like a maze.

For the sake of simplicity, think of florists in the following categories.

Rose-and-carnation shops. As their name indicates, these shops carry a limited variety of flowers, though they may say they specialize in weddings and offer package prices. For the most part, they don't have access to suppliers of more unusual flowers, because the focus of their business is on volume rather than on creative or original design. Even if your floral needs are simple, take a close look at what you'll get for your wedding dollar here, and remember that neighborhood shops with talented owner-designers often provide the same service at the same or even lower prices, with better flowers and more interesting design. Rose and carnation shops often do not have designers you can meet, and the person who sets up your wedding will not be the person who sold you the flowers. They often specialize in the catering hall wedding with table centerpieces of two carnations, dyed to match the bridesmaids' dresses.

Small shops where the owner is the designer. You can identify these shops by their high level of taste. Look at the flowers in the shop's cooler. If they are garden flowers and the popular wildflowers and greens, along with some sculptural branches, you know that this shop has access to interesting flowers. As for the shop's design talents, talk to the owner and ask to look at pictures of his or her work. At these shops, the owner or manager will either deliver and set up your flowers, or will be there to supervise the work.

Bucket shops. Called this in the trade, they carry a wide variety of flowers displayed simply in buckets, and often have plants and unusual greens. Everything is sold cash-and-carry. Blooms may range from garden-variety flowers to exotics from far-off lands. Judge their work by the designers who do weddings for the shops. Many owners of these shops do not want to specialize in corporate work or labor-intensive weddings, and have set up their businesses in this format for just this reason. Although bucket shops are wonderful places to buy flowers, they may prefer not to do weddings because they are not staffed to handle the work involved.

Florists as artists. These florists may also be painters or sculptors, and they bring an artist's eye and creativity to the business of flowers. A San Francisco florist who designs whimsical wire and flower jewelry is one. A Long Island florist who also sells interesting decorative arts and antiques and specializes in the country-garden look is another. A Chicago florist who is a graduate of the Art Institute and who uses flowers as her medium is yet another example of this type of florist. Some of these floral artists have retail shops filled with specialized wedding equipment.

Flower Girls

Is there anything more charming than a flower girl wearing a Kate Greenaway-style dress and carrying flowers as she precedes the bride down the aisle? Flower girls can wear garlands of flowers in their hair and carry a small nosegay, or scatter rose petals (or potpourri) from their own flower-decorated baskets, or carry hoops decorated with flowers. The hoop has a historical connotation: when toys were simple, it was a childhood favorite. Although hoops have not been seen in weddings for years, florists say flower-decorated hoops have enjoyed a comeback since Princess Diana's flower girls carried exquisitely decorated hoops.

Others work from loft spaces or even their own homes and get business via word-of-mouth referrals. They may or may not have access to risers, lighting, wedding canopies, etc.

Sophisticated, often urban, and always upscale florists. Not only do these florists design centerpieces and floral decor, but they can create an entire design and floral atmosphere. The English country garden with perennials is popular, but these florists can create an atmosphere tied to many periods in history or to a certain design influence or feeling. One of these top-level florists could create, for example, the look of an Italian villa with trellises and grapevines, flowers, fruit, and vegetables, which would make a show-stopping wedding motif. They work at high prices and often won't do weddings for less than $5,000 or an even higher base price. Most have an elaborate stock of aisle risers, lighting supplies, wedding canopies, trellises, and other props.

Except for the rose-and-carnation shops, the lines separating florists into these categories can be hazy. An artist-florist may, for example, love creating an entire atmosphere with flowers and have enough workers available to handle the most sophisticated, high-cost wedding. The little neighborhood shop owner may stretch her design capability and set-up and delivery staff for a special client. And the fanciest, most expensive florists may take on a smaller, less costly wedding than what they usually do for a bride they like who has ideas they can easily handle.

And it may not matter which florist you like. Some wedding site managers will specify the type of florist you must choose. Big city hotels, for example, will caution you against using small, neighborhood florists, whose delivery, setup, and removal of goods after the wedding – their systems, in other words – don't quite work within the hotels' larger scale.

Before choosing a florist, you may want to visit several. If it's a full-scale retail shop, look in the flower coolers on a delivery day. If you see buckets of the most ordinary flowers (carnations, gladioli, and roses), then that's what they sell and also what they buy from their suppliers. In smaller shops, an owner's style is almost always apparent in the design and decor. I warm up to shops that are overflowing with flowers and interesting baskets, vases, and other floral accessories. These shops feel like something you'd stumble across in London or

Paris. I'm also open to a flower shop that resembles a gallery, with stark, uncluttered white walls and flowers and branches displayed in laboratory-clean, clear glass vases that are sculptural objects. Remember that many floral designers do not have retail spaces.

Make sure, however, that the florist you choose has the equipment you need. Risers to hold centerpieces above the table, pillars or aisle stands for aisle flowers, special lighting effects, and wedding canopies are not insignificant expenses for a florist. Most florists have some wedding equipment; others have more; a few have a great deal. Decorators and designers who specialize in weddings are another option. They may have equipment and sophisticated ideas, and often work with a florist or a wholesaler who supplies flowers. Don't expect them to work with your florist. If you plan to use a designer, hire him or her first, since he or she will undoubtedly have personal florist preferences.

My Favorite Snotty Florist Story

The opposite of the florist with wedding packages and no personal attention is the florist who wants to dictate every phase of your wedding but whose attitude tells you that he or she is bored to death by mere weddings.

One such florist told a bride that he simply would not decorate or provide linens or flowers for a gift table for the reception. "Darling, you shouldn't have friends who do such a tacky thing as bring gifts to a wedding. Refuse to accommodate those people!" The bride, taken aback, said nothing. But later, accepting that some of her relatives would, indeed, bring gifts to the reception, and that there was no way of stopping them (even if she had wanted to), she stopped payment on the florist's deposit check and wrote him a letter canceling his services.

Ask to see photographs. Most florists have snapshots in small albums, for which they apologize profusely. But even these pictures can give you an idea of their work. Big, elegant florists, of course, who work on fancy budgets, often have oversized photographs of their work, which are fun to look at. Avoid, at all costs, the oversophisticated florist who has seen and done it all, and therefore may not be able to offer you fresh ideas.

CREATE YOUR OWN STYLE IN FLOWERS

Before your first visits to florists, analyze your needs. How much decoration does your church, temple, or wedding site need? Will flowers already be in place? If you bring in baskets or urns of flowers for each side of the altar, for example, can you then remove them to use at the reception, or are they part of an expected donation to the church or temple? Visit the space where you will hold both the ceremony and the reception. Find out what other brides have done and what is customary. Some churches are filled with flowers at certain seasons, or they have stained glass and elements of decor that make extra flowers redundant. For the ceremony, consider aisle or pew decorations, and flowers up front. Jewish weddings are held under canopies that range from simple to elaborate. Churches often look fine with two oversized floral arrangements, one on each side of the altar. Some allow no decorations at all beyond what they provide. Very few allow lit candles to be used as part of the decor or in floral arrangements.

Think also about the quantity of flowers at the reception. Elaborate

---

Three Wedding Flower Problems

If you have a grownup attitude about your wedding, almost no floral mishap could be labeled a disaster. I've witnessed several disappointments, however, and know they occurred because of a florist-client mismatch or, in one case, because of a florist with more attitude than skill.

- I watched my young friend open the oversized white flower box at her wedding. She carefully slipped off the bow and looked inside with anticipation. Her face fell. Too busy to think about flowers, she had hired the florist recommended by the catering hall where the wedding would be held. At their one meeting, my friend gave her almost no instructions. After looking through a book of common flower arrangements and bridal bouquets, she chose a fairly standard, all-white bouquet, asking the florist to make it look "looser and less arranged" than it did in the book. "I want something beautiful," she said, assuming the florist would know what she meant. When she got a stiffly wired, over arranged bouquet of roses and carnations, she was disappointed, but it was too late to make any changes.
- One bride hired a popular and trendy florist, a two-man team. From the start, she had problems. The florists didn't return her telephone calls. They didn't send the contract for months after they agreed to. They didn't get back to her with details after meetings. On the one hand, she may have been overly perfectionistic, a bride who quit her job to devote all her time to planning her wedding. On the other hand, the florists didn't know how to calm her fears or increase her confidence in them. She allowed their reputation to reassure her.

  The day of the wedding, they delivered over $5,000 worth of flowers, a truckload, to the mansion in the country where her wedding was being held. One of the florists abruptly approached the bridegroom and demanded a check. The bridegroom was appalled and more than a little annoyed. "We won't even unload the flowers if you don't give us a check," the florist said nastily.

The bride forgave them, though, when the flowers were in place. They were perfect, tall and regal in their graceful Italianate candelabras with their built-in vases. But the worst was yet to come. During dinner, the beautiful but top-heavy centerpieces began, one-by-one, to topple over. After the second one crashed into someone's food, the wedding consultant quietly explained the situation to the bride and bridegroom and then she went around the room and removed the flowers from every one of the containers. Rumor has it that the same thing happened to the same florist, with the identical containers at another wedding several months later in a downtown hotel.

- When a friend was married several years ago in Denver, she hired a florist she'd known for some time. She didn't know a lot about flowers, since before she began planning her wedding she had needed little more than an occasional arrangement or funeral basket. But she had grown to like the man in the neighborhood shop who always helped her.

  Again and again she told him she wanted her bouquet to look "wild" and loose. Two weeks before her wedding, she realized that the florist didn't understand the style she was talking about. Just before her wedding, while on a business trip to Chicago, she bought $30 worth of flowers in a downtown bucket shop and flew home with them. She took them to her florist and showed him exactly the kinds of flowers she wanted at her wedding, especially in her bouquet. His response showed his confusion: "Where in the world will I find Queen Anne's lace and black-eyed Susans?" She wound up with lovely flowers, arranged in a loose, simple way, but they were not even close to what she had hoped for. Her neighborhood florist did not have access to the unusual flowers she'd had in mind.

---

rooms may need few flowers. Some rooms will look barren without the softening effect that flowers create. Ask the catering director or manager what is customary here, too.

For the flowers themselves, if there is a bucket shop in your city, visit it and familiarize yourself with the names of your favorite flowers. Think about the atmosphere you want to create at both your wedding ceremony and your reception. The woman who is attracted to sharp-edged exotic flowers in intense colors will not want anything softly romantic or Victorian. Clip photographs of flowers you like and dislike from wedding magazines and from home and fashion magazines (anywhere centerpieces and flowers are used as accessories). Bookstores carry excellent flower books with beautiful, full-color pictures. Think in terms of developing an educated sense of design, color, and scale in flowers.

Have in mind the colors you'd like to use. Remind yourself that becoming obsessed with finding flowers that match dresses or linens will unnecessarily complicate the process. Think about nature's colors and how they all blend and complement each other. Purple or blue flowers will work with blue linens or attendants' dresses if they're approximately the same shade. Whereas there is a wide range of red and pink shades in flowers, there are very few peach-colored blooms. Don't insist on matching any two shades. And never, ever dye flowers.

Whites need not match. What makes an all-white room or ensemble interesting is a variety of textures and shades. The same is true of bridal bouquets. Flowers come in every shade of white. Even at the center of the purest white rose, the color is creamy. All-white bridal bouquets, with only the whitest of orchids, look flat and uninteresting. The trend today is toward using color, ranging from pastels to more vivid combinations of flowers, even in bridal bouquets.

Doing Your Own Flowers

Priscilla Kahan did her own wedding flowers in suburban Connecticut and she did not have an easy time. Priscilla envisioned herself arranging flowers the morning of her wedding when she thought she would have nothing to do. She also thought that by keeping busy, she would avoid feeling nervous. What she didn't plan on was how physically wearing the job turned out to be. Nor did she expect the mansion where her wedding was being held at 4 P.M. to be locked at noon.

"Since I envisioned loosely gathered summer bouquets as centerpieces, I thought I could do them myself, get exactly what I wanted, and spend less on flowers than I would if I worked with a florist," says Priscilla, 34, a top retailing manager who had once worked in the display department. Priscilla ordered about $300 worth of fresh flowers and vases and spent an hour or so talking to the owner of her favorite flower shop. A week before the wedding, she returned to the florist to make a selection of the specific types of flowers. The day of her July wedding, she and her maid of honor met for coffee as planned and drove to a friend's house to borrow a station wagon.

"I had my first misgivings at the florist's. She showed me how some flowers had to be cut on a slant and others straight across, and she explained which was which. She loaned us cutting tools, but didn't have anyone there to help us, so we loaded about ten buckets of flowers into the car. Those flowers were heavy."

When they arrived at the mansion, every door was locked. By then, Priscilla remembers it was hot, so they unloaded the flowers and put them in the shade, and they sat down under a tree to wait for the maintenance crew to return. An hour later, they started cutting flowers. As they cut, they put them carefully into vases with a small amount of water since they didn't have much. "All the time, I'm wondering if they'll wilt in the heat," says Priscilla. Finally, the maintenance crew showed up.

Priscilla and her maid of honor carried the flowers into a room where they could finalize the cutting and arranging. An hour later, after rushing through the work, the centerpieces were ready. It was now just past three, and the bride's and maid of honor's bouquets needed to be arranged. At 3:30 P.M., Priscilla realized that she had no time for a shower and would just barely be able to fix her hair and get into her wedding dress.

"I was a wreck. Doing flowers is a lot more physical than I imagined. The only good thing was that it kept me from getting nervous. What would I change about my wedding? I'd pay someone to do the flowers."

Gail Sarni, on the other hand, did her own flowers and is happy she did. "We had two huge urns with flowers in them delivered to the church, and my father moved them to the house we rented for the reception. I'd only invited family to the wedding, but had a gang coming to the party, so this was a good way for us all to keep busy. My mother and my sister and I put the flowers into ten centerpieces. I'd allowed an hour, but the whole thing took less time than that and was fun," she says.

Gail's mother had bought baskets and taped pieces of floral clay into each one. Gail put together one centerpiece they all used as a model. "We broke down [florist's lingo for took apart] the big vases, which were made up of eight different kinds of flowers. We pulled them out by type. One person did all the ferns, another all the red and pink flowers, another all the purples and blues, etc. I was the head of the team and did most of the cutting. We followed my sample, so we knew exactly how many of each kind of flower to use in the centerpieces. One of us counted out all the flowers and the other two put them into the baskets. It was a snap. My flowers were perfect. It gave me something to do other than sit around and worry," she adds as an afterthought.

Gail had called a handful of florists in Boston before she found one who was willing to work with her. Cost was important, but Gail wanted beautiful flowers. Since she had been in the hotel catering business for years, she had watched florists work and knew exactly how to organize the task.

The florist provided the bridal bouquet, as well as three bridesmaids' bouquets. Gail's bouquet was all white roses, which cost $75, and the bridesmaids' were multicolored, at $45 each. Total cost for the wedding was about $500.

Use Your Bouquet Again

You may want to show off your bouquet throughout the reception, but resist carrying it around with you. Brides who carry loose-tied bouquets with stems that are not wrapped or immersed in water (in small, individual water-filled containers attached to each stem) may ask for an ice bucket or vase to hold their bouquets near them on the wedding table.

Bridesmaids' bouquets and a mother's nosegay can be treated the same way, as extra flowers at their tables.

Be prepared, too, to give florists an approximate amount you are prepared to spend for flowers. More than any other area of wedding costs, brides often end up spending more than they anticipated for flowers, because they so enjoy the process of learning about and selecting them. But be forewarned: The flower business is far more complicated than pretty blooms, and you will never learn as much as your florist. A certain amount of trust is mandatory.

Therefore, work with a florist or designer you admire and respect; then trust him or her. There are dozens of variables when it comes to flowers. The weather is a potential source of problems. If a florist tells you that the lilacs are not good the week of your wedding because it's been an extremely dry spring, ask if they can be found at any price, then decide whether it's worth the extra cost. Bringing in lilacs from France can be expensive. If the florist is reputable, you'll be told the truth.

If you're interested in saving floral costs, consider going with what is called a "market buy," which means using whatever flowers are good and plentiful the week of your wedding. An important factor is which markets retail florists have access to. Those that deal with specialty or major floral suppliers can obtain flowers from around the world, and wildflowers and garden flowers as well.

Ironically, the most common flowers are often the most difficult to find. If you crave peonies, be aware that the domestic blooms are available only around Memorial Day. They may be available from the southern hemisphere at another time, but expect to pay dearly for them, and the supply may be limited so that only the biggest florists can buy them. The same is true of lilies of the valley, violets, and other short-lived, garden-style domestic flowers. Roses, even the recently developed, fist-sized blooms, are available year-round, at a range in prices, if a florist has developed resources and can get them. The price range in roses is wide. A small rose will cost far less than a bigger one; and roses from a florist who knows how to nurse them to their full perfection for the day of your wedding will be more expensive than cash-and-carry roses.

Apple blossom branches are fragrant and sculptural in quality. But they are fragile and must come from a nearby apple tree. If you have a wonderful garden or orchard, look for a florist who is willing to combine his or her talents and flowers with some of your own flowers. Or find a florist who has access to these flowers (perhaps from his or her own garden) and then hope for perfect growing weather.

A WEDDING FLOWER CHECKLIST

When thinking about wedding flowers, be aware of whom you want to have flowers on the day of your wedding. Here is a checklist similar to the one used by most florists to help you organize what you'll need. To save your own and your florist's time, you may want to have the information in each category organized and ready for discussion at your first meeting.

Bride

color and style of gown, with fabric sample if possible

style of bouquet and flowers

bouquet for tossing, unless you plan to throw the real one

floral headpiece or other flowers

Bridal party

color and style of gowns

quantity and style of bouquet and other flowers

Flower girl

color and style of gown

style of bouquet or basket of petals to drop

floral headpiece

Boutonnieres

number and style of flowers for bridegroom, best man, groomsmen, ushers, ring bearer, fathers, grandfathers, and others

Corsages or other flowers

number and style for mothers, grandmothers, godmothers, aunts, cousins, teachers, mentors, neighbors, and other important guests

Decorations for ceremony

main altar decorations

aisle and pew decorations

foliage, rental greens, or props such as canopy, candelabra for altar, or aisle runner

length of aisle and type required

Decorations for reception

place-card table

centerpieces (number of tables and size, linen style and color)

cake decorations and flowers for cake table

Miscellaneous tasks

delivery and setup

removal

Appreciation or thank-you flowers

WHAT YOU'RE PAYING FOR

Expect to spend about half of your flower costs for labor. Labor costs cover a great many unseen parts of every flower bill. This starts with the ordering of the flowers from carefully developed resources. Once flowers arrive, they are prepared by someone who removes bruised or dead leaves or thorns. Then, in what can be a days-long process, they are nursed into perfect condition. Finally, in the single step that consumers see, they are carefully combined in ways that show off their beauty.

Then, and this is a major procedure for weddings, the fragile flowers are delivered at peak condition by a work crew that is competent and well trained to set up your wedding. After the wedding, unless you are purchasing containers such as vases, baskets, risers, lighting, canopies, etc., or you keep arrangements simple so the containers don't have to be returned, someone will pick up those pieces that were loaned or rented to you and return them to the florist.

Those florists who are firmly anchored in the upper price range have teams who specialize in every phase of the floral business. Chicago florist Virginia Wolff, a creative and enthusiastic designer, says the single biggest secret to her success is the team of competent, loyal workers she has hired over the years. In fact, Wolff herself, who is hardworking and exceedingly charming, can be seen checking the condition of every flower in every arrangement minutes before a wedding begins.

She gives tremendous credit to her labor force. One of the men on her staff is the buyer. He has learned, in years of experience, how to get flowers from Colombia or other far-off lands at peak time for weekend weddings. If storms keep planes from taking off or landing, he knows alternate resources and routes for just about every flower on earth. "Roses have to come in on Wednesday for a weekend wedding," explains

Wolff. "They're like tight little bullets when they arrive and have to have their stems cut every day. In the meantime, they must sit in an immaculately clean bucket of water that is just the right temperature. That's how you get roses to open perfectly. Once they're open just right, they go into the cooler to crisp."

Look for florists who take time to explain what they can do for you and what kinds of weddings they have done in the past. They should be able to offer information about the type of flowers available at the time of year when the wedding is being held, and some preliminary design options for your wedding. You will want approximate prices and, if you're spending more than $800-1,000, detailed and specific prices for each phase of your wedding. Also ask florists about their set-up and delivery crews. Negotiating the labyrinthine back passageways of big city clubs and hotel banquet facilities takes time, experience, and patience, and not every florist knows how to do it. Asking who will set up the flowers on the day of your wedding is a reasonable question. You need to feel confident that the florist you hire can carry out the last detail of what you contract for him or her to do.

Depending on what you spend for flowers, how detailed your plans are, and how you balance your own demands with time constraints, expect to meet with the florist between one and four times. If you're spending more than $3,000-4,000, three or four visits may be necessary (although one busy bride who spent over $5,000 arranged everything without any meetings because she trusted the florist).

Can you negotiate prices with your florist? On the actual cost of flowers and labor, not much. There may be room for compromise on the type of flowers you choose, and on the number and size of centerpieces and bouquets. The biggest, fanciest florists often suggest using flowers as backdrops for photographs, or recommend other costly special effects. A fancy, impressive floral piece on a pedestal by the receiving line does look great in pictures but is not a necessity. On estimates, some florists suggest mounting curtains, trellises, and gates covered in flowers. If you cut back on those, you can cut costs considerably.

There are ways to decorate weddings without flowers. Choosing a garden site that is already filled with blooms is one way to save. Using less costly flowering plants or greens as centerpieces rather than cut flowers is another.

OTHER DECORATIVE EFFECTS

The trick when decorating a large space is to think big. Colorful table-

The Best Thing About Our Wedding

"I had a very casual, very warm and beautiful wedding in a small country town in Connecticut in December, and it was 60 degrees and a perfect day. But what I'll always remember is how friends decorated our car and wrote funny and obscene things all over it, and my parents had to drive the car back to Brooklyn with all the writing and everything hanging off it. We still laugh about that."

Evan Brookstein, 27, first-time bride.

The Best Detail About Our Wedding

"The antique bird cage I provided to hold gift-checks was a nice detail. Because we knew guests would bring checks, I wanted a system better than wearing a white satin moneybag. We placed it on a table next to the cake table, and had two envelopes we'd received ahead of time in it, so people knew why it was there, and then guests just slid their envelopes through the bars.

Bette Jelinek, 29, first-time bride.

Advice from the Florists

Ze Ze (who uses only his first name in both his business and his personal life) on East Fifty-second Street in New York, a Brazilian-American who is frequently featured in national magazines, says brides should hire someone they like and trust. "I usually tell them I have to see the site, and then we need to talk about their ideas and my own. I like to be practical, and love working with businesswomen who are practical too. We can sometimes take the money from one part of the decor and put it into another part, and I don't mind thinking that way."

"We really have to be selective [about clients]," says Ric Harris, manager of Grassroots in Las Colinas, an upscale planned community in Irving, a suburb of Dallas, Texas. "We can do only so many weddings and we want to reflect the bride's personality. The worst kind of client is someone who says, 'Let us see a wedding book.' They might need to look for someone else. We want to work with the individual and with the family if they're involved. Colors are important. If a bride wants a sense of earthiness, for example, we might mix herbs in with her bouquet. If she wants something more formal, then we'll do that. We want to do whatever it takes to reflect her personal style and feelings. That's how the best florists work today."

Maria Vella at Bomarzo in San Francisco says, "Flowers are like every element of design. There are grownups who are so tied to convention that they do the same thing over and over and never develop a design sensibility. On the other hand, I worked with a very young bride recently who knew exactly what she wanted. She chose a wedding site that didn't make her feel constrained and wore a beautiful apricot silk lace gown. She had great taste and wanted to do things her own way, with her own wonderful artistic sensibility."

"Weddings are my favorite things," she explains. "But the people I like the least are the ones who carry around wedding books that tell them exactly how to do things, and who are so afraid of making a mistake. I almost never like the most formal weddings. They're usually no fun."

"Some people come in and it's as if they're in a store shopping. They say, 'I'll take one of these, this aisle stand, this *chuppah,*'" says Virginia Wolff in Chicago. "That's not the way to do it. I want clients to tell me what they think about in terms of their wedding. Sophisticated with candles? Romantic, soft with tulle? A garden wedding? How do they want their weddings to feel? Are they having the kind of band that changes clothes for each set? Or something more sedate? Then, once I know that, I can create an entire design built around their dream, their image."

cloths or flowered print fabric draped or arranged in swags on tables can change the entire appearance of a room. Sculptural branches in oversized wine buckets with a few flowers could create memorable table centerpieces. A white trellis in a garden setting could be decorated with vines. One big city florist chose huge, fluffy white feathers as centerpieces and for years sold them to brides as unique in the world. In a wedding with an Italian vineyard theme, grapevines can be used to construct a trellis, and vine wreaths with fruit and vegetables can be placed at the center of each table. For autumn weddings, pumpkins and gourds along with fall leaves and a few flowers would be appropriate. And dried flowers are sometimes used to create color and a memorable effect.

When decorating with or without flowers, think in terms of props. One bride who had virtually no money for flowers tells how she covered boxes with beautiful gift-wrap and put one at the center of each table. Before the wedding, she asked one person at each table to come up with a "gift" of a quality needed in marriage. Then, in addition to toasts, guests took turns telling what their gifts symbolized and how the quality would help the bride and bridegroom have a good marriage.

Balloon and party accessory shops often have ideas for wedding decor, mainly built around what they sell. Not only can you buy goods from them, but you can also pay for delivery and installation. Jack Margarella, owner of Celebrations, a party accessories store on Chicago's north side, talks about using all kinds of materials other than flowers to decorate tables. For example, a lighted building was placed at the center of each table at an architect's wedding. "We sometimes use light or glow sticks twisted into shapes such as hearts. We've done a single rose in a balloon. Once we did piñatas, which sell for about $15 each, with balloons and flowers." Outside of flowers and fabric for linens, the single most popular decorating item is balloons, in arches, bunches, pastels, and brights. Margarella lists the kinds of props he uses at parties, some of which might be suitable for a special-interest wedding: old 45 rpm records, individual cakes, musical props such as instruments, magic props.

Weddings are not the time for crepe paper streamers, but thin paper party streamers could be interesting draped around an object with oversized glitter scattered on the table for a festive, party atmosphere. Remember, too, that candlelight softens everything. And yards of tulle can make almost any site romantic. As for themes, it bears repeating. The wedding is the theme. Leave "Arabian Nights" to the prom-decorating committee.

CHAPTER SEVEN

The Wedding Feast

Americans have never been more knowledgeable or enthusiastic about what they eat. Food today is often sophisticated and as likely to be international as regional – a style that is a creative amalgam of influences and tastes, interpreted in a confident, lighthearted way that is typically American. Today's brides and bridegrooms are often well traveled and have brought home an appetite for excellent, high-quality food with dramatic flavors.

Combine those trends with the fact that men and women have always commemorated special occasions by providing guests with the best food and drink they could afford, and you will understand today's wedding feast, offered as a gesture of generosity and hospitality.

RECEPTION TIMING AND COST

The first influence on the type of food served is the time of day the wedding reception is held.

The traditional **wedding breakfast** has always been lunch, although you could follow an early morning wedding with a lavish country-style breakfast (city-style breakfasts are often brunch). Breakfast dishes are frequently served at brunch wedding receptions, although lunch can as easily be Chinese dim sum as omelets or eggs Benedict. (Wedding cake and champagne can be served any time of day.)

More popular as a wedding celebration meal than breakfast is what Americans call **brunch,** a combination of hearty breakfast and lunch foods. At a midday wedding celebration, this meal could start with champagne or mimosas and juice drinks, and might include a variety of fresh fruit, muffins and sweet breads, possibly omelets, crepes, side dishes, and dessert. The meal could then be followed with wedding cake and coffee, and possibly a coffee station serving a variety of flavored coffees.

The **wedding lunch** bears little resemblance to the usual American midday meal. It is a light, elegant dinner rather than a hearty lunch. Luncheon weddings usually last for two to three hours, including the ceremony.

The wedding followed by a **cocktail party reception** differs from the dinner buffet party only in the quantity of food served. The menu can be limited to finger food, such as appetizer dishes and hors d'oeuvres, or it can provide a buffet that might include an entree such as roasted and sliced filet of beef or a chicken or fish dish and a pasta or rice side dish. With today's lighter appetites, guests get plenty to eat at the cocktail party reception. What distinguishes the cocktail party from the dinner reception is the seating arrangement. At a cocktail party guests expect to stand, sit, or perch wherever they can, to wander and talk to other guests, but not to have to spend an entire evening in the company of one group of tablemates or even to remain seated for the entire party. Cocktail parties start from late afternoon to early evening.

The **wedding tea** can be a dessert buffet or combination of tea sandwiches, dessert, and wedding cake, served with champagne and wine or with coffee and tea. This reception could be held in the late afternoon, earlier than a cocktail party, say from three or four to five or six on a Saturday or Sunday.

The **dinner party** reception is the most expensive wedding reception, whether it's a seated service or a buffet. Guests at evening weddings expect to spend four to six hours with their hosts. It is not unusual to attend a wedding at 6 P.M. and not leave a dinner dance until almost midnight, although many couples prefer to condense the wedding into four hours, starting the marriage ceremony at 7 or 8 P.M.

In terms of the exact timing of receptions, there is no hard-and-fast rule. Some couples will have ceremonies in the morning no matter what kind of reception they choose, even if that means an entire day separating the two events. Others wouldn't think of having the reception separated by more than the time it takes to move from the ceremony site to the reception space, whether that's two steps or two miles. Generally, brunch is in the later part of the morning or the earlier part of the afternoon, while lunch is a slightly later version, similar to an early dinner. The duration of the reception depends on the activities planned.

What I Would Change About Our Wedding

"I loved it but there were a few dumb, practical things I overlooked. I didn't serve hors d'oeuvres with cocktails. I don't know why someone didn't bring it up. I planned the menu with one of the best caterers in town, and he never mentioned it, maybe because he thought I would say something if I wanted to serve them. And my father-in-law's attitude about dinner was that there wasn't enough food. I married into a culture where food is very important and abundance counts, and my caterer was sort of chic and he didn't understand that. And neither did I at the time."

Jennifer Jackson, 29, first-time bride.

Dancing keeps guests at a party longer. Whatever time you schedule the reception to begin, make sure that service begins early, since there may be guests who skip the ceremony and go directly to the reception.

As for the type of service, some events – and certain spaces – seem appropriate to buffets, others to sit-down service. Caterers and catering managers often have insight into how and why the different services work with different age groups and times of day, and within specific spaces.

Expect to spend from 50 to 60 percent of your total wedding budget on food and beverages.

AMBIENCE AND ATTITUDE

A major trend in American food, as it has long been in Europe, is what successful restaurateurs know – that ambience and attitude are almost as important as the food itself. Today's American food professionals know this and have taken food service a step further. There is almost nothing more impressive than a lavish American buffet, set up in a variety of serving dishes on different levels, beautifully decorated with greens and flowers and with a wide choice of well-prepared, attractive foods.

Menus today are as much about attitude as they are about taste. In restaurants, this is conveyed in a variety of ways in addition to the quality and style of the cuisine: graphics and style of menu, skills, attire, educational level of waitstaff, and decor of rooms. The wedding feast, the most important and costly menu most brides and bridegrooms will ever choose, is often a synthesis of all these trends. Wedding feasts tell guests a great deal about their hosts. The best are made of excellent ingredients, displayed with care and served with style.

One popular choice in food service today is the buffet, for reasons that are intrinsic to grownup weddings. Buffets display food generously and in an interesting way. Guests move around a reception and do not feel trapped at a table all evening. San Francisco caterer Meme Pederson, owner of Edible Art, tells about a wedding party she set up. "After we brainstormed with this couple they decided to hold the reception in a greenhouse. We found a beautiful one and totally redid the displays of orchids so that all the same kinds were together, and then we put them under spotlights. We displayed the platters of food on rolls of sod, all on different levels. At that party, we did a carving station and a Mandarin pancake station. The food was good, familiar food, not terribly out of the ordinary. But the display was so wonderful that it made the party."

Another couple chose a winery for their wedding, and Meme tells how it overlooked the vineyards during a time of year when wildflowers were everywhere. "We do our own canning and displayed the jars so the sun came through them. It looked like stained glass. This was in mid-September, so we had big fruit and vegetable displays like piles of tiny champagne grapes and wonderful ripe peaches. We had things in big, copper containers and we had flowering kale and greens everywhere. It all emphasized the naturalness of a fabulous northern Italian buffet with food set up in two rooms so guests could move around."

Even fairly simple weddings often feature unusual food. "Everyone loves hors d'oeuvres and desserts, but they've changed over the past few years," says Philadelphia caterer Robin Rovner Barg. "It used to be that hors d'oeuvres had only to be salty and desserts were sweet. That was enough for them to be successful with less sophisticated palates. Today, Americans want both ends of the meal to be interesting, with strong flavors in very, very small portions."

New York caterer Catherine Schubert says that when choosing the food for a wedding there's more involved than picking the menu. "Brides should find someone whose food skills they respect, but also someone they trust. Then, they must relinquish control. Women in business are so used to being in charge that they'd better find people they respect or they'll drive themselves crazy," she says.

Meme Pederson agrees. "The best thing to do is tell your caterer,

The Best Wedding Decision I Made

"I decided to hold my wedding at a downtown private library with a ballroom. That meant I could hire my own caterer and focus on making the food really special. So many times people are bound by hotel or banquet facilities' policies and standard procedures, whereas this gave me a lot more autonomy and control in having exactly the reception I wanted. There was a lot of work at the last minute, but I had such a beautiful and different wedding that it was worth it."

Katie Chalmers, 26, first-time bride.

Carvery Stations

To keep guests moving, individual service and carvery stations at buffets have become a hit from coast to coast. Edible Art, a caterer in San Francisco, lists seven "Performance Station Options" for an hors d'oeuvre reception. In each case a chef in spotless white is stationed at the buffet to help guests.

The Classic Seafood Bar offers Pacific Coast oysters shucked to order and Gulf prawns poached in wine with champagne mignonette and traditional cocktail sauce. The Caribbean Curry Station includes spicy chicken curry stewed with coconut milk, tumeric, fenugreek, and chilies, served with traditional unleavened bread and mint-cucumber raita, pineapple chutney, spice-roasted peanuts and other condiments.

There is also an oyster bar, a mandarin pancake station with two fillings, a sushi bar, and a tostada or quesadilla bar with upscale Mexican-style ingredients. Prices range from $7 to $11.50 per person and cover two hours of service for 100 guests or more and include the menu, service and kitchen staff, and equipment (tables, linens, china, silver, etc.).

---

or whoever is in charge of food, what you're interested in, and come up with a range of costs per person. Everyone is used to working within budgets. Do everything possible so that you can enjoy your own party. That's the most important rule to remember."

But doesn't everyone do that? Not necessarily, say all three caterers. "People get scared away from their own instincts. Don't do that to yourself," Meme says. "We had this mother and bride recently who said, 'We don't want people to be stuck at their tables, and we don't want dinner to be crowded.' They then proceeded to choose a six-course dinner and put ten people at each table. I felt terrible for them, that they didn't have the courage to go with their gut feeling about what they wanted to do, and then stick with it."

Memorable and Personal Wedding Receptions

Polished and Elegant Overlooking Phoenix

Polished and *elegant* describe Melissa and Michael Moore's wedding in Phoenix, in the Mansion Club, a home built as a gift for his wife by chewing gum magnate William Wrigley, Jr., in 1931. Built on a six-acre hilltop and used as a club and conference center, it commands views of Phoenix and the entire Salt River Valley.

The couple—in their late twenties, the bride being married for the second time—wanted a small wedding and limited the guestlist to 60 close friends and family members who had been part of their four-year relationship. The wedding Melissa describes as "storybook, Camelot, as perfect as any occasion could be" was held outdoors on a terrace. It began when the bride walked down a long, stone staircase with her father to the music of a brass ensemble. After the service, performed by a minister, a string quartet took over and champagne, wine, imported beer, and spring water were served as guests left the receiving line. A lavish, artfully displayed buffet was followed by a dessert buffet. The sophisticated display of food included oversized silver platters of attractively arranged fresh vegetables and fruit, roast beef, and a smoked turkey in carvery stations, small lamb chops grilled and served butler style, shrimp, and a variety of salads. Melissa ordered a cake from a bakery that specializes in unusually delicious wedding cakes. One tier was strawberry rum, the other banana rum cake. It was frosted in white icing and decorated with fresh flowers.

Cost: $4,000 for food, beverages, service, and music for 60 guests, or $67 per person (music was included in the club's wedding package).

An Exuberant Russian Dinner and Dance in Chicago

Lisa Berger, 25, wanted a wedding that was different from the hotel weddings that were the norm for her crowd. She wanted to reflect her husband Gabriel's Russian heritage and she loved the spirited feeling of the evenings they had spent in Chicago's Russian nightclubs.

The couple rented a suburban women's club with room for the ceremony and dinner dance. They then hired the owner of a Russian restaurant to cater the food and a band to play lively Russian music. After the wedding ceremony, champagne and hors d'oeuvres were served, then guests were ushered to tables in the ballroom as the band struck up a spirited Russian song. Eight platters of hearty, cold hors d'oeuvres ranging from smoked fish to a robust Russian potato and vegetable salad had been set on each table. Vodka and wine toasts were made. After each of the courses, guests got up to dance. Just after 10 P.M., grilled chicken and steak entrees were served. At 11 a sweet table was set up and guests were served slices of wedding cake.

Cost: $10,000 for food, beverages, and service for 125 guests, or $80 per person.

A New England Sit-down Picnic Lunch

When Mary and Charlie were married, they were 25 and not in any position to pay for their own wedding. Still, they wanted a less formal atmosphere than they knew their parents had in mind. At a seashore house they had rented over past summers, they erected a tent. Mary's parents, who paid for most of the wedding, put one condition on the wedding food service: they wanted a sit-down, served meal. "The caterer grilled chicken and beef, Armenian-style, to reflect Charlie's heritage, and made huge pilafs and great salads," Mary explains. "A friend who is a pastry chef made the wedding cake and it was a really delicious carrot cake decorated with beautiful leaves she made out of marzipan and painted." When Mary's brother offered to set up a bar of raw in-season clams and oysters as his wedding gift, they accepted, but had to sign a waiver with the caterer that if anyone got sick, she would not be responsible.

A string trio of a cello, bass, and violin played during the ceremony and meal. The wedding and reception were over by 6 P.M. Then young couples pushed the dinner tables to the side of the tented platform, put on tapes for dancing—and later that night ate wedding leftovers on paper goods bought especially for the occasion. This was the casual party the newlyweds had craved for all their college friends and close family members.

Cost: $11,000 for 200 guests, or $55 per person, for all food, equipment rentals, and service of six waitstaff (including two for the shellfish bar), two bartenders, and two supervisors. Waitstaff doubled as cooks at grills.

Cocktails and Dinner at Home in Chestnut Hill

MaryAnne and Sam, age 47 and 52, respectively, and being married for the second time, had in mind a more elegant version of the kind of party they might give once a year. After their marriage in a Chestnut Hill, Pennsylvania, Episcopal church, about 60 close friends and family members returned to the couple's home. A string quartet played as hot and cold hors d'oeuvres were served with champagne in elegant flutes. On the house's two porches, open bars offered full service. After an hour of cocktail service, dinner was set out on a flower-and-greens-decorated, multitiered buffet in the dining room. Just before dinner, the bridegroom gathered everyone in the living room and made the first toast—to his bride. A round of intimate and witty toasts, as many by women as by men, were made.

Cost: $2,500 for food and service by one bartender, three waitstaff, and one supervisor. Additional costs: $350 for rentals of chairs, dishes, glassware, and serving pieces; $475 for a small tent to cover the deck; $300 for liquor; $150 for a wedding cake. Total: $3,775 for 60 guests, or $63 per person.

MaryAnne and Sam's Wedding Menu

Hors d'oeuvres

Cherry tomatoes stuffed with pesto, garnished with toasted pine nuts
Tiny crisp quesadillas with a dollop of salsa
Bacon-wrapped scallops with a bourbon marinade
Ruffle-edged, spicy pork dumplings with Thai dipping sauce
Tiny potato fritters, topped with creme fraiche and caviar
Huge baskets of crudites piled high with spinach dip served in hollowed-out vegetables
A whole brie, top removed, spread with mango chutney and almonds, then warmed, served with thin slices of Granny Smith apples and rye crackers

Buffet Dinner

Gazpacho mold
Poached salmon with dill sour cream
Roasted vegetable strudels
Pasta stir-fry with shrimp and Oriental vegetables
Filet of beef served with tomato chutney, miniature twist rolls, and horseradish cream
Caesar salad
Coffee, Tea
Wedding cake

The Tea Dance and Dessert Buffet

Karin and John were both 40, and it was a second marriage for both. Money was limited, Karin explains, "and I think everybody hates sitting through those long evenings at wedding dinner dances anyway. But we have a lot of friends and decided to have a tea dance with champagne and a huge dessert buffet in a country club ballroom that is now owned by the city park system."

A caterer provided service, equipment, and some elegant desserts. Family bakers provided the rest. The bride and bridegroom are competition ballroom dancers and so dancing started right away with a waltz by the newlyweds. "All afternoon we did two of the things we love the most: we danced and we ate dessert," says the bride, who wore a white competition ballroom dancing gown. This was a midwinter wedding and the bride wanted everything to look elegant. Silver trays and serving dishes were rented, along with dozens of small plates, glassware, and coffee mugs. The bride made ingenious centerpieces for each table out of white feathered doves and two tall tapers intertwined with greens. Candles were lit as it got dark in the late afternoon.

Cost: $2,200 for 300 guests, or less than $7.50 per person, including food, beverages, service, and rentals.

Karin and John's Dessert Menu

Prepared at home by family:
Huge trays of oversized fresh strawberries and ladyfingers
with white and dark chocolate sauces for dipping
Melonballs with fresh mint leaves and kirsch
Madeleines and pecan bars
Six rhubarb pies
A wide assortment of brownies, including amaretto, turtle (with a layer
of caramel and nuts), German chocolate, and raspberry

Provided by the caterer:
Heart-shaped pink petit fours
Tiny cream puffs with hazelnut and cognac filling
Several platters of carefully arranged fresh fruit, especially melon,
garnished with fresh grapes, whole pineapples, and mangos
Lemon tarts with raspberry garnish
Bread pudding in cake cups, with whiskey-caramel sauce
A multitiered chocolate wedding cake

The Potluck-with-Love Wedding Dance

SaraJane Arneson is an actress in her forties. Her husband is a part-time college professor and political activist. They have, as SaraJane explains in her basso profundo voice, "about a million friends." For their wedding, however, they had 20 members of both families and a handful of friends at a small wedding and restaurant dinner. "After the wedding, we got serious about having a party to celebrate with all our friends," says SaraJane. "I looked into my checkbook and figured we could pay for a band or food but not both. I chose the band." In the wedding announcement and invitation they wrote themselves, they invited friends and conveyed their attitude about the party, which SaraJane says, "and I'm being objective," was one of the best parties she's ever been to. Guests agree.

A graphic artist friend designed the invitation, which came in several parts. On the cover sheet, the marriage was announced. As the invitation was opened, confetti and rice fell out. The copy continued: "And we're still celebrating. Please join us on (date). Pick a time. Arrive at 2:15, 3:12 or 8:10. We'll be receiving all day. Pick an attire. (We're doing casual and we want you to be comfortable too.) Pick a food. And prepare it. Please bring a dish full of food to share. (Don't you just love potluck?) Pick a little, talk a little, pick a little, party a lot. We look forward to your presence."

Guests arrived all day and brought a wide range of food. The bride says the party worked on many, many levels. "I got a great band and we took up all the rugs and danced and danced. I couldn't believe how much beautiful food came into this house, and how fabulous and delicious it was. Either our friends are great cooks or they know where to buy fabulous food. People raved about what a great, loose party it was." SaraJane reflects that what makes parties like these so much more fun than the more formal kind is that "people today love to participate. Our friends enjoyed bringing food for us. They often gave the bowl or the container as a wedding gift. I don't like passive parties. I want to dance, do something. I've been eating and talking for years and people get bored with that. I used to give those kinds of parties, but I want something more interesting now. This was perfect."

Cost: $200 for wine and beer, $30 each for two servers, $600 for band. Total: $830 for about 150 guests, or $5.50 per person.

A Caterer's Wedding Fantasy

Catherine Schubert, 30, is a New York caterer known for providing trendy food at moderate prices. Although her own wedding is still a fantasy, her ideas are worth listening to.

"I've been involved in so many weddings and can tell what works. Parties that are drawn out, where people get a chance to relax and dance and have great food are the best," she says. "I've been influenced by two friends' weddings. One was a weekend in Indiana at an old, reconstructed Utopian colony. There were lots of events, including a prenuptial party given by the groom's family, a picnic, and then the wedding dance and a beautiful buffet. By the end of that weekend, we'd all made new friends.

"The other great wedding was in Spain, at the bride's parents' second home. It was a real family thing. They got fabulous tarts and patés from across the border in France and set them out so they looked beautiful. Then people danced and drank wine and talked and later they had a barbecue. It was spectacular to be eating this unbelievable food and drinking good wines on a terrace with a view of the Mediterranean.

"I think about my own wedding almost daily, mainly because I've finally accepted the fact that my parents probably won't pay for it, which I used to think was the worst thing that could happen. But then I realized I want to call the shots. And I know from all the weddings I cater that it can be a very difficult and trying day when parents pay for everything, when it can become their party and may not be that much fun."

Catherine believes that food today is about resources, which means finding the best of each kind of food. "Your wedding cake should be the most delicious cake you can find and even something as simple as bread should be the best money can buy.

"For my wedding I'd have the best caviar I can afford—I'll get it wholesale—with vodka and champagne. And I'll have a bunch of fabulous hors d'oeuvres served to guests, the kinds of things where they say, 'What is this? It's the most delicious thing I've ever eaten.' Then we'll dance, dance, dance all night, and end the party with a barbecue. Not dripping ribs. This will be a European barbecue where the entire meal is grilled. I'll serve it late, when people are famished."

Catherine Schubert's Fantasy Wedding Reception Menu

Caviar, Vintage Pol Roger or Veuve Cliquot, Vodka
Wedding cake

Evening meal
Meats grilled in the Italian fashion, over herb branches:
lamb marinated in red wine, garlic, and rosemary;
chicken breasts marinated in lemon, olive oil, and rosemary;
filet mignon marinated in red wine and garlic;
guinea fowl with thyme
Grilled vegetables and wild mushrooms
Grilled polenta with sundried tomatoes and goat cheese
Warmed focaccia

CHOOSING A CATERER

Before you interview caterers in person, spend a few minutes on the telephone with several. Many caterers have preprinted sample party menus that give you an idea of their style and price range. Pick two or

Never Watch Your Caterer Set Up

Most professional caterers are unflappable men and women who can pull together a party faster than you can remember the menu. They work fast. Watching a caterer set up for a wedding reception is unnerving for all but the most stoic brides. Most caterers work down to the last possible minute of their deadlines. Under these pressures, they will not value your last-minute suggestions. Watching your caterer set things up could be the final detail that tips you over the edge into wedding insanity.

three favorites and make appointments to interview them. If time is a priority, choose your one favorite from menus and by reputation, interview her or him, and decide without seeing others. If you lack confidence, remember that you will learn more about the business with each meeting.

Know your caterer by reputation. Check references or get recommendations from friends. If you like the food at a party you attend, ask for the caterer's name and check with the chair of the event or with the host about what it was like working with the caterer. Big-name caterers don't always have big-time prices. They often are famous because they're reliable and serve wonderful food in interesting ways. Small caterers can also be excellent. They often work harder, have competitive prices while they're getting started, and may be more open to suggestion than the more seasoned professionals. Never work with a temperamental caterer. There are too many excellent caterers to risk working with a prima donna. If possible, sample your caterer's food. Some caterers run restaurants or take-out food shops, which makes sampling their menus easy.

Make sure the caterer or catering manager is someone with whom you are compatible. You won't spend much time with the caterer on your wedding day, but you need to share his or her taste and style, and know that he or she is hardworking and responsible.

Check with caterers about what their prices include. Caterers all estimate jobs differently. Some break out individual costs; others provide package prices. Here's what is usually part of an all-inclusive price.

- *Food.* This means ingredients along with the purchase, transportation, and preparation.
- *Equipment.* This includes the rental of tables and chairs, serving pieces, plates, glassware, silver, and linens. Most caterers will tell you that before you eat a bite of food, you need to pay a minimum cost of $3 to $10 for equipment rentals, depending on the elaborateness of your service. Some caterers own their own equipment and do not make this a separate cost.
- *Service.* Experienced caterers have their own waitstaff on call. They also have formulas for how many servers you need per 100 guests, for both sit-down and buffet service. Since kitchen help is the backbone of any catered event, do not scrimp on service. You don't want the effect of your menu spoiled by harassed waitstaff who can't get the food out to your guests, or who serve it on messy trays because they can't take the time to return to the kitchen and replenish the food as well as tidy up

the servings. One or two extra waiters can make all the difference between a slow service and an unattractive buffet with partially filled dishes, or smooth service with inviting tables and trays.

THE WEDDING CAKE

American bakeries have undergone a revolution. Big cities and their suburbs and many smaller towns have bakeries that specialize in high-quality cakes made in small batches from the best ingredients available. The difference between the old-fashioned corner bakery's cakes and these new concoctions is vast. Today's best cakes are often worth every extra penny. They are literally the best cakes money can buy. There are traditional multitiered cakes, flourless chocolate cakes, moist double-chocolate mousse cakes, apple-whiskey-walnut cakes, various cheese-cakes, pumpkin, carrot, and zucchini cakes, and delicate white and yellow genoise cakes with fresh fruit fillings.

In choosing a wedding cake, there are several factors to consider. One is price: Neighborhood bakeries still supply wedding cakes at reasonable costs. They keep costs low by using cake mixes and by avoiding high labor costs. Baked goods from gourmet bakeries, on the other hand, are made in small batches from carefully developed recipes and are therefore more expensive.

Why are cakes so expensive? Wedding cakes involve more work than even good amateur bakers imagine. Take a close look at the bottom layer of a multitiered cake. For even a medium-sized wedding cake, this is baking on an impressive scale. The cake must be level and perfectly balanced in order to provide a sturdy foundation for all the remaining layers. Wedding cakes, with fillings, frosting, and the tools of their construction, are heavy. They are built very precisely, with nary a tilt or bit of extra frosting to unbalance them. Three graduated sizes of simple cake layers, a 15 inch, a 10 inch, and a 6 inch, if purchased separately from a good bakery, might be priced at $50 to $100 for all three cakes. If they are to be used as wedding cakes, each is a double layer (two layers, rather than one twice as thick, which wouldn't bake in the middle). These same three cake tiers, when decorated, constructed, delivered, and assembled into a multitiered wedding cake, can run two to five times that cost.

Wedding cakes range from $1.50 per person, a low-end price usually available only from a home baker or a neighborhood or small-town bakery, to $10 per person. A high-end cake by a well-known baker who custom-decorates it can run even higher.

In-house and Outside Caterers

The managers of many rental spaces have learned, through experience, which caterers they can trust and which they cannot. They often have in-house caterers or lists of those they recommend. Their aim is to make sure service goes smoothly and that the space is clean after its use. Listen to them, but if you have a preferred caterer, approach the club or hotel's management in a businesslike way with your request. You may want to attach reference letters or a list of noteworthy parties your caterer has managed. Often, managers will allow outside caterers in their spaces if they believe they will do a good job.

The other major considerations in choosing a cake are the type of cake and its aesthetics. If you want a multitiered cake, you need to think about the relationship of tier sizes. To see how different sizes work, try stacking pan sizes for effect. You would not, for example, put a 6-inch tier atop a 14-inch cake. Think too about the kinds of separators used to hold tiers. They range from simple and sophisticated to the wedding cake equivalent of gold shag carpet. There are clear, heavy plastic pillars, or the commonly used white plastic pillars with or without swans, flowers, swags, etc.

Of course, not everyone wants a wedding cake. Brides today may choose the typical French wedding croquembouche, which consists of layers of cream puffs in a conical shape held together by a caramel glaze. Fruit and chocolate fondues have also become popular. Or brides might serve the American favorite, gourmet brownies, or a dessert buffet that can range from simple to elaborate, or can include the more typical buffet of small pastries and fruit. Ice cream buffets may sound like a good idea, but they melt quickly and can look messy and inelegant.

Groom's Cake

The tradition of having a smaller, more strongly flavored (often chocolate) groom's cake than the (white on white) wedding cake is seldom seen at weddings in the United States. When the groom's cake was common, it was because the wedding cake was consumed at the reception and the groom's cake was sliced, packaged and sent home with guests. This was the slice of cake single women were to put under their pillows to inspire sweet dreams of the man they would marry.

The same variety in taste is true of the bride and groom figurines that once were de rigueur atop a wedding cake. Casually painted plastic couples are still sold, and china figurines reminiscent of those from the 1930s and 1940s are available from trendy gift shops. Another cake-top decoration is the photographic replica of the bride and bridegroom created by a photographer, but this can be complicated. Do you really want to dress up in your wedding finery and have a photo taken to be duplicated for the top of your cake? Or does the photographer supply the gown, veil, and tuxedo? Could he put your heads on another bride and bridegroom photo? Or you might dress in something that reflects your interests, such as riding or scuba-diving outfits, for a less conventional approach. One mother of the bride, who is an artist and gallery owner, chose artist-designed ceramic figures that symbolized the couple's interests for use on the tiers of the cake. One older couple bought doll-house bride and bridegroom figures and placed them in various poses all over the cake.

If there is a single noteworthy trend in wedding cake decoration, it is the use of fresh flowers along with frosting. The most expensive florists sometimes assign one person to the cake and cake table, and this attention to detail shows in the beautifully decorated cakes and display tables. Wedding magazines frequently run photographic spreads on wedding cakes which can give you design ideas. A creative family member or friend might like to manage this detail for you. Careful planning can elevate the cake and its display to something special that can easily be the centerpiece of your dance floor, if the space is large enough to guarantee the cake's safety.

Baking, building, decorating, and delivering a wedding cake are not for the inexperienced or fainthearted. My theory is that one of two individuals should be in charge of delivering and setting up your cake: the baker or the owner of the bakery. Delivery requires great attention to detail. Fragile cakes are sometimes delivered in specially outfitted vans or in boxes cut to accommodate the bottom tier. In some cases, the cake is delivered unassembled and put together on site. Each layer of a multitiered is first affixed to a sturdy material like a piece of heavy cardboard or light wood and is often held in place with icing. Then, double-edged tape holds the base on another, stiffer base, and finally, dowels are fitted into the pillars that separate the layers. Most bakeries send along a repair kit with extra ring and flowers and all the tools needed to repair any damage the cake might have suffered en route.

Most caterers buy wedding cakes from bakeries or expert home bakers. They may or may not be able to arrange a cake tasting. Some will allow you to bring in your own cake; others will not. Many of the biggest hotels have their own bakers and are proud of their baking and design skills. Thus, they may not allow any cakes to be brought in from outside bakeries. Most, however, will simply add a fork charge for serving. Preference, cost, and quality are factors to be considered.

A final word of advice: Beware of catering halls and hotels that assume you will not serve your cake, but will wrap it and send it home with guests instead. For dessert, they frequently serve an ice cream concoction made ahead by the thousands and frozen. If your cake is delicious, by all means serve it as dessert. But be sure to discuss serving sizes, since many wedding cake serving charts provide only minuscule

The Best Thing About Our Wedding

"My father and grandfather were German bakers and they went all out for my cake. It had tiny grapes and beautiful flowers and was the best work they could possibly do. It was a very rich devil's food cake that they knew had always been my favorite. It was exceptionally beautiful and really tasted good. I'll always remember that cake."

MaryAnne Marks, 25,
first-time bride.

Cake Decor Options

Today's wedding cakes can be decorated with frosting in the shape of ribbons, swans, and butterflies as well as incredibly lifelike flowers, berries, and grapes. Some bakers use a basket motif, or will duplicate the lace and embroidery of the wedding gown (which strikes me as obsessive and labor-intensive for a fairly forgettable detail). The most common icings are buttercream and stabilized whipped cream, but cooked fondant and rolled frostings are also fairly typical of today's upscale wedding cake frostings.

Wedding Cake Savings

To save on wedding cake costs, have a smaller size cake made than what would serve your guests, and display it. Supplement this cake with sheet cakes of the same flavor and frosted in white. The sheet cake can be kept in the kitchen and easily sliced and served to supplement the cake on display. Example: If you are having 200 at your wedding, order a wedding cake for 150, plus enough sheet cake to serve the extra 50 guests.

servings. Thus, an actual dessert serving may be two or three times the size of a tiny slice. To enhance cake as dessert, you might want to accompany it with a fruit or other sauce.

Here are some of the most delicious and creative cakes I've seen at weddings.

- A dense chocolate cake with fresh raspberry filling, covered with chocolate ganache (a mixture of chocolate and cream), again in white chocolate frosting, and decorated to look like Antoni Gaudi's Guell Park in Barcelona. This cake was displayed on a huge silver tray covered in full-blown roses and peonies in shades of pink.
- A five-tiered, rich yellow cake filled with frozen souffle filling, a different flavor in each cake: lemon, strawberry, amaretto, chocolate, and raspberry. (For lighter cakes, fresh fruit fillings can be made with little or no sugar.)
- A hazelnut dacquoise (meringue) cake with custard filling, frosted in stabilized whipped cream (not for a humid day).
- An Italian canolli cake, frosted in rum-flavored buttercream.
- A three-tiered wedding cake that comprised an entire buffet. One tier was carrot cake, another blueberry cheesecake, and the third a rich devil's food cake with white-chocolate frosting. The cakes were sliced and served with a variety of fresh fruit and several sauces on a buffet.
- A delicious yellow *genoise* filled with buttercream, covered in royal icing that was allowed to dry for an hour or so, and then covered with white fondant, all made in the classical European manner.
- A black and gold, art deco cake to match the wedding's design motif. This rich carrot cake with cream cheese filling and frosting did not take a backseat to its decoration.
- A delicate white cake tinted pale pink, frosted in white buttercream and decorated in pink and white lifesize marzipan roses and candied violets. Smaller marzipan roses were made so that every guest got one alongside the cake serving.
- A four-tiered, triangle-shaped, rich chocolate cake, frosted in marbleized fondant frosting. This cake was prepared by an artist-pastry chef who decorated it with thin triangles of chocolate—each hand-splattered with white on dark chocolate or dark on white chocolate. It looked like a Jackson Pollock painting.
- An artist-designed cake covered in white-chocolate leaves, each hand-painted in delicate shades of green and decorated with fresh flowers.

Americans are drinking less than ever before, both for health reasons and out of fear of mixing drinking and driving. Whereas the open bar with full liquor service is still expected at many weddings, there is growing preference for what is called the soft bar: champagne, wine, soda, mineral water, beer, and coffee and tea. Dinner-dance weddings may include an open bar as part of their service but clubs, hotels, and caterers are aware that guests drink less than they did in the past and that consumers want to keep close track of bar bills.

For those brides and bridegrooms who are having small weddings but know of one or two guests who will want martinis or Scotch, making sure that a waiter is earmarked to serve those few guests can be less costly than providing an open bar for everyone. If your budget is tight, or if you have a strong preference, don't be afraid to limit alcoholic consumption. By greeting guests with trays of champagne and perhaps mineral water, you can save a hefty percentage on the cost of an open bar or avoid having one altogether. If guests are offered champagne or wine, one-third to one-half will never approach the bar for a mixed drink made with hard liquor. Remember that an increasing number of wedding hosts serve what they normally would at their own parties, which is often wine, champagne, beer (possibly a choice of imported or regional American beers), and mineral waters.

As for quantities served and bar costs, allow six to eight glasses per bottle of wine or champagne. Plan on serving two or three drinks per person during the first hour, one per hour after that. Children and teenagers sometimes drink more soda than you thought possible. Whatever you can or cannot provide, avoid a cash bar. It is better to serve a limited amount of beverages.

Caterers know that certain ethnic groups drink more than others. They also know that younger guests, within two to four years of college, drink more than any other age group, until guests hit their midfifties, when they again drink more heavily. Some people drink more wine than mixed drinks. Others won't touch wine, but head straight for the Scotch, bourbon, gin, or vodka. Ask their advice about your guestlist.

Many caterers allow you to buy your own liquor, or buy it and bill you at cost plus a small percentage for labor. If you arrange this yourself, remember that picking up and delivering cases of liquor and soda is time-consuming and heavy work. Also remember that unused liquor cannot

The Best Thing About Our Wedding

"I loved my wedding cake. I thought if I could get a great and unusual cake, everything else would work too. The food at the Stockton Inn in Bucks County, Pennsylvania, is excellent. The cake was a hazelnut dacquoise with buttercream frosting and decorated in fresh flowers. It wasn't like any other cake, and it sort of set the tone for the kind of wedding I wanted—really different with a lot of attention paid to the details. It was out of this world."

Joan Mayhew, 38, first-time bride.

The Best Thing About Our Wedding

"We had lemon meringue pie for dessert, which is our favorite dessert, and that made it so different and fun. We got about a dozen pies and loaded them into our car for the trip to our country cottage where we were married. Also, a friend and I went out and picked armloads of wildflowers the morning of the wedding, which she thought was insane. I bought flowers to go with them, and we arranged them together, which was fun and kept me from facing what a nervous wreck I was. Oh yes, and we ate before the ceremony. Doesn't that seem right? To get married over dessert?"

Betsy Miller, 34, first-time bride.

usually be left at your wedding site. Make provisions to have it stored, delivered somewhere, or handled by the caterer. Even some major hotels will allow you to serve your own wine, for a per-bottle corkage fee. One bridegroom realized that the least expensive champagne on the hotel's list would cost more than a higher-quality champagne he bought on sale and paid a corkage fee to serve. That is, if a hotel charges, say, $25 a bottle for inexpensive champagne and $5 a bottle for you to bring in your own, you may be able to get an excellent case price for a high-quality champagne at $18-20 per bottle.

Homemade Wedding Food

A few caterers will allow you to mingle homemade wedding dishes with their food. Those who will not explain that they must consider insurance. If someone became ill, for example, who would be liable? Others simply don't want your best efforts mixed with their own products. Small catering companies who are attached to a church and cook in the church kitchen will be the most easygoing. Big-name caterers may be insulted if you ask.

As for having a family member prepare wedding reception food, this is entirely dependent on the atmosphere you hope to establish and the skills of the amateur caterer. Excellent cookbooks are available on quantity cooking. But that's just the beginning. Can the cook manage the purchase and organization of massive amounts of ingredients? Can he or she prepare and store the food? (Home storage of food for even a small wedding of 50 guests can be a problem.) Is the home cook prepared to deliver, serve, and clean up? Are that person's attitudes and skills appropriate for what you have in mind?

Home-style weddings can be warm and welcoming. But even if the bride and her mother are experienced hosts, they may not want the work of managing the wedding food service, even if they don't do the actual cooking.

If the couple or family manages the food, they must do so with the same forethought and planning as a professional caterer. It is guaranteed that the bride and bridegroom won't want to be bothered with the logistics of what to do with leftovers, for example, when the wedding is over.

On the other hand, hiring a professional caterer who is a friend or family member can be an effective way to save money and control quality, perhaps combining their work with your own but hiring them to handle all service.

TABLE LINENS

Your caterer may be able to provide unusual linens to create special decorative effects. Or you may prefer to work directly with a linen rental company that provides a wealth of sophisticated choices for dining and serving tables.

Plain colored linens, in pastel, bright, or dramatic dark colors, either floor length or long enough to look finished when chairs are pushed in, are the simplest and lowest cost linens available. Prints and specialty fabrics such as plaid taffetas, satins, and moires cost more. Lace overlay tablecloths are romantic and feminine, and tables draped and swagged in tulle can be beautiful. Some brides cover chairs in simple white or off-white slipcovers. Rectangular tables can be draped and swagged in matching or complementary fabrics, and layered with other linens for effect. Call a linen rental company for creative ideas and cost estimates. In major markets, you can find competitive prices. If decor is important to you, be sure to coordinate this with your florist and caterer, or let them handle it for you.

CHAPTER EIGHT

Music: The Key to Timing, Emotional Tone, and Energy Level

Bandleader and jazz pianist Peter Duchin, one of the few musicians in the United States you can hire for your private party who has immediate name recognition, plays at wedding receptions and says there are two kinds. "The first is the wedding where the bride is either very young or still in awe of her mother's organizational skills," he says, "so the entire wedding, including the music, is dictated by the mother."

The other kind of wedding, Duchin says, is more fun. "It's either a second marriage or the professional woman marrying the guy she's been living with. The music is more contemporary, the wedding less formal, and yet it has an old-fashioned, romantic edge. These are the couples who really seem to be in love, not the young ones." And the music is better, too, he says with a laugh. "You're wiser at 30 than you were at 21, and you obviously have better taste and more to synthesize than you did when you were younger, which influences everything," Duchin explains.

Society bandleader Don Cagen and his vocalist wife, Becky, in Chicago, are the kind of couple who finish each other's sentences and who, at least in public, never disagree. They say that sophisticated couples are fun to work with. "They've traveled. They've been to the Caribbean and have brought back a taste for the music. It's vacation music to them. They like rock and its subtleties. If the hip bride makes one mistake it's thinking that she and her guests won't get out on the dance floor and really boogie. The thing is you have to talk to your bandleader and articulate your vision. But then he has to make it work within the larger frame of the party. If it's a dinner dance, the bandleader's job is to fill the dance floor. It's that simple."

THE RANGE OF MUSIC

Because weddings combine the formality of ritual and tradition with expressions of intimacy, love, and commitment, they are filled with emotion. And no aspect of the ceremony is more tied to feelings than music, for the simple reason that it can be profoundly moving.

Music (as well as the serving of liquor and food) controls the timing of the wedding reception. More than any other component, music sets the emotional tone and the energy level for both the ceremony and the celebration. Whether you envision an intimate, elegant occasion or one where guests dance the night away, the style of music and the type of musicians are key to how your wedding works.

The range of music available for each of the wedding's various components is wide: from stirring classical music at the ceremony to cheery, uplifting popular songs during cocktails, to lively rock music at the dance. Each can have a place in a wedding. Jazz is mellow. Big bands are exuberant. Blues are funky and hip. String quartets can have a lush, old-fashioned sound that is romantic and thus tugs at the heart. A brass quartet sounds important, inspiring, and powerful.

Before making decisions about music, consider what is customary, what your own style is, and what you can afford to spend.

WHAT IS CUSTOMARY

Music at wedding ceremonies, whether it's an organist or a string quartet, starts about a half hour before the ceremony. This is called the prelude.

Vocal or instrumental solos are usually performed before the processional, during the prelude, when most guests have arrived and the bridal party is being lined up in the rear of the church or temple. There can also be vocal solos during the ceremony, at an appropriate prearranged time. During the final part of the prelude, generally there are a few minutes of silence before the bridal party enters the sanctuary or marriage site. This announces to guests that the wedding is about to begin. The music often changes or is played with more volume when the bride or bridal couple enters.

Whereas processional music, played during the wedding procession, is uplifting, with a march tempo and a sense of anticipation, cere-

Ceremony Favorites

Although couples sometimes say that they know it's become a cliche, they wouldn't feel married without the stately "Bridal Chorus" from Wagner's *Lohengrin* ("Here Comes the Bride") as their wedding processional, and they also may want the traditional recessional, the "Wedding March" from Mendelssohn's *A Midsummer Night's Dream.* Are your musicians bored with such traditional music? Has the organist played it at thousands of weddings? It's your one and only (or at least your last and best) wedding. Insist on the music you want.

Bear in mind that some Catholic churches and many Jewish congregations bar both of these pieces, the Catholic church because they are secular works written for the theater (which is why, no doubt, they have such dramatic, theatrical impact), and rabbis because of Wagner's well-documented anti-Semitism and Mendelssohn's conversion to Catholicism.

Other processional classics are Pachelbel's Canon in D and the wedding march from Mozart's *The Marriage of Figaro.* The processional choice of Prince Charles and Princess Diana, now widely known and recognized as "The Prince of Denmark's March," is Jeremiah Clarke's Trumpet Voluntary in D, which, of course, was written for a trumpet. Also popular ▸

mony music is nearly always traditional classical music. Recessional music, played after the marriage ceremony to accompany the now-married couple back down the aisle, is upbeat and festive.

Most churches and temples have specific rules governing what can and cannot be played at weddings. Some do not allow secular love songs during services. Clergy members have ideas about what is appropriate in the services they conduct. Be sure to discuss this long before the ceremony. The communal singing of hymns, for example, is a frequent part of wedding ceremonies that take place in houses of worship. The singing is part of the service and according to the custom of the church or temple. At weddings in other locations, group singing often feels overly intimate and somehow unsuitable.

Music during cocktails should never be so loud that it overwhelms conversation. On the other hand, some volume increases the excitement level, especially at the beginning of a party, and gets a celebration off to a good start. There's nothing wrong with having to speak up to be

---

Music – The Best Thing About Our Wedding

"Martha did not want what she called a wedding band," recalls her mother Jill, who planned most of the wedding for her lawyer daughter and son-in-law, since they came home one week before the ceremony. "From the beginning, Martha and Graham said they wanted the original renditions by the real artists. They worked hard on the music list they gave the disk jockey, and I added a few golden oldies and a rhumba and fox-trot or two. We told the deejay not to talk much, and definitely not to do any kind of shtick. This was a wedding, not a bar mitzvah, we said, and we wanted him out of the spotlight, with no light show or anything tacky. He was sort of hurt, but agreed.

"But the big hit at the wedding was a roving group of musicians led by a violinist I'd heard at another wedding and hired on the spot. They played everything including old Jewish songs I loved and more contemporary songs too. They could play requests and if they got a song they didn't know, they handled it by improvising in a very cute way. The leader was completely charming, and there was a bass player and guitarist who also played a horn. During dinner, they went from table to table. They were terrific."

Martha Eskoll and Graham Cahill, 27 and 28, first marriage, were married in the elaborate grand ballroom of a downtown hotel. Total cost: $30,000, including $400 for a deejay and $750 for three hours and $150 for one-half hour of overtime for the live musicians who played for the ceremony and during cocktails and dinner.

---

heard, as long as the high-decibel level doesn't last the entire party.

Experienced musicians have ideas about what is and is not appropriate music for wedding ceremonies and receptions. They are aware of the proper times for musical fanfares, those musical introductions to special parts of the reception, and of the kinds of music and songs they prefer for different parts of the wedding ceremony. Be sure to discuss your own musical preferences. Musicians will often learn a special song or two, if they're given plenty of time and the sheet music, or are told how to find the music or an arrangement you like.

MAKING MUSICAL CHOICES

Before hiring musicians and choosing music for the various parts of the wedding, consider the following factors.

- *The feeling you want to create.* Think about the time of day and the tone you want at your wedding as well as your own style. Formal or informal? Restrained or exuberant? Elegant or casual? Sweetly romantic or completely unsentimental? Afternoon or evening? Dance music or background music? Spirited ethnic or sedate classical music?
- *Your musical preferences.* Classical or contemporary? Jazz or blues? Classic rock or Motown? Big band society swing (heavy on the foxtrots)?
- *Your budget.* Can you afford romantic, old-fashioned strings or a resounding brass ensemble for the ceremony? Is the cost of an authentic big band or a professional rock group within your financial framework? Do you want an organist at the church and a pianist at the reception? Do you prefer a restrained, somewhat elegant disk jockey, a traditional take-charge deejay, or someone completely anonymous to play the right tapes at the right time in the party? Costs range widely between big cities and small towns, and by region. A string quartet can be hired in Atlanta for under $400. The same caliber of musicians may cost more in New York and Chicago, or on the West Coast. Bands range from $700 to well over ten times that. Beginning bands may charge less for their first engagements than they do when they become well known and have a following. Disk jockeys, depending on their equipment, expertise, and the overhead they need to cover (advertising, marketing and office help, special effects such as light shows, an assistant), can cost from as little as $200 to as high as $1,500.

Once decisions are made about the type and style of wedding music, you will want to hear musicians, either live or on tape, or meet with a disk jockey. When you meet with musicians or a deejay, ask about

are Handel's *Water Music,* and Bach's preludes and chorales for the organ.

At the end of the ceremony, Sir William Walton's "Crown Imperial March," Beethoven's Ode to Joy from his Ninth Symphony, and Purcell's Trumpet Tune in C are appropriate.

Because of renewed interest in Jewish heritage, songs from Israel or from the eastern European (Ashkenazic) or Sephardic cultures are often used in Jewish ceremonies. In ancient times, a flute was always played to introduce the bridal couple. And music set to poems from the Song of Songs is frequently heard, including "Dodi li" ("I Am My Beloved's"), which is especially beautiful.

As for vocal solos, most singers have a long list of their favorite pieces and happily offer choices for use at various times during the ceremony. This, too, must be discussed with your wedding officiant.

their style even if it seems fairly obvious. Remember, you're trying to develop a vocabulary that will help make you a better consumer and judge of talent. Ask also about the kinds of weddings where the musicians or deejay have worked. The deejay or bandleader who is experienced at lively ethnic weddings may not know how to be quiet and discreet and play background music. The opposite is true as well. One bride tells how, after interviewing several professional disk jockeys, she and her fiance hired an amateur. "We didn't want a light show or someone who had to be center stage. We really just wanted a disk jockey who was low-key and sensitive to the flow of the party and knew when to play different kinds of music. The guy we hired cost a little over $200 and was perfect."

Advance Listening

Most bandleaders acknowledge that their tapes of wedding music are far from perfect. Nevertheless, be persistent about hearing their work. Remember, when listening to a tape, that the music is not being performed under ideal studio conditions. Pay attention to the quality of the vocalist, the type of music, and the level of musicianship. "Tapes may not be good," says bride Betsy Fox, "but I have the ability to keep that in mind, and it shouldn't interfere with the quality of the playing. Even if there's a lot of static, you can still hear if the trumpeter can play or if the vocalist can sing."

Bandleaders may discourage you from observing the musicians at someone else's wedding by explaining that weddings are private events. If you do attend someone else's wedding, wear appropriate dress.

Describe the type and style of music you're thinking about to the musicians or disk jockey, then ask them to describe, from their point of view, what they consider the ideal wedding. Be prepared to listen to musicians, who often know a great deal about how parties work. Also be ready to describe the atmosphere you hope to establish at your wedding. If the disk jockey or musicians don't ask you questions about your expectations, or if they seem so experienced that they don't welcome your ideas and opinions, keep looking.

Be prepared to provide them with the following information: size and site of your reception, approximate age range of guests, and your own musical tastes. When you first meet musicians or deejays, be prepared to describe your favorite musical styles and some specific songs that you especially like. Identify your favorite radio stations, and explain your choice. Although there is nothing as exciting as a good live band, any style of music you want can be played by a deejay with a good ear and knowledge of music.

Musicians and deejays for both the ceremony and the reception should be familiar with the sites, the instruments provided such as an organ or piano, and the type of wedding service, and should know whether the available electrical services are adequate for the sound equipment.

There are general rules of common sense for the size of the room and the number of musicians in the group as well as for the type of music played. A string quartet or small group playing classical music will generally not be heard throughout a large ballroom without a good sound system. A loud rock band might be inappropriate if you have a large contingent of elderly relatives and lack a comfortable adjacent room, even a lobby space, where they can escape. Then, too, eight musicians may be three or four too many for a medium-sized hotel room or a club or restaurant space.

Dancing is appropriate at afternoon weddings, but unless you're in a windowless or heavily curtained ballroom, it will never be as exuberant as at an evening dinner dance. Still, luncheon and tea dances, especially with the service of champagne or wine to liven up the crowd, are festive and fun. If you want a set of spirited dancing at the wedding, make this clear to your bandleader and insist that the exuberant dancing take precedence over the kitchen's needs. Some bandleaders, knowing they have to please the hotel catering manager more than individual clients (in order to get referrals), will interrupt a lively set of dancing for the dessert service rather than incur the wrath of the catering director.

Musical Resource

The American Guild of Organists has a book with over 400 music titles appropriate for weddings in churches and synagogues and a tape with a variety of pieces played by organist Robert Anderson. They are available from American Guild of Organists, 475 Riverside Drive, suite 1260, New York, NY 10115, 212-870-2310. Prices (as of 1993 and expected to stay the same for a while) are $12.95 for the book and $8 for the tape, which include handling, shipping, and tax.

Know Your Instrument

"I heard this fabulous piece of music on the huge pipe organ at our church and loved it," says Page Whitney-Borg, a bride married in New Jersey. "So I got the name of the piece and gave it to the organist at my hometown church, where the organ was much smaller. It sounded awful played on that organ, because the organist wasn't as talented, but also because the instrument was completely different."

A Bandleader Who Wouldn't Listen

Lisa Berger and her husband still argue about their band's playing of the wedding processional. The recent expatriate leader of the Russian band insisted on playing "If I Were a Rich Man," from *Fiddler on the Roof* saying he played it at all Jewish weddings. "Everyone loves it," he said. The bride had no intention of walking down the aisle to the theme song from the popular show and in fact had a hard time not laughing at what she considered a ridiculous idea. "I would have had to skip to keep time," she said.

The bandleader dug in his heels. He didn't know any other processional music and kept pushing the bride to go with his choice. Lisa bought sheet music for "Ice Castles," from the movie of the same name, for the musicians. She gave it to them in plenty of time for them to learn it. She grits her teeth every time she hears the processional music on her videotape. "They played it so badly," she says. Still, she is the first to admit that she never heard the music at the wedding. "It's amazing. When I was walking down that aisle, I didn't hear a thing."

As in every other area of wedding planning, for every rule there seems to be an exception. One elegant, carefully planned birthday dinner for 40 close friends was a huge hit because the 20-piece orchestra raised the roof. The band played requests and ended up being part of the event. Several guests sang their favorite numbers, one guest, a jazz pianist, got to lead the band, and the drummer flirted shamelessly with all the women. The big band was the perfect size for this party and would have been just right for a certain kind of intimate, off-beat wedding.

If you're hiring musicians or a band, make sure all the specifics of the agreement are clear. Most should be put in writing. Bands often have standard contracts and either trustworthy reputations (that you are aware of) or references (that you can check). Here are the kinds of specifics you'll address.

- How many musicians will be at both the ceremony and the celebration?
- Is there a leader and, if so, what role will he or she play in making announcements?
- What time will musicians arrive?
- What time will they depart?
- Are the musicians familiar with the sites for both the ceremony and the celebration or are they willing to visit them?
- What information do they need for setting up equipment?
- Do they expect to play on a platform at the receptio? If so, who is responsible for erecting it?
- Will they stay overtime, and at what cost?
- Will they play continuous music?
- If they take breaks, how long will they last and how often will they occur?
- What will they wear?
- Should you provide them with meals?
- Who will cue them at the beginning of the wedding ceremony? (This has a tremendous potential for problems that can result in serious delays. The musicians wait for the clergy member, who waits to be cued by the family, who waits to be cued by so and so, etc.)
- What kinds of fanfares, if any, are they prepared to play and at what points in the reception?

STYLE OF MUSIC

Cultures that developed close to the Mediterranean, and those that have

A Wedding Music Disaster

"We were lucky to get the church we wanted for the date we had in mind, but since it was not located where we now live, I didn't have a chance to hear the organist. My brother-in-law sent me a tape and this organist was so bad," says Toni Prima. "I was incredibly busy at work at that point and couldn't manage to find another organist and negotiate with the minister long distance about using someone else, so I let it go. For the processional, he wanted to play a Bach piece, which should have been somewhat marchlike, and he played it really pastoral and slow and I knew I could not walk down the aisle to it, it was so embarrassingly, badly played. The only other thing he knew was a Purcell trumpet piece, and he said, 'Oh, all you girls want what Princess Di had,' which annoyed me, but that was what he knew and he didn't mangle it too badly.

"At the reception we had a small band trying to play a big-band sound, which was our big mistake. For our first dance, we chose a Buddy Holly song, "True Love Ways," which is a ballad. I asked the band if they would learn it. They said fine and I didn't think another thing about it. When they played it, it was sort of up-tempo, Lawrence Welk swing. They massacred it. And we said to each other, 'What is this?' Our band got great reviews from several sources, which just shows you that word of mouth isn't always foolproof." Toni was married in her own and her bridegroom's hometown in Ohio, even though they now live in New York City. After the wedding, she said, "I think clear communication is really important. If you're relying on word of mouth, remember that everyone's aesthetic and taste are different."

Toni Prima, 34, first-time bride.

evolved from them, frequently have a tradition of exuberant dancing at weddings. Italian and Greek musicians and Jewish klezmer bands know the spirited songs of their cultures that get crowds onto the dance floor at weddings. Dancing the tarantella or hora is fun for everyone, both observers and dancers. The Jewish chair dance, where the bride and bridegroom are lifted above the crowd in chairs held aloft by a quartet of strong guests, is a combination of heart-stopping sentiment and lively fun.

As for American perennials, most grownup brides and bridegrooms wouldn't be caught dead having the chicken dance or the hokey-pokey played at their weddings, although it's wise to remember that they exist because people love to be lured onto the dance floor to get involved in

A Bandleader's Advice

"There's one way I know that the party won't be a great one," says Chicago bandleader Don Cagen. "If the bride's not interested in and not thinking about her wedding music. The bride who can barely choose the music for her first dance? That party is in deep trouble and I always know I'm going to have to work extra hard to get people dancing and make things work.

"The other extreme is the client who wants to give you a line-by-line playlist. "That doesn't work either, because they don't know how to make parties work, what to do to get things going, how to calm them down when food has to be served, how to get things rolling again, etc. My advice is to hire someone you trust and then let them do their work."

What I Would Change About Our Wedding

"I would have had a three-piece orchestra instead of the organist that came with the church. He was awful. I would have visited the churches before making my choice. This was a long-distance wedding and I had to take others' advice on the church. I heard raves about the one we used, but I didn't like the way it looked and ended up taking minimal pictures there. I didn't see it until it was too late. I should have heard the band or a tape of their music. They were mediocre although they got great reviews from several sources, which shows that word of mouth isn't always foolproof."

Barbara Jenkins, 32, first-time bride.

uninhibited dancing, even at the risk of looking slightly foolish. The problem with these two catering-hall wedding classics is that they make guests feel far too self-conscious. For exuberant American dancing, consider rock and roll, which may be the closest thing to the spirited dances of our collective ethnic pasts. Not everyone will enjoy sets of rock and roll, because to be played properly, it has to be loud enough to drown out conversation. Part of its power is its volume.

"We played a recent wedding for a 34-year-old stockbroker and a 40-year-old banker," says New York bandleader Peter Duchin. "They didn't want any rock and roll, for two reasons. They preferred show tunes, jazz, and swing because she wanted soft music so that her guests could talk. She understood what is absolutely true. In order to work, rock and roll has to be loud. I have to say this again and again to people. You can't play rock and roll softly. It doesn't work. People don't always believe me, but it's true."

As for the first dance, most couples choose something either romantic and slow, or their favorite song, or a traditional waltz, fox-trot, or tango with some sweep. When planning the first dance, think show business, because when it begins, all eyes will be on the bride and bridegroom. One image is of the couple gliding out onto the dance floor, waltzing gracefully with the bride's gown billowing like Anna's dress in the famous waltz scene in *The King and I.* If that's your fantasy, it's sure to take some work to pull off. Some words of warning: Not every ballad is a waltz. Make sure that you can dance to the song you've requested or, even better, that you request a song you can dance to. Some couples take lessons, or rent a ballroom dance video and practice at home.

If you expect to make your first dance into a real performance, remember to think big. If your dance floor is oversized, start at the center or most of your guests will miss the production, and move around the floor. If it's a tango, make it exaggerated. If it's a waltz, dance grandly, so the movement of your dress is imposing. For this, even if the rest of your wedding is simplicity itself, you may want to think Hollywood.

CHAPTER NINE

Wedding Photography and Videography: Preserving the Memories

The strong wish to make a wedding or other milestone less transient than the events of a single day or even a long weekend is understandable. What will be retained when the wedding is over? The memories, of course. But memories need cues, and photography and videography are the best ones available.

Recording a wedding is complicated, however, especially because brides begin planning their weddings by thinking that the images they carry in their minds are simple. By the day of the ceremony, they have realized how elaborate their fantasies can be and how strongly they can conflict with the ideas of others.

Traditional wedding photographs capture the simplest myths: starry-eyed couples stopped in the middle of all the excitement they're causing, glamorized and distanced from reality. In real life, today's grownup brides and bridegrooms not only have the time of their lives at their weddings, but they are also in control, certainly of themselves, if not of every detail. What they want recorded on film is simply what occurs at the ceremony and celebration, rather than some idealized version of themselves as a make-believe queen and king carefully posed in full-dress costume.

Weddings are photographic settings that provide wonderful, natural opportunities for the right photographer. There is tremendous excitement and emotion. There is an atmosphere usually containing lovely settings and flowers, attractive food and drink, and an elegantly dressed wedding party and guests. The bride and bridegroom are at the center of all the activities, feeling happy, looking great. It is difficult, therefore, to understand why many wedding pictures look so similar, like stock shots following a specific, traditional formula.

No other wedding service is as fraught with frustration and disappointment as photography. One reason is that we are surrounded by highly sophisticated images. It is safe to say that no one's wedding will look as joyful on film as the average, upbeat 60-second commercial.

Guests and participants are seldom as beautiful as models in perfume ads. How many wedding portraits feature brides posed and lit as sensitively as the fashion shots seen in print? Almost none. Electronic and print ads may take days of shooting to arrive at refined images. But we are influenced by these ads because they are what we see every time we turn on a television or open a magazine. Expectations can become out of touch with reality. For the most part, wedding photography has not changed even though weddings have. It is easy to see how frustration occurs.

Lisa Garrett, a New Yorker, hired a well-known, traditional wedding photographer and spent between $3,000 and $4,000, with the cost of enlargements and reprints, for her photographs. To say she was disappointed is to greatly understate the case. "Since then, I've been to a lot of weddings and have watched the photographers. I get the feeling they're all burned out because they've shot a thousand weddings and don't care about any of them."

But the studio she hired is changing, probably in response to complaints like her own. When a friend used the same company, she worked closely with a newly hired woman photographer who took pains to get to know her and the bridegroom so she could individualize their photographs. "My friend's pictures were much more interesting than ours. The photographer followed what was happening at the wedding and got great candid shots," Lisa explains, noting that her photographer followed his checklist and shot everything in the most traditional way. But what she envies most are her friends' wedding portraits. "They put on their wedding clothes a few weeks after the wedding, which was fun, and went out on the beach. They were so relaxed and happy. The wind was blowing and the atmosphere was just beautiful and their portraits are out of this world."

THE RANGE OF PHOTOGRAPHIC STYLES

At one end of the spectrum is the traditional wedding album filled with clichéd shots of the bridegroom looking at the bride's ring, the couple standing stiffly in front of the camera, the bride attempting to gaze, awestruck, at her own bouquet, and even corny double exposures of the wedding couple in a cameo, superimposed on some bare spot in another photo. At the other end of the spectrum is the artistic photographer who looks at everything through a wide-angle lens that slightly distorts the wedding and guests, and makes them look highly ironic, perhaps even a

How to Get the Wedding Photographs and Videos You Want

Here are some tips to ensure that your filmed record is as good as the wedding itself.

- Look at the wedding samples by several photographers and videographers before deciding on who you want to hire.
- Check with your wedding officiant about rules concerning the taking of photographs and videos during the ceremony.
- Be sure your photographer and videographer understand what you want. You may want to be fairly specific, for example, about the percentages of candids and formal images you want taken at your wedding.
- If you want a full range of formal family shots, consider doing them before the ceremony, since you do not want to lose the feeling you have after the ceremony and delay your arrival at the celebration.
- Provide your photographer and videographer with a brief list of moments, individuals, and groups you want recorded at the ceremony and reception.
- If the photographer or videographer is unfamiliar with your wedding and reception sites, suggest that he or she visit the sites a week or two before the wedding.
- If you are worried that your photographer or videographer will not shoot enough, offer to pay for extra film. In the final analysis, once you have hired a photographer and videographer, film is the least expensive part of the job.
- If you have a long list of family members and friends to be included, ask a friend or family member who knows the key players in both your own and your bridegroom's family to point out key individuals to the photographer and videographer.
- If you want documentary-style photographs or video, make sure the photographer or videographer comes to your home early in the day and can stay as late as necessary at the reception.
- If you want photographic portraits, think about possible sites at the ceremony and celebration and in your area. You may want to have portraits made after the wedding ceremony on another day in order to get something unusual and special.
- For special effects in a video, consider adding childhood photographs, family scenes at various ages, and parents' wedding photographs.
- To get a fairly accurate record of guests, ask the photographer to shoot about the same number of photographs of guests as you have guests at the wedding.
- When you arrange your own photo processing, you will not want to entrust the photographer's film or negatives to the corner drugstore processor. Instead, get recommendations of professional-caliber processors to handle every step of developing and printing. The difference in quality is significant.

One Photographer's Favorite Wedding Images

"The bride had arranged for a beautiful gold, black, and white art deco wedding cake, and the cake designer and bakery owner had a broken arm when he came to set it up. I got him with his assistant who had to do everything, including touching up the icing that had gotten a little damaged in the transportation. They were working with incredible concentration on this extraordinary cake and there's a sequence of pictures that shows all of this.

"I got the most beautiful shot of a bride walking up the grand staircase of an elegant downtown hotel, with her entourage of attendants and the consultant around her, but sort of all at a distance so that the photo is focused on her alone with them very much in the background. And she has this great smile and is puffing up her dress and completely unaware of the camera. The photo tells so much about this happy day for her and how she was feeling. That's a great shot. It truly happened.

"One of my favorites was an incredibly lucky shot. I shot a bride being held aloft during the Jewish chair dance and she's laughing hysterically while being held up by four guys and everyone around her is dancing and clapping and kind of blurred. I just held my camera up, aimed it at them and shot lots and lots of exposures.

"At another wedding, there were hours of preparation beforehand. I tried to get a sense of all the hustle and bustle of the wedding. The bride's mother was there directing everything, and the bride, who was a physician, said that for once this was okay with her. I got a photo of a helper, a young man pressing her veil, which had a twelve-foot train and was like clouds of tulle. He was pressing it on a wide windowsill with trees right outside the room—a very delicate and beautiful shot. Before the wedding I tried to be a fly on the wall and get all the behind-the-scenes preparation.

"A portrait of another bride in black and white was then hand-tinted in pastels. Two years later we shot her with her first child as a surprise gift for her husband, and wrapped the baby in velvet. Both were very soft. Very contemporary."

Mary Beth Cregier, F-22 Studio, Chicago

little grotesque. Think of wedding photography by an artist as uncompromising as Diane Arbus.

Most of today's sophisticated bridal couples want a style in between the two extremes of the creation of the corny wedding fantasy and the harsh depiction of reality. Thus, the photojournalistic style is becoming increasingly popular. Emphasizing realism and naturalness, it accurately records what happened at the wedding, while attempting to make the event and its participants look beautiful. In candids that capture the day, shots of family members, and perhaps some portraits taken before or after the day of the wedding, beauty is tempered with reality.

Before hiring someone to photograph your wedding, be aware of the wide variety of photography and photographers in today's market.

The traditional wedding photographer. For the most part, this photographer is experienced at shooting weddings and is either the owner or the employee of a studio that specializes in wedding photography. When you think of buying a package that includes an album with a certain number of photographs, and of formulaic shots by someone who orchestrates the events, you have the traditional photographer in mind.

Traditional photography costs range widely. Clients usually pay an extra cost for each print or enlargement beyond the set number they receive for the basic fee. The advantage to choosing a package is that you get a completed album. The initial cost can be fairly low, since wedding studios make their money on reprints. One studio owner went so far as to say he did not want upscale or sophisticated brides, because he couldn't make any money on them. "My bread and butter is the working-class girl's wedding where every aunt and uncle orders a big photo and both sets of parents want their own albums."

The irony with traditional wedding photographers is that the more experienced they are, the higher the likelihood of burnout. There are exceptions – wedding photographers who stay fresh for a lifetime – but the only way to be sure is to meet with the actual photographer who will shoot your wedding and discuss your needs. The problem is that many studios discourage this, and if they do allow a meeting, it will take place after you have signed a contract.

Big city photographers generally have wedding packages that start somewhere over $300 at the low end and $1,000 to $1,500 at the high end. The fee includes an album with a set number of shots and a limited number of reprints.

The classical wedding photographer. This photographer specializes in expertly set-up and well-lit portraits at a cost above the middle-market

The Couple Who Hired Two Photographers

Because the aesthetics of Nancy and Ed's wedding were so important to them, they wanted to capture design details on film. But they also wanted a traditional wedding album. To make sure they got all the photographs they wanted, they hired both a traditional wedding photographer and a commercial pro.

Sensing that the traditional wedding photographer wouldn't be happy about this (he wasn't), they told the wedding consultant to be aware of potential problems and to make sure any disagreements were kept out of earshot.

There was conflict between the two photographers ("Don't get in my way," the wedding photographer told the commercial photographer), but the couple got the pictures they wanted of their lavish flowers and elaborate food along with loads of unexpectedly beautiful candids. "Our wedding pictures are absolutely perfect," they say. "The traditional photographer got all the predictable stuff, and the photojournalist captured how everything looked and did fabulous candids. Our album is the best, and it was worth it to have them both there."

range. He or she may also do family shots and some candids at the wedding, but their overall image of your wedding is one of elegance and restraint and the resulting work is somewhat more formal than that of other photographers. Those known as "society photographers" usually fall into this category. The advantage of using them is that they know how to shoot beautiful studio or home portraits and are unobtrusive at the wedding reception. Their portraits, bound in a leather album, present an idealized, often heavily retouched view of a wedding.

Prices for the successful, well-known classical wedding photographer are at the high end of the traditional photographer's price range, $1,200-1,500 for an album and a selection of portraits.

The photojournalist. This is the trend that is changing wedding photography. These photographers pride themselves on recording the event and shooting whatever is taking place rather than on orchestrating wedding events. In other words, they follow the action rather than create it. Most try to record weddings in the most natural, unobtrusive way possible, and they blend into a wedding, shooting only what they think is dramatic or touching or unusual.

Most photojournalists also take group shots of the wedding party and family members, although a few suggest hiring a more traditional wedding photographer for this task. Depending on the size and length of the wedding, some bring an assistant to help with the arrangements of large groups. The advantage to hiring a photojournalist is the use of natural lighting and the spontaneous feel of the photographs.

Many of these photographers charge an hourly fee plus expenses that include film and processing. Often, they provide a 3 by 5 proof print of every shot, along with a set of negatives and the name of a high-quality printer. You then pay for enlargements and may put together your own album, which lowers your costs.

Photojournalist's fees usually are from $750 to $1,000. You must add in the price of your own album and of reprinting from the negatives.

The commercial photographer. You almost never see shots of flowers or decor or carefully lit photographs of food tables in wedding albums, even though time and money might have been lavishly spent setting up the ambience of the event. For high-quality magazine-page still-life shots or portraits, you may want to hire a professional photographer who specializes in this kind of work. Top-notch commercial photographers whose main source of income is advertising, editorial, or catalog work may photograph a small number of weddings a year. They know that shooting a buffet table or tray of food means using a tripod, long exposures, and supplementary as well as ambient lighting. Their photographic samples indicate the specific skills needed to record your thoughtfully planned scenes in equally beautiful photographs.

Most commercial photographers charge regular freelance fees, which means their hourly cost plus expenses. They provide proofs and negatives so that you can arrange for your own reprints and enlargements, but they almost never do albums.

The photographic artist. This photographer shows his or her work in a gallery and takes pride in artistic shots worthy of framing and hanging on a wall because of their aesthetic value. The photographic artist often shoots only in black and white. He or she almost never takes traditional shots of family member lineups, but may consent to work alongside a photojournalist or traditional photographer. What you can expect from the photographic artist is beautifully composed and printed photographs that are suitable for framing, delivered matted or dry-mounted in a portfolio. This style is for the art or photography buff, not for the bride who wants a wedding album.

The potential problem is that photographic artists may prefer to use wide-angle or other special lenses that result in shots more distorted than pretty and of more appeal to your sense of humor than to any romantic image of how weddings should look. Photographic artists often resist prettifying their photographs and may want to deliver a gritty wedding image.

The widest range in costs is among photographic artists, who may do a wedding for $500 or charge over $3,000. Their prices are tied to their view of their own talents rather than to the wedding photography market.

The amateur photographer. I advise against using an amateur, if that means, for example, a brother-in-law, friend, or relative, because it is

The Guests Who Took Their Own Pictures

One photographer bride bought disposable cameras for guests and displayed them in two oversized, flower-decorated baskets. Interested guests shot photographs of their children and families, and since everyone was dressed in their finest, they liked having the chance to take their own pictures. The bride didn't buy enough cameras for everyone, and not everyone took a camera, but those who did later told the bride how thoughtful it was to receive this unexpected photographic gift, and they sent her prints they thought she might like to have.

Another bride, a friend of the photographer who was married a few months later, liked the idea so much that she put a camera on each of her guest tables for ten, and she too got prints of some candid moments and group shots she might otherwise not have had.

often difficult to make that person accountable. If you hear of a photographer, though, who works hard at his or her craft, who takes his or her small business seriously, and who keeps prices low because he or she works at home, it can surely work. See the photographer's samples and make sure the work is up to your standards.

Cost for the amateur is the lowest of all, of course, which is part of the appeal. Many decent photographers think shooting your wedding is a fine way to spend an afternoon and take photographs for well under $300, with you in charge of the printing and organization of photographs into an album.

These categories may be slightly overstated. There are, for example, many fine traditional photographers who like weddings and are willing to spend time shooting candids as well as stock shots. The photojournalist may also be an artist who can take traditional photographs as well as commercial, still-life and art shots. And as Lisa Garrett observed about the traditional wedding studio she used, many studios are responding to the need for change. Then, too, there are photographers who have mastered every phase of their craft, from candids to still lifes, from portraits to family lineups, and who willingly shoot everything with great finesse. But it is wise to remember that your wedding photographs will be the result of the skill and the attitude of your photographer, and of your ability to clarify your desires and needs.

The Best Wedding Gift

"Our best gift was a videotape of the ceremony and reception, which I thought we were too old or too sophisticated to want. But friends hired their cousin to film everything and we love it because it really helps us remember how we all looked and how much fun the wedding was."

Sonya Reeves, 42, second-time bride.

A PHOTOGRAPHIC PRIMER

Candids. Usually unposed and somewhat unexpected shots that capture the spontaneity at wedding events and may be amusing or touching, rather than photographs taken by stopping the action and staging an activity.

Enlargement formats. Common sizes of enlargements are 5 by 7, 8 by 10, and 11 by 14.

Fixed-fee prices. A set fee that covers a certain number of hours at a wedding spent shooting a specified number of rolls, and possibly providing you with a certain number of shots and an album. Extra rolls or more time can often be added if your needs change at the last minute.

Formals. Posed family groupings and shots of the bridal party: you and your bridegroom, all the bridesmaids and groomsmen; your parents and his parents; members of your family, with the newcomer; members of his family, with you; all the aunts and all the uncles; your complete, extended family.

Full-flash photography. Photographs taken with a flash to eliminate the shadows of natural light.

Hand-tinted portraits. Black and white photographs that are hand-tinted, often with colored pencil. This soft technique used in the 1930s and 1940s has again become popular.

Hourly prices. Some photojournalists and commercial photographers charge an hourly fee for weddings, plus a per-roll cost for film and processing. They may provide clients with a complete set of 3 by 5 or 4 by 6 numbered proofs (numbering is of major importance in the reordering process) and all negatives of film shot at the wedding.

Natural-light photography. Using illumination that ranges from bright sunlight to softer light from a window, these photographs have a natural and realistic appeal, complete with shadows.

Package prices. This includes a set number of photographs and usually an album, shot during a predetermined number of hours and at pre-established locations. Extra prints or enlargements involve an additional cost.

Photo sequence. A series of photographs portraying the action of an event.

Portraits. Specially posed and lit photographs of the bride, or bride and bridegroom, that are often taken before or after the wedding.

The Best Thing About Our Wedding

"The disposable cameras were great. I hired a photographer, but some of the best shots were taken by guests. They're priceless. No photographer can be everywhere and people today love to have a role in occasions like weddings. I think it made guests feel included, rather than just observers. They had fun taking pictures. Everyone got into the act."

Shannon Hartwell, 31, first-time bride.

Proofs. Individually corrected for color and contrast, these are somewhat more expensive to process than snapshots. In the past, photographic proofs faded. Most wedding proofs today are processed as permanent photographs.

Special effects. Double exposures, cameo effects, haloing of individuals, etc. There is usually an additional charge for these photographic gimmicks used by highly traditional wedding photographers.

Stock shots. Taken by the photographer who carefully stages wedding events as photo opportunities. They show the subjects smiling into the camera as they greet a guest, cut the cake, throw the bouquet, remove the garter, or engage in other wedding events, rather than capturing the day as it unfolds.

Advice from a Photographer

Mary Beth Cregier is a successful commercial photographer in Chicago and co-owner of F-22 Studio. She specializes in national food ads, catalogs, and magazine layouts. She began to shoot a few weddings every year after her own wedding, when she found it difficult to hire a photographer who could satisfy all her photographic needs.

"I advise brides to hire a photographer who is knowledgeable about different styles of lighting. The still-life quality of a beautifully set table and the food and candlelight will not come through if a photographer walks up to a scene and shoots a picture with the strobe on the camera. You have to use a tripod, leave your shutter open, and use ambient lighting. If people want really excellent photographic lighting, hire someone with a good assistant because one person can't do it all in the time frame of a wedding.

"To get pictures that really tell a story, wedding photographers have to think like photojournalists and be there to record what happens rather than causing it to happen. Hire someone you can spend some time with before the wedding, and then encourage them to shoot as much film as possible. There's nothing less expensive than film. It takes just one frame to get a fabulous picture. Good commercial photographers shoot Polaroids before the actual shot, but at a wedding there's no time for that, so you have to shoot and shoot to get the exposure, composition, and feeling right.

"Set time aside for the posing and lighting of portraits. Unless you'll be happy with a great candid shot enlarged to portrait size, don't expect to shoot good portraits on the day of the wedding. They are a totally separate kind of photography. What most consumers and photographers don't realize is that simple flash photography can almost never produce portraits, which include background and environmental lighting, or a backdrop. I don't like plain backdrops because they say nothing about the ambience of the wedding day. For me, the best portraits include natural lighting with some backlighting from a natural source. I then might fill in with flash. I may bring along big lighting boxes to get soft, flattering portrait lighting. Portraits are done at studios for a reason, because it gives the photographer more control over the surroundings and equipment. If there's time, I like to take a couple out after their wedding and shoot them in beautiful surroundings or maybe take them back at the site of their wedding, which can be fun."

VIDEOTAPING YOUR WEDDING

Brides and bridegrooms may remember their wedding day as flying by and wish they had a video image of their vows and other highlights. Videotaping the ceremony and parts of the celebration can let you relive the excitement and help you remember the high points.

When interviewing videographers, make sure they have commercial-grade equipment that is as similar to state-of-the-art (network television camera) quality as possible. This means that videographers can be unobtrusive, using few lights and often positioning the camera ahead of time and leaving it unattended. Anyone with a few hundred dollars can go into the wedding video business, and this new field is full of people who have done just that. They are often untrained, unskilled, and in and out of business faster than you can say "I do."

Videographers with good equipment need little more than normal indoor light to produce a clear image. In contrast, the least expensive video cameras require strong lights that can spoil the feeling you want at your wedding. Churches and synagogues with rules against videotaping are usually familiar with the first cameras that were disruptive. Newer cameras can be set up ahead of time and run without anyone to monitor them, and are almost unnoticeable.

Prices for wedding videos vary greatly, ranging from the lowest I've heard of, $200 by a skilled amateur on the East Coast, to $1,500 for a professional in the Midwest who owns top-notch equipment and also shoots commercials. For your fee, you will usually get one or two tapes that can be used in most VCRs. Beyond equipment, what you are buying is the experience of the camera operator and the time the crew spends editing the tape. Paying for editing is worthwhile because you may want to avoid getting a rough-cut tape of everything shot at the wedding, which can be from three to five hours. Editing is what will ultimately make the tape interesting. Visit a few videographers and look at their wedding videos before hiring anyone.

But remember that even if you have a makeup artist, hairstylist, and excellent videographer, without a producer, writer, and entire camera crew your wedding tape will never have the quality of a national ad, which may have taken weeks to script, hire, plan, and then shoot.

Advice from a Photographer

Denis Reggie is based in Atlanta but shoots all over the United States, and is known for his candid photographs of celebrity weddings, including those of Kennedy family members. He was called by the *New York Times* "a storyteller with a camera... the hottest wedding photographer," featured by *American Photo* magazine as "America's premier wedding photographer," and distinguished by *Harper's Bazaar* as "the best of the best."

"Get someone to photograph what actually occurs, not what people wish were occurring. People who hire a photojournalist want to have everything look beautiful, but they do not want an enhancement, what they *wish* were there. I shoot real, genuine, nonfictional weddings, as they really happen."

Reggie gives photography seminars around the country where he tells photographers how the entire wedding photography business is changing. He sees consumers (brides and bridal couples) as either leaders or followers, and divides wedding photographers into the same two categories.

"The younger bride is not at a point where she is a leader so she needs a photographer who determines how and when things happen. To create this artificial presence, she should hire someone who knows how to run things. The reality is that those brides have little say in what happens at their weddings.

"My clients are decision makers. They lead their crowds and do not want a photographer who is telling them and their guests what to do. They want someone who follows the action and is a quiet observer, who believes the bride is wonderful just as she is, not as she is told to be. The leader bride needs a professional, quiet photographer who observes and documents. I may be a leader in my industry, but I wear a different hat at weddings and let the bride run the show, or just let things happen. This is not to say I don't get traditional pictures. They should take a few minutes, no more than five minutes.

"Candid means taking your cue from what's already there, and then recording that reality with an added dose of artistry. More and more brides are waking up to the notion that posing is not all that much fun. A bride shouldn't be treated like a model unless she is one. Above all, you must be yourself at your own wedding. This is the wrong occasion to play 'pretend' and try to be someone you're not. Choose a sensitive photographer who will instinctively feel and capture the moment. This requires mental effort, rather than a pat formula."

Still, if professionalism is important to you, be aware of special effects such as voice-overs, overprinting of your names and credits, and the use of music to set the tone and mood. Background music can introduce the video, separate it into parts, and stylize the presentation. Some videographers excel at interviewing family members and guests and getting their best wishes on tape, or they may record guests' insights on marriage or use other documentary-style techniques.

Skills are an important quality to look for in hiring your photographer and videographer. Just as important, never, under any circumstances, hire someone you don't like. The relationship between you and your photographer or videographer on the day of your wedding is too intimate and the results are too specific for you to waste time on someone with whom there is the potential for conflict. The photographer who won't listen during the initial interview will not turn into a thoughtful, sensitive person by the day of your wedding.

In hiring a videographer and photographer, it is wise to remember that when the flurry of activity preceding the wedding is over, what remains are the memories . . . and the on-film record of what really happened, how everything looked, and how you, your family, and your guests enjoyed themselves.

CHAPTER TEN

Decisions and Priorities

You both work and time is at a premium. You don't want to get obsessed with every detail of planning your wedding and the idea of quitting your job to make your fondest wedding dreams come true is more than a little impractical. You want to save time, plan efficiently, and spend money wisely. You also want a beautiful wedding. How and where do you begin?

Standardized checklists almost never work. Grownups may not set their wedding dates a year in advance, and they don't need to be reminded of certain obvious wedding purchases and choices. When I think about standardized checklists, I think of one that prompts brides to drop notes to their bridesmaids the week before the wedding reminding them to be sure to bring extra pantyhose of a certain color and brand to the wedding. Checklists also fail to take into consideration the economic level of the bride and bridegroom, the degree of formality or informality of their wedding, the amount of help they can hire, and the professional level of the wedding vendors they choose.

How best to allocate planning time, as much as what to do with that time, may be the most important logistical factor.

WHERE TO BEGIN

By now you have a clear image of the feeling you want at both the wedding ceremony and the celebration. When it comes to the actual planning, the wedding cake provides the perfect metaphor. Think of the stages of decision making like tiers of a towering wedding cake. The first tier must be substantial and sturdy enough to support the rest of the cake. It must be complete before the other layers are added. Without that first tier, there can be no wedding cake. For example, without knowing the budget and financial commitment you have from each other, in savings, or from parents (a first-tier decision), you cannot hire a band or florist, which are decisions to make during the second tier of planning choices.

First-Tier Decisions Each of these decisions is part of developing an overview. Every other decision rests on them.

- size of guestlist
- time of year and time of day
- wedding officiant
- locations for ceremony and reception
- budget and financial commitment (who pays for what)

Second-Tier Decisions These choices give style and individuality to the wedding ceremony and reception.

- style of wedding attire and accessories for yourself and the bridegroom
- style of attire for attendants
- menu and beverages
- musicians, band, or disk jockey
- florist
- photographer and videographer
- invitations and other printed materials
- wedding assistance on the day of the wedding and possibly beforehand

Third-Tier Decisions These details can make your wedding unique.

- schedule for wedding day
- readings during ceremony
- choices of ceremony and reception music
- final flower selections
- special events such as introductions, toasts, first dance, bouquet toss,
- garter ceremony, etc.
- gifts for attendants, parents, special friends
- wedding gift for the bride and bridegroom
- seating for reception, if it is a sit-down dinner with assigned seats

Seating Instructions

The Bride's Table. The bride's table is usually set apart by flowers, decor, or location from guests' tables. The bridegroom sits to the left of the bride. The best man is to the bride's right, the bride's honor attendant to the bridegroom's left. Then, attendants or attendants and their escorts or mates are arranged around the table, alternating men and women. If there are few attendants, other close friends are invited to be seated at this table. In one case we know of, the bride and bridegroom chose to have a beautifully set table for just the two of them at their wedding.

The Family Table. Generally, the parents of the bride and bridegroom sit opposite each other at a table, with grandparents, godparents, clergy member and his or her husband or wife, and closest friends also at the table. Grandparents, of course, may prefer to sit at their own tables with their closest friends.

How to avoid confusion? For all but the most casual wedding, a schedule of times for events is a necessity. If your catering manager inspires confidence and assures you that this is not necessary, trust him or her but still go over approximate times.

If time or confidence is at a premium ▸

How far in advance must wedding sites, bands, photographers, and florists be booked? If you're being married on a Saturday night during the most popular wedding months of the year – May, June, September, and October – they must be hired as long as a year before the actual wedding date. If you want a specific church or temple for the ceremony, a particular ballroom, or a well-known bandleader or florist, call first. Talk about general availability and specific dates, and build your wedding around what is most important to you.

Here is a rough timetable for how much time to allot to various tasks within different time frames. All schedules are based on planning a wedding of small to moderate size, from 50 to 150 guests.

- *With one year to plan,* set aside the first one to two months for first-tier decisions. Move down the rest of the list, writing out a brief schedule for second- and third-tier decisions within the next several months. Allow no more than two to three months for all second-tier decisions, which include hiring most wedding service providers. Then, during the next two to three months, you will have time to finalize your choices of ceremony events such as readings and musical selections. Move on to final floral choices, the use of traditions, and the seating of guests. With a year to plan a wedding, you may be able to do nearly all the work on weekends and during evenings and lunch hours.
- *With eight months to plan,* four weeks should be earmarked for the key, first choices. Devote one to two months to second-tier decisions, and allow yourself the same time for third-tier choices. With eight months to plan a small to medium-size wedding, you may be able to do most planning chores on weekends, evenings, and lunch hours.
- *With three months to plan,* allow about two to three weeks to set the guestlist, find a site for both ceremony and celebration, engage an officiant and order invitations. Have your budget well in mind before you begin planning. Then, move down the checklist fairly quickly and do one or two tasks per week. You may need to take a few days off work, as well as plan meetings on evenings and weekends.
- *With one month to plan,* make first-tier decisions within a week and move quickly on to the others. Prioritize, and don't try to concentrate on every detail. Take a day or two off work, one during one week for phone calls and the scheduling of appointments, and another day the following week to meet wedding service providers. With one month to plan a wedding, there is little time to comparison-shop. Get references ahead of time and be prepared to hire the first service providers you meet.

and you use paid assistance, hire this person early in the planning process. Alternatively, think about hiring someone to work for you the day of the wedding to oversee details. Then, one person will report to you because you have told all your wedding vendors to see her, or in a few cases him, the day of the wedding. Once this is done, don't think about details. Let them all happen around you.

Planning Timetables

Amelia, 27, and Tom, 28, a sensible, well-organized couple, allowed eight months to plan their wedding, the first for both of them. They hoped to accomplish everything during lunch hours, weekends, and evenings over eight months. The bride took four days off to arrange for blood tests for both of them, get the marriage license, interview one wedding vendor who was only available on weekdays, and handle a few other details. Amelia also took off three days just before the wedding. Cost: about $8000 for 90 guests, or just under $90 per person, for an afternoon lunch and dance party in a garden setting with optional indoor seating.

Amelia says, "If you have eight months, you can do almost everything on weekends. With less time, you'll have to take more time off. If you don't have a close friend or a mother who can help, as mine did, then you need more time. I couldn't have pulled things together without my parents' help. My dad had just retired and he helped with a lot of details, including choosing the wines. He organized two wine tastings for us. One was for champagne and the other for wine and they were a lot of fun.

"I set priorities. Flowers were not crucial. The garden we were married in was overflowing with flowers in August. Food and wine choices were very important because we love to eat. We wanted good music and since we couldn't afford a great band, we went with an amateur disk jockey who didn't have to be a personality. We had jazz and big-band music during hors d'oeuvres, classical music for lunch, and then 1930s and 1940s dance music.

"What would I change? I took three days off right before my wedding and the last day was too stressful. My mother and I wrapped pots of wildflowers in lace and tied a blue ribbon around each pot, which we expected to finish in an hour. The ribbon wouldn't stay in place and we finally had to jam drapery hooks into the soil to get it to look right. They looked fine, but it took forever. And then guests from out of town kept coming over to spend time with us. I'd left a few errands to do and ended the day feeling really stressed. Too much was going on.

"My advice: Plan to do one thing, or maybe even nothing at all, the day before your wedding."

Pat, 39, and Jimmy, 49, wanted a cost-conscious but aesthetically beautiful dinner dance in a hotel ballroom. This was the bride's first wedding, the bridegroom's second. Total time spent on planning was about three hours per day, three or four days a week, for eleven weeks before the wedding. Cost: $11,000-$12,000 for 110 guests, or $100 to $110 per person.

You Need a Mother

Annie Morrow, 27 at the time of her first marriage, says, "I couldn't have done it without my mother. I know a lot of women don't get along with their mothers, and I think that's too bad. We worked together really well, and she had a lot of great ideas about how to save money and how to make things look beautiful.

"The day before my wedding, we were putting the centerpieces together, and having a lot of trouble. They didn't work, but she wouldn't let me get upset. She never interfered but she was there to help. Both she and my dad let me make my own choices, or we made choices together. Everyone should have parents like mine."

Pat says, "Jimmy didn't think it could be done, but I planned our entire wedding in less than three months. Once we decided to get married in January, we chose April 7, since that's my grandparents' anniversary.

"People who give themselves a year to plan their weddings are out of their minds. Work expands to fill time, and they end up crazed because they have too much time to be indecisive, to always look for something better. I chose the hotel, went there twice and didn't second-guess my choices.

"My dress took the most time. I didn't want anything too traditional. I finally tried on one dress I loved but it was extremely expensive. It was by a local designer, so I went to her factory and showroom. We ended up buying all our dresses—my own, my mother's, and the bridesmaids'—from her. Once that decision was made, everything seemed to fall in place.

"What would I change? I'd give a list of 'must' photos to the photographer, who missed some pictures I thought were incredibly obvious, like me with my mother. And we paid for an open bar, but the bartender put a cup with money in it on the bar, for tips I guess, and guests might have thought it was a cash bar. That annoyed me.

"My advice: Once you decide to get married, set a date and get it done."

Donna, 37, and Richard, 41, an exceptionally successful and busy couple, were marrying for the first time. The bride spent less than ten hours in the planning of her lavish wedding at a private club. Cost: $34,000 for 160 guests, or $212.50 per person.

Donna says, "I hired a wedding consultant, took her suggestions and loved everything. We had just set up a business and it wasn't convenient for me to do much myself, although under other circumstances I would have done more. One funny thing was how the florist and the consultant kept expecting me to be more involved in things, and I simply trusted their judgment. They were used to working with brides with less confidence. I found a photo in a flower book with the mix of flowers and colors I wanted and I told the florist to copy it exactly, which she did.

"I paid the consultant to look for rooms in hotels and clubs and she reported back to me with a checklist we developed. That way I didn't have to leave my office until the final cut. I saw two places and picked one.

"By that time I trusted her and had her pick out a few dresses after I told her what I wanted, and that saved a lot of time. All in all, I figure I spent about eight or nine hours in choosing the menu, at fittings for my dress, and in handling details. My secretary helped. I hired someone with nice handwriting, another secretary, to address all the invitations and I kept track of responses. I couldn't have done it without the professional, paid help.

"My advice: Make wedding decisions as if they were business decisions. That takes some of the emotion out."

MaryAnne, 47, and Sam, 52, wanted to be surrounded by loving friends and their four grown children in their church and at home to celebrate their second marriage. MaryAnne, a magazine editor, frequently plans promotional and marketing events and pulled her wedding together in less than three months without taking any time off. Everything was done during lunch hours, weekends and evenings. Cost: $6,000 for 60 guests, or $100 per person.

MaryAnne says, "There wasn't anything difficult about any of the decisions. The one really time-consuming part was the fittings for my custom-made afternoon dress. Now I know why well-dressed women don't do anything else. I had four fittings and the designer-dressmaker said it wasn't enough. She has some women there all afternoon a couple of days a week.

"In our area there are a lot of beautiful places to be married in, and we looked at two mansions and several private clubs, but nothing felt right. Once we decided to be married in our church and have the reception at home, everything fell into place. I found a caterer whose restaurant I'd eaten in, and met with her once at her place, and she gave me menus and price lists. Then she came to our house for one brief visit. We decided where the food would be assembled, how it would be served, where things would be stored and how much equipment was needed. The florist was familiar with the church and visited the house once.

"I got the musicians through the caterer and the photographer was a photojournalist friend. The person we spent the most time with was our Episcopalian priest. We talked a lot about the service, and it was beautiful. He recommended certain kinds of music and readings for our children, who loved being included. I loved my wedding.

My advice: I had a friend watch over things on the day of the wedding. She said she didn't do much, but having her there made me rest easier."

Under most circumstances, good wedding vendors can be found at just about any time of the year. Pat, who put her wedding together in three months, found a well-known bandleader who was not booked on a Sunday evening in April. She not only booked him, but negotiated his price. In fact, unless you need name brands, you can always find talented wedding service providers, if you're willing to be

Keep Your Notes

If for no other reason than that your children (or you) will be amused some day, keep your wedding notebook with its ideas, menus, comments on wedding vendors, and all the other minutiae that go into planning a wedding. Prices and styles change, and your children or grandchildren may welcome the chance to look back on behind-the-scenes information. I can hear them now: "Mother, you paid what for your wedding gown?"

a little flexible on time of day and day of the week.

Planning a wedding in three months or less? If it's the busiest time of the year, be flexible in scheduling the day and time. Allow yourself two or three half days of doing what reporters call "working the phones," which means making enough contacts so that you are sure to hear back from someone. Once you have wedding vendors on the telephone, gather as much information as possible, keeping it organized and orderly to simplify the decision-making process. Make a rough checklist or list of questions and information necessary for each decision. Vendors don't return calls? Call again. After three unreturned calls, take them off your list. If you're in a huge rush, always call more than one vendor in each category but decide via phone which vendors you want to meet. Reward people who return calls promptly. Not only are they being polite, but they're interested in your business.

Putting together a wedding in less than a month? Get help: friends, staff, a relative, a paid consultant. The savings in time, effort, and emotional stress may be worth the expense of hiring someone to assist you. Professional wedding planners know what is booked and where to get answers fast.

Many invitations can be ordered and received within a week. For most weddings, addressing and mailing can be done in less time than it took you to get the list together in the first place. Allow an uninterrupted day or two, or several long evenings. If you're using a calligrapher, reserve that person's time early and allow plenty of hours of work.

What a Friend, Sister, Maid of Honor, Best Man, or Your Mother Can Do

- Help with a specific task such as handing out corsages and other flowers, pinning boutonnieres, meeting the caterer and answering his or her questions, checking in with the photographer and giving him your list of "must" photos.
- Pass out checks to wedding vendors, musicians or vocalists, and the wedding officiant.
- Do a reading at the ceremony or reception.
- Handle the guest book by positioning it outside the ceremony, or by making sure it is passed to guests at the reception.
- Have breakfast with you on the morning of your wedding and hold your hand in case you feel pressured or stressed.
- Watch for the special needs of elderly relatives or friends.
- Spend time with the flower girl and ring bearer ahead of time so they have someone other than their own mother and the bride in charge.

Enjoy Your Day

If brides and bridegrooms share one complaint after the wedding is over, it is that the day flew by and that they hardly remember it. How to savor your own wedding? Avoid getting caught up in details and your own schedule. The morning of your wedding make sure no details are left to be handled. Stop, sit back, take a deep breath, and look around you. Again. And again. Remember what it's all about. The two of you. Your marriage. A lifetime. Let events happen without taking part in any choices. The cake isn't exactly what you ordered? Mention it to your mother or to one friend if it's something that can be changed now or addressed later. Then enjoy whatever it is. Sip your champagne or juice or mineral water. Take another deep breath, and look around at everyone you have invited to help you enjoy this milestone occasion. Look into each other's eyes. Make a private toast. Kiss the bridegroom. Kiss the bride. Enjoy.

In traditional Jewish weddings, the bride and bridegroom are encouraged to spend ten or fifteen minutes alone, after the ceremony and before the reception. Anita Diamant, writing in her thoughtful and thought-provoking book, *The New Jewish Wedding,* explains *yichud,* or seclusion, in this way. "It is time to exhale, embrace, and let what has happened sink ▸

in. It is also an important respite from the strain of being the center of attention for a whole day. It is an island of privacy and peace before the public celebration begins."

She suggests that while breaking the traditional fast, couples should eat something they will enjoy since they may not have the time or inclination to eat much during the reception. She says that although this may make it impossible to assemble a receiving line immediately following the ceremony, it keeps the emphasis where it is supposed to be in a Jewish wedding—on the joy of the bride and bridegroom rather than on the expectations of the guests.

Do You Really Want to Work with Friends?

There are two potential sources of conflict in hiring a friend, say a florist or caterer, to work at your wedding.

The most obvious is objectively assessing the level of your friend's skills. If he or she were not a friend, would you hire him or her anyway? Most friends won't take kindly to being asked to show you samples of their work. They expect you to trust them implicitly.

Equally important are your expectations and your ability to make demands on a friend. Will you feel comfortable spelling out your needs? If you're a stickler for details, will you be angry if something goes wrong? If your friend doesn't return calls immediately, will you be frustrated? Are you both professionals, able to handle emotion and not let friendship interfere with business, or business with friendship?

Sylvia Kokolj, a florist and the owner of Montbretia in San Francisco, says, "It's better to make a friend out of a client, than a client out of a friend"—a sentiment echoed by other professionals.

On the other hand, Nancy Pirie, 29, hired a caterer friend whose abilities she respects, and they had a wonderful time planning her wedding. Nancy also hired a designer and onetime photostylist she had worked with to oversee all the details and make them look beautiful. She had complete trust on the day of her wedding not only that her two friends would do a good job, but that they would like working for her. Any regrets? None whatsoever. "No one could have done what they did for me. What I like is that Bobbie, the designer, now stays with JoHanna, the caterer, when he goes to New York. They met at my wedding."

TIME SAVERS

Here are ways to save precious hours, days and weeks.

- Do your reading and learning early. The learning curve must peak in the early stages of planning a wedding. As soon as you set a date, get a book or two and pick up some magazines for ideas.
- Be prepared to make quick decisions. Go to each interview ready to sign a contract and leave a deposit. If you want to think about your choices for a day or two to avoid making a mistake, set your own deadlines ("I'll have a band within a week") and stick to them.
- Limit the amount of comparison shopping. You don't really have to interview six florists if you like the one you visited first or second and are confident of that person's design and delivery skills, as well as price.

You Need a Friend

Molly McBride, married for the first time at 36, puts it this way: "What every bride needs is a good friend whose taste is impeccable, who loves her, and who knows what's right and what's wrong. And it would be nice if she had an aunt with a close friend on 47th Street.

"My friend took me to a designer fashion show where I saw the most divine dress, white panne velvet. Of course it was being worn by a beautiful black model who was six feet tall and weighed about 94 pounds, but it was the dress I wanted, and she helped me get it. Not wholesale, but less than retail.

"She made me wear her pearls, which were beautiful. She said, 'I know you and you'll buy some dumb little white dots and you need something important.' So she loaned me her big, matched Hong Kong pearl earrings with a beautiful clasp and they were perfect."

"She asked if I planned to dye my white shoes to match my white dress. I didn't know what she was talking about, so she took me to Peter Fox on Thompson Street in Soho [in New York City], who sells nothing but bridal shoes. He has everything. And he dyed my white shoes another white to match my dress. I think back to all the things she knew and I didn't, and the time she spent with me ▸

- Split the work. It takes two to get married. Your bridegroom can interview photographers while you see florists. You visit sites together, but he is responsible for the music while you decide on the invitations.
- Delegate tasks. Your mother, sister, best friend, mother-in-law, or favorite aunt may be eager to assist, or at least willing to help you make decisions or do some shopping for you. If she offers, take her up on it. If she doesn't offer, ask tactfully for help.
- Never second-guess yourself. Be positive about your choices. Once you've selected a site, stop thinking about other, better locations. Once you've chosen a band, do not continue to do research.
- Hire help or get a friend or family member's promise to help, especially on your wedding day. If you hire a professional, find her early in the process.

The Day of the Wedding

Before you make too many decisions, and especially before you add many third-tier choices, consider the day of the wedding and who will be in charge. If you have ever managed a project or special event, you know that those you instruct or hire will consider you the boss.

Let's say you have arranged for a friend to handle the guest book at the wedding. And you have given the florist a list of who gets which flowers, including the corsages for two mothers, three grandmothers, and your godmother, along with all the boutonnieres that need to be pinned onto the men, the bouquets that must get into the hands of each attendant, the basket for the flower girl, etc.

The day of the wedding dawns. Your friend arrives and asks where the guest book is, and wonders whether she should stay with it. And by the way, what's the best spot for it so it won't be ignored? The florist comes at that moment, needing identification of each person on your list so she can pass out flowers. Attendants would like to run through the ceremony, if you haven't had a rehearsal the night before. Where is the text for the ceremony readings you carefully typed and copied for everyone? And who, asks the lead musician, will give the signal to the priest, minister, or rabbi, along with the musicians and the bridal party, to prepare themselves to begin the wedding? Right now. You have become the bride manager.

In the wedding business, I saw both the potential for confusion if there's no one in charge and the tendency to rely too much on outside help if there is. Both can be avoided. Whether or not you hire a wedding consultant, the wedding day can run perfectly smoothly when you delegate tasks.

Here's how it can work. Tell your florist ahead of time to look for someone specific other than you when she arrives with wedding flowers. Have that person ready either to help the florist find everyone or to do the handing out and pinning of the flowers herself. Get the guest book in advance to the person who will be in charge of it and instruct him or her how it should be handled. Find out, before the wedding day, if your minister, priest, or rabbi will be in charge of starting the ceremony and whether someone should notify him or her exactly when this should happen. He or she may take total control of everything, but on the other hand may not. Some churches and synagogues have their own wedding consultant or advisor.

Officiants in secular surroundings—which may be unfamiliar territory—seldom take charge in the same way as clergy members do in their home church or temple. In this case, work with someone else, possibly your mother, your maid of honor, or a friend with a take-charge personality, to manage the important half hour to one hour before the ceremony when it can feel as if a thousand details need to be handled. Be aware that weddings frequently do not begin exactly on time. You may want to wait for last-minute guests to take their seats, for an errant violinist to return from the bathroom, for the lost groomsman to be found "just outside the door" where he has been waiting to be notified while he enjoyed a last-minute cigarette, for the flower girl to be located in the church's garden. Someone should always be in charge of cuing everyone, and it should not be the bride or bridegroom.

At the reception, the catering or banquet manager will handle many routine tasks in the absence of a wedding consultant. He or she should be aware of when the musicians will arrive, when you expect first guests to arrive, and when you want hors d'oeuvre and beverage service to begin or bars to open. Will you be introduced or do you expect to set up a receiving line, or both?

on the phone and at all those lunches, and I wonder what I would have done without her."

CHAPTER ELEVEN

The Perils of Perfectionism and How to Avoid Them

Working to have the wedding you want and being satisfied with the results are very different from setting standards so high that they instill panic and, ultimately, a sense of personal failure.

Unfortunately, not until brides, bridegrooms, and their families are immersed in the planning process do they recognize the perils of perfectionism. Some brides, though, say they could sense themselves, and sometimes those around them, becoming obsessed about everything, and they didn't know how to prevent turning into a fascist bride, who feels out of control with anything short of perfection. They may be aghast to find that planning a wedding takes more time and far more emotional energy than they had imagined. Given that everything must be shopped for and found, then negotiated for and purchased, and that at least two families may be involved in the public declaration of taste and financial wherewithal, couples or brides (or families) with high standards can easily find weddings an emotionally loaded business.

Communication skills between the bride and the bridegroom, the bride and her family, and the bridegroom and his parents are often tested in the extreme at a time when these individuals – especially the bride, if she's taking on most of the planning – may be suffering from physical and emotional overload. How to avoid this? Hearing about some near calamitous weddings may help.

THE WEDDING ROLLER COASTER

Linda, an old friend from the West Coast, moved to Chicago where she met her fiancé. They decided to get married, and Linda wanted to hold her wedding in her new home city. Her parents are retired and live in Arizona, and since she didn't want to be married there, her new home was a logical choice. Both Linda, who was in her late thirties, and her mother are known for their fabulous, drop-dead taste. My friend's parties always have the trendiest food, and her apartment is finished down to the last detail. Every fabric matches every wallpaper. Every table matches every chair. She is always exceptionally well dressed (in a matching sort of way) and admits that her father still helps with monthly expenses, because she can't quite manage on her own salary. She was married the first time at 21, but since the marriage lasted only a few months, it is never spoken of. This was treated as a first wedding.

Linda was excited about her wedding. She always wanted to plan a really beautiful occasion and admitted that she wanted things to be so perfect, so special, that her mother would finally be in awe of her taste as well as her organizational and hostess skills.

About a month after Linda began planning her wedding, I could see her getting overwhelmed. She had a three-ring binder bulging with menus, costs, telephone numbers, and other notes. Linda couldn't make any decision without wondering what her mother might do differently to make the wedding more exceptional. "She's way ahead of me in style," Linda confided, adding, "I'm their only daughter," as if to explain the hovering attitude of her parents. Clearly, Linda saw her wedding as a chance to show off for her mother and her parents' friends, and to win their approval.

You know what's coming. Her friends saw it happening. Only Linda was impervious to her own competitive behavior. She hired a nasty florist who specialized in intimidating insecure women. She interviewed eight bandleaders. She and her bridegroom looked at a dozen small ballrooms in hotels and clubs, after Linda had prescreened twice that number of sites to save her fiance's time. Yet there was something wrong with every location. The bathroom wasn't nice enough. The ballroom wasn't close enough to the entrance. She didn't like the catering manager, or the food wasn't beautifully served or sufficiently delicious.

Linda had become the unwitting fascist bride. She couldn't tolerate criticism, and her standards were so impeccably high that nothing, but nothing, satisfied her.

By the time she was ready to make the decision about where to be married, two of the three spaces in the best hotels in town were booked on the date of her wedding. Should she change the date? Or should she take the third space, even though this was an admission that she had no other option? She was paralyzed with indecision. Everything looked incredibly complicated. Emotions accelerated. She was in a constant state of near panic.

The Best Wedding Decision I Made

"I chose a place that I thought would encourage a casual, lively, and fun party and it did. We were married in a church but the reception was at a beach club. The combination of everyone being really well-dressed but just inches away from these beautiful, sandy beaches was unexpected. People danced like crazy and had a good time, which was very important to me."

Daniela Gomez, 29, second-time bride.

On the day of Linda's wedding, everyone was anxious about it. A friend and I took a bottle of chilled champagne into the dressing room and served it to Linda, her mother, her sisters-in-law, and a few friends. The wedding consultant Linda hired at the last minute seemed to be in control of every detail. Linda drank a very little champagne (she usually doesn't drink at all), relaxed, and later told me her wedding could not have been more perfect.

Gail, a mutual friend of Linda's and of mine, promised that this would never, ever happen to her. She decided to have a party to announce the marriage, several weeks after the wedding would take place in Aspen, Colorado, with 20 close friends and family members. For the big party, which she considered her wedding reception, Gail planned to spend about $15,000-20,000 for 200 guests. But after seeing Linda's self-inflicted frustrations, she cut her guestlist to 100 and the budget to $10,000, about $5,000 for food, cake, and bar, and called it a day.

She met with one caterer, they chose the menu, and she refused to worry about it. Whereas she wanted her wedding to be intimate and personal, she wanted the big celebration to be exuberant and lively. How did it all work out? It felt exactly right, in part, I believe, because Gail had decided it would be wonderful. The band was not perfect. There was a mixup in the linens at the last minute, and Gail had to send a friend to a nearby store to buy tablecloths. But both Gail and her husband loved their party. "If I hadn't seen what Linda did to herself, I might have been tempted to go that route," she says. "I could feel myself getting carried away like Linda. There's something about a wedding that is intimidating. It makes you think you have to have the best, and then some."

The truly unforgettable wedding, in every way, involved a middle-class bride of 28 named Cindy, a successful professional who married someone from a rich and well-known family. In her heart, I believe, she worried that her middle-class background would show and that she would look ridiculous. Because of her bridegroom's own insecurities (in spite of his family name and money he's never succeeded at anything), he did not inspire her with confidence.

Cindy had what some brides dream of: unlimited resources. Her fiancé and his widowed mother offered to pay for the wedding, telling her they thought about $40,000 should cover a wedding for 200 guests. Cindy thought she'd need $50,000, and decided that if costs exceeded that, she would make up the difference.

Instead of being liberating, the lack of financial limits created too many choices. Cindy did not appear to be intimidated by the choices as much as overwhelmed by all the merchandise and services she was seeing for the first time in her life. When she mentioned prices to her future mother-in-law, who controlled the purse strings, the older woman was aghast. Ten thousand dollars for flowers and linens? Twenty-five thousand for food and a little champagne? Cindy loved everything she saw. She interviewed the best florists, the toniest photographers, the most creative table linen designers, the most elegant bandleaders. She took fabulous recipes from cookbooks to her meetings with the caterer, not to one meeting but to three. Seeing that the bride was a monster in the making, the wedding vendors began to envision huge profits and compete for her business.

Cindy became increasingly overwhelmed. Her notebook was filled to bursting with information. The logistics were staggering, and planning the wedding began to feel like producing a movie, but without the aid of the movie company's staff of worker bees to pull it together. Three months before her wedding, she quit her job so she could work on the wedding fulltime. Not surprisingly, she ended up having four kinds of music, each provided by a different group, which made sense to her. "I want a brass ensemble with a big sound for the ceremony," she said, "and a great jazz combo for the cocktail part of the reception and dinner, and dancing that older people will like for the first part of the reception, and real hip music for the young people who stay late."

Getting her invitations into the mail took days of concentrated effort. They were designed by a graphic artist on beautiful handmade paper. The enclosures had enclosures. She found the world's best calligrapher. She had a special seal made to go with the wedding's theme, and sealed every envelope with sealing wax. To save on messenger fees, she hand-carried everything herself to and from the stationer and the calligrapher.

The day of the occasion was finally at hand. The wedding was held in six rooms of a city mansion with a beautifully landscaped yard. Everything looked beautiful. The chairs were covered in white slipcovers. The tables were covered with floor-length, peach moire tablecloths and lace

What I Would Change About Our Wedding

"We threw our own pre-nuptial party the night before our wedding and took care of details such as renting the party room in our apartment building and decorating it, getting the food delivered by a caterer, buying champagne and hiring waitstaff and all that. We forgot one detail: we didn't hire our servers for long enough, so they could clean up. At Midnight, my husband and I were still cleaning up. Even with disposable everything, there was a lot of work. A definite oversight."

Gail Park, 30, first-time bride.

Magic Moments

- At Caryn Brown's and Henry Tomson's wedding, they wrote a brief presentation ceremony and gave a trophy to the mutual friend who introduced them. "For loving attention above and beyond the call of duty..." it began. Guests loved it. Their friend will never forget it.
- It's called the Krenzl in Yiddish, and it was a touching moment for everyone when Lisa Berger's and Gabe Foshay's parents were seated back to back in the center of the dance floor and the entire crowd danced around them wishing them well, now that their last child had married and was away from home. This celebration of the end of parental responsibilities is a happy, lively song, and is usually accompanied by the Krenzl, or crowning, where the bride and bridegroom crown their parents with floral wreaths to show their appreciation.
- When Jenny Powers's and Ken Clause's college friends unrolled their calligraphed banner wishing the couple well and signed by everyone there, the words were only part of what the couple loved. The effort that went into this banner made it a special possession, something they pull out for New Year's Eve parties and other family celebrations. Next is "a christening party," says the bride.
- The California commissioner who married Amelia and Jeffrey didn't want to include in the ceremony the statement, "If anyone knows any reason why this union should not take place, speak now or forever hold your peace." The couple insisted that the commissioner ask the guests and then pause. "We had to force her, but she did it. There was a long, dramatic pause and dead silence. We turned around and everyone was wondering if something had gone wrong. Then we slowly turned back and the commissioner said, probably with some relief, 'I now pronounce you husband and wife.' It was wonderful," says Amelia, still laughing at the memory. "It was like something right out of a Victorian novel and we loved it."

overlays. Tulle was pouffed artfully around each table and was caught with clusters of pale peach roses. They looked exquisite, like a movie set. More tulle and roses draped each and every bush surrounding the patio. There was no question that everything was designed to look incredibly romantic, and no one suspected the agony that had gone into the planning.

Behind the scenes, however, the various musicians were arguing about how and where to set up their equipment. A design consultant, a one-time florist and hairdresser hired at the last minute to oversee things, fought with the florist, who was mad that he hadn't received his final payment. And they drove the wedding consultant crazy.

As for the couple themselves, they were oblivious to it all, happy about how beautiful everything looked and how loved they felt, right? Wrong. Three months after the wedding, they were still arguing over the food bill. "The meal was nothing like what we ate at the sampling," says the bridegroom. The bride tells stories of someone's brother (his? hers?) fighting with the chef in the kitchen. The bridegroom blames the consultant for some unpleasantness with the florist (over his final payment), and Cindy confesses that she secretly took out a loan to pay for extras she didn't want to tell her husband's mother about. She is now repaying it on her own, knowing that her husband would never approve.

I should be able to add a horror story about a less costly wedding. I don't know of one, though, which says something about weddings and money. I have never heard of a wedding that cost less than $10,000-15,000 that was a disaster. Of course, when sky-high prices are not being paid, standards do not aim for perfection. And smaller weddings are not as difficult to organize. Perhaps brides who *choose* to have simpler weddings avoid the problems that come with spending too much and reaching far beyond what they already know. Most women, after all, can choose flowers that cost less than a king's ransom without getting overly anxious. Working to keep a wedding in scale with normal life, keeping it in proportion to how we usually entertain but making it nicer, might be the answer to avoiding becoming a fascist bride.

Why look at wedding disasters? Because I have seen the potential for destructive, perfectionistic behavior in too many brides who create their own psychological pressures and end up being overwhelmed by what should have been fun. Details become overimportant. A need for affirmation from the outside substitutes for the goal of having a beautiful, loving wedding. Clearly, these two wedding nightmare stories relate to the brides' fragile self-esteem.

Something beyond the fairly obvious insecurities many individuals bring to the planning of a public occasion is at work here. It seems clear to me that brides who obsess over every detail are, in some way, avoiding thinking about the marriage by focusing on the wedding.

Melissa Moore explains the different feelings at her first and second weddings and says there's no doubt that she had to be in control of every detail of her first wedding because she felt out of control of the marriage. "This time my mother and four aunts were in the room when I was getting dressed and I was so happy and at peace and eager," she says. "At my first wedding I cried uncontrollably. I was weeping so hard that I couldn't see anyone because I knew I was doing the wrong thing. I didn't actually know that, but my subconscious was telling me I was out of control. I had to try to be in charge of everything around me so I could focus on that rather than on the fact that I was marrying the wrong guy."

OBSESSING AND HOW TO AVOID IT

In weddings where the marriage is not the problem, perfectionism still can exist. How to avoid it? Here are a few reasons for wedding obsessiveness. Each focuses on an attitude that exists in the world of business but is significantly different in the world of weddings.

The Unspoken Image. In the world of business, employees work with clear, established goals. Although brides may begin with a vision of the perfect wedding, their goals are fluid. In shopping, they are constantly bombarded by service providers who claim they can improve that vision.

The solution: In business you hire professionals you like and respect and encourage them to do their best work. You are clear and specific with them about instructions, and then let them do their jobs. On another level the answer is even simpler: Pick a style and believe in it.

Experience Shortfall and Work Overload. In the world of business, there's a training period and a support staff. Employees are given plenty of experience in the lower ranks before they take charge of projects. On the other hand, most brides have never planned a wedding or any kind of celebration of this size and importance. Even professional women in upper income brackets who know better can get bitten by the perfectionism bug and struggle to plan the perfect wedding.

The solution: In the world of business you hire or listen to people who have more experience than you do, which helps compensate for your limited experience. And you delegate tasks, which relieves the burden of work overload. In arranging your wedding, though, you may be unable or unwilling to do either. Instead, allow enough time for planning, giving yourself extra weeks or months if you want to do more than a little comparison shopping to educate yourself about the market. Accept help, from your bridegroom, mother, sisters, friends. Give them clear ideas of what you want. Listen to them and trust them. Or hire a wedding planner.

The Emotional Overlay. Everyone involved in a wedding can have some emotional stake in it and may try to influence you accordingly. As difficult as it can be to defend your opinions in business, it is even more difficult to prioritize and compromise when dealing with your family, where even adults are seen as children. The ambivalent or insecure bride faces more problems because of unresolved emotional issues that influence her choices.

The solution: This is an especially difficult area, because it's not easy to separate cause from effect. Family dynamics can thrust members back into childhood behavior patterns. It can be a struggle to communicate in a calm, rational way or to compromise to keep family peace. Try to stay in control and not give in to anger. Be clear in your mind about issues that are worth fighting for and those that can be compromises – before they become sources of conflict. If your family is unwilling to allow you to do what you are sure you want, back off and organize the wedding yourself – before you and your family alienate each other.

The Bride Is the Center of Attention. In business projects, the planner is behind the scenes acting as manager of operations. During the entire wedding ceremony and celebration, however, the bride is the focus of attention. Women, especially those beyond the starry-eyed-bride stage, may have mixed feelings about this role.

The solution: The bigger and the more formal the wedding, the more this happens. If you're serious about wanting to avoid being in the spotlight, have a less formal wedding. (But if you love the idea of being the focal point of the entire day, disregard this as a potential problem!)

Working within a Budget. Even some brides who have been responsible for finances in their business settings can have difficulty working within a specific budget dictated by their own and their bridegrooms' and families' financial limits.

The solution: If you make an actual budget, be realistic about costs. Be practical. Stay within your price range when you see vendors. If you

What I Would Change About Our Wedding

"I didn't have many friends at my wedding. Now, I know lots of people and would have loads of friends to invite, but it was a funny time in my life. I hadn't kept in touch with my high-school friends and because I lived at home I hadn't made close friends in college. So I had a few of the teachers I taught with at my wedding, and everyone else was family. It was wonderful and warm, but I envision a wedding being surrounded by friends and I wasn't. That still sort of makes me feel bad."

Virginia Miller, 29, first-time bride at 25.

can't afford your city's most elegant band or use the most popular florist, don't meet with either one. Be content with what you can afford. Treat some decisions as if they were business choices. And never, ever, under any circumstances, defend or explain your choices to guests. Do what you can afford and let it go at that.

The Best Wedding Decision I Made

"For my peace of mind, the best decision I made was what to keep firm control over and what to delegate. I controlled my choice of wedding gown, rings, flowers, church music, wedding cake, some of the ceremony, and the wording of the invitations. Because we were being married in our hometown in Ohio, rather than in New York where we now live, I had to delegate the choice of menu, photographer and photos, band, favors, groomsmen's outfits, and bridesmaids' dresses. In these cases, I was consulted on the choices, but often bowed to others' wishes and expertise. And it all worked fine."

Toni Prima, 34, first-time bride.

For every ten brides, there is probably one who will succumb to obsessiveness. Besides driving themselves and everyone around them crazy with their perfectionism, obsessive brides tend to squeeze all the life out of their weddings, a good reason to avoid perfectionism in the first place. The confident woman, of course, plans her wedding as care-

---

The Ten Commandments for Grownup Weddings

1. It's your wedding.
   It's not your parents' or his parents' wedding, and not a public occasion meant to live up to (or down to) community, family, or neighborhood standards. It yours and his. Make your wedding personal by individualizing it with a style that's all your own.

2. Your wedding should reflect your deepest feelings about marriage and married life.
   Remember what you're there for. It's not a show. You're there to celebrate your love and your future together. How you plan your wedding will demonstrate how you will live your life.

3. You should have a good time at your own wedding.
   Your wedding is not New Year's Eve, with the pressure to have a good time even if the gaiety rings hollow. Surround yourself with the people you care about and with the food, music, flowers, and other elements that will make you happy. Your pleasure and joy will naturally shine through.

4. Your wedding should be in keeping with your financial limits.
   Your own or his or yours together. Your parents' or his. Set a budget and stay within it. Choose the best you can afford—within your limits.

5. Pick a few details and concentrate on making them unusual.
   Make a special poem part of your ceremony, find a baker who will use your grandmother's recipe for the cake, spend time with your mother choosing both of your dresses, or make sure your wedding vows reflect your sense of partnership in marriage.

6. If you tend toward compulsiveness, obsess about only one thing at a time.

   During the planning stages, break large areas into smaller, more manageable portions. For example, think of the wedding reception in parts—the music, the dinner, the toasts. Remember, this is not a grand opera production with weeks of dress rehearsals.

7. Everything possible should be done beforehand so you can avoid the pressure of handling details on your wedding day.

   Prior to the day of your wedding, delegate as many responsibilities as possible to others. Make a schedule. Let the caterer worry about the food, the florist about the flowers. Ask friends to watch details, or hire a consultant.

8. Every marriage is a mixed marriage.

   He's male and you're female, and beyond that most differences pale by comparison. Don't assume that, because you belong to the same faith, your decisions will spring from your shared cultural background. This is why defining what's right for each of you and for your families is necessary.

9. Don't invite Emily Post.

   Etiquette exists to make social occasions easier, not more difficult. Today's smartest couples are rewriting the rules with confidence, dignity, and style.

10. Set aside family conflicts on your wedding day.

    Your brother-in-law is a jerk? Haven't seen your father for years? Can't stand your Aunt Thea? Give them a big hug anyway. Guests and family members will almost always reflect your loving attitude and add to your day's joy.

---

fully as she can within the framework of her time and budget, and then allows some room for spontaneity.

MAKING IT ALL WORK

Maybe having a successful wedding comes down to qualities of character. Kindness and tact combined with a willingness to compromise. Confidence. Knowing who you are, along with understanding the significance of your roots and the relative importance of your own independence. Prioritizing and clarifying goals so you can stick to your guns when it counts. Learning to trust others, but not being overly influenced by them. Not worrying about transgressing unwritten community rules and standards if you want to substitute your own style. In the long run, mature and thoughtful brides and bridegrooms have grownup weddings.

"You can get sucked into the 'shoulds,'" says Scott Johnson, a lawyer bridegroom in his midthirties who was very involved in the decision-making and planning process of his wedding. "If you avoid all the advice about things you absolutely must do, most of it goes away. We called our parents a lot and got their input, so they'd feel like they had participated, but we did things our way."

Scott and his bride, also an attorney, hired professionals they trusted. "We knew that when you act as your own general contractor, it can become a disaster because you're doing all of this for the first time and trying to get everyone to cooperate," he says. "We listened to the hotel's catering director, and he was there at the hotel the entire time of our wedding." He said, 'Talk to me. It's my job to take care of everything.'

"People who want to go out and do it all themselves," and he stops, sounding exasperated, "we hear them on the phone negotiating about every detail – 'Is that the time the ice sculpture is delivered?' – and they end up crazed. They're so inexperienced they don't even know what they don't know. My idea was to find the best help there was and trust them, and it worked. We had a wonderful wedding."

The mother of a bride, a young professional woman working in Los Angeles, while her wedding was being planned in one of Philadelphia's most elegant suburbs, says she did most of the work for her daughter and son-in-law, and that they had constant conversations about details so she'd be sure they'd love their wedding."

In retrospect, she says she thinks too many people get carried away with the theatricality of their weddings and lose sight of what a wedding is all about. "The reason everyone thought it was such a wonderful wedding was not the flowers, the tablecloths, or the food, but because there was a real feeling of joy and happiness, and you can't fake that. My daughter and her husband got married at seven in the evening. They and all their friends played tennis that day and were around the swimming pool all afternoon. At four, I looked at all the bridesmaids and the groomsmen in their swimsuits and said, 'We're now turning into a wedding. Let's pretend that *House Beautiful* is coming in 30 minutes. We have to get everything ready for the photographers. Towels up, and take them to the basement. Get dressed and be back here by five. A hairdresser was waiting to help everyone with their hair, so an hour was just enough. And they were all ready on time, and relaxed, and had a good time."

"People get too overwrought about weddings," Ellie Richards says.

The Best Thing About Our Wedding

"Everyone knew everyone else. There were about sixty of us and we were all pals and the warmth and love we both felt from everyone was incredible. A lot of our friends from politics were there. We had worked together on campaigns, which really gives you a bond. We wouldn't have had any other kind of wedding."

Dixie Vance, 34, second-time bride.

"My daughter was in a wedding, and the mother told all the bridesmaids they had to have special designer panty hose of a certain color that cost $12.50, which is so unnecessary. People get too wrapped up in the details. Who cares about matching stockings? Nobody. I hate weddings where everything is so packaged. 'Now you have to do this. Now you have to cut the cake.' Let things come naturally. People ought to be happy that they're seeing all their friends. Being loving and gracious and natural is what's important. What weddings are really all about is the couple at the center, and about the hospitality of welcoming friends to celebrate one of life's happiest occasions with the bride and bridegroom and their families."

Think of it this way: Unless you're professional actors or the kind of individuals who love being on stage, weddings are not theater performances. In a very deep sense, weddings reveal who we are and how we feel about love and marriage and the important ceremony that is a hallmark in most of our lives. The couple who wants to have fun, who is relaxed and enjoys each other's company, will have a wedding that expresses those attitudes. The couples with loving family ties and roots and a sense of community along with personal confidence will bring those feelings to their weddings. Those are the weddings that have genuine joy and happiness without being strained or artificial. Not surprisingly, they are what everyone really wants. They are the best kind of weddings for grownups.

Index

About the Author

Carroll Stoner writes about women's issues and about subjects related to roots, family, and community. She is a co-author of *All God's Children* (Viking/Penguin), a book about cults, and she originated the ideas for *Reinventing Home* and *Reinventing Love*, collections of essays by a group of women writers on domestic and personal life. As one of the first women managers in the newspaper business, she was involved in changing women's pages to feature sections at the *Hartford Times*, *Philadelphia Inquirer*, and *Chicago Sun-Times*, where she was an assistant managing editor and won the Penney-Missouri Award as editor of the nation's best feature section. After leaving the newspaper business, she was cofounder of The Wedding Company, a workshop-seminar/consulting business geared towards working women. She is married and the mother of a grown son and pre-teenage daughter and works in an office decorated with her collection of antique wedding gowns. She is an avid Chicago Bulls fan.